FAMILY LAW AND SOCIAL POLICY

LAW IN CONTEXT

Editors: Robert Stevens (Haverford College, Pennsylvania),
William Twining (University College, London) and
Christopher McCrudden (Lincoln College, Oxford)

Family Law and Social Policy

Second edition

JOHN EEKELAAR

Fellow of Pembroke College, Oxford

WEIDENFELD AND NICOLSON
London

To My Family

© 1978, 1984 John Eekelaar

First published 1978
Second edition 1984

All rights reserved. No part of this
publication may be reproduced, stored in
a retrieval system, or transmitted, in
any form or by any means, electronic,
mechanical, photocopying, recording or
otherwise, without the prior permission
of the copyright owner.

George Weidenfeld & Nicolson Limited
91 Clapham High Street, London sw4

ISBN 0 297 78274 6 Cased
ISBN 0 297 78275 4 Paperback

Photoset by Deltatype, Ellesmere Port
Printed in Great Britain by
Butler & Tanner Ltd.,
Frome and London

CONTENTS

PART THREE: LAW AND PROTECTION

PART FOUR: LAW AND SUPPORT

CASES

STATUTES

PREFACE TO THE SECOND EDITION

My purpose in writing this second edition was very different from what I was attempting in the first. The first edition was a response to what was then perceived to be a shortcoming in the way much family law was taught at the time. Courses concentrated on the legal rules and paid little attention to their social setting, still less to what empirical knowledge then existed as to how they actually worked. The result was a book which organized its material around the main areas taught as family law. It was an attempt to provide, as it were, a background illumination to the standard family law course.

That approach has been abandoned in this edition. A major reason for this is that the central family law textbooks have themselves reacted to the 'law in context' movement and provide much fuller reference to the data on such issues. I have taken this development as an opportunity to free this book from its relationship to any family law course and instead to use it as a vehicle to re-think many of the basic principles on which family law operates. In doing this I have selected those areas which seem to me to be most relevant to my theme. The book in no sense seeks to treat all legal questions, nor even to deal comprehensively with all legal materials relevant to those areas which are discussed. It is, however, an attempt to put forward a coherent and principled theory which might underlie what I consider to be some of the most important problems with respect to the state's role in relation to family living.

In doing this I have retained some of the features of the first edition. In particular, I have kept the division of the exposition into three sections, corresponding to the major functions family law is seen as having: adjustment after breakdown, protection within the family and support of family living. The argument for doing this is developed somewhat more fully than in the first edition. It should be stressed here that this classification is considered subordinate to the major

xviii PREFACE

thesis developed in the book. This is an explicit theory about children's rights, although it can also be seen as a wider political or social theory. The materials drawn on include some foreign (mostly Commonwealth and United States) legal material and a wide range of research data. In a rapidly moving field such as this, where co-ordination of knowledge is particularly difficult, some relevant material may have been overlooked. If so, I have to offer my apologies.

This edition could not have been written without the opportunities provided by the Faculty of Law of the University of Toronto during the academic year 1981/2. To its faculty members, students and secretarial staff I owe an immense debt of gratitude. I have also to thank Pembroke College, Oxford, for granting me the leave to enable me to take the opportunities offered, and once more to my colleague, Dan Prentice, for shouldering the burden. My debt to my research colleagues at the SSRC Centre for Socio-Legal Studies, Wolfson College, Oxford, particularly Robert Dingwall and Mavis Maclean, will be obvious from the text. I know I have benefited immeasurably by the insights from their own disciplinary standpoints (one of the unique contributions the SSRC Centre has been able to make to learning) and I only hope I can pass these on in some way. But, of course, I alone am responsible for the imperfections of the finished product.

April 1983   John Eekelaar
                                          Pembroke College Oxford

PART ONE: THE FAMILY, LAW AND SOCIAL CHANGE

I
Marriage, Family Living and Family Law

The epicentre of family law has always evolved around the institution of marriage. Marriage is the basis of the legal family and has therefore provided the framework in which legal obligations of the adult parties towards each other and their children have been set. There are, however, many indications that marriage is losing this central position. Other forms of living arrangements which can broadly be considered 'familial' are becoming more common. Marriage is still the most significant of these, but it is becoming difficult to see with clarity what are the characteristics which distinguish it from other modes of family life and correspondingly harder to know what legal responses are appropriate to each of them. The first purpose of this chapter, therefore, is to provide a rough social profile of the different forms of familial living as they seem to be emerging in Britain in the early 1980s. Reference will also, however, be made to data from some other (mostly) western societies, sometimes for fuller illustration and sometimes to sharpen the picture by way of contrast. In this way those members of the population who constitute the actual or potential 'clients' for family law and their distinctive problems can be identified.

The rise and 'decline' of marriage

The first half of the twentieth century saw a significant expansion in the proportion of the population of western European countries (except Ireland) who had experienced marriage. In Sweden, the

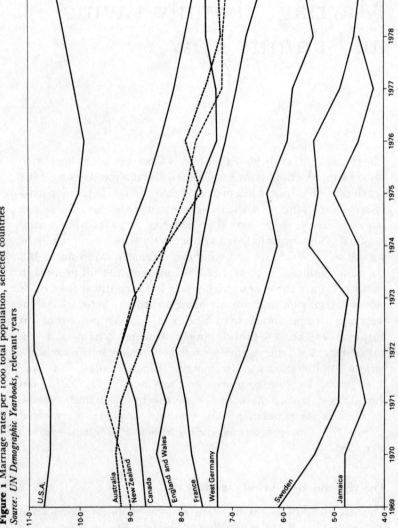

Figure 1 Marriage rates per 1000 total population, selected countries
Source: UN Demographic Yearbooks, relevant years

proportion of women who had ever married by the age of fifty rose from 77.4 per cent in the period 1886–90 to 91.4 per cent in the period 1936–40; in England and Wales the corresponding increase was from 83.6 per cent to 96.0 per cent.[1] Although the marriage rate began to rise from the early 1930s, the most notable feature of this marriage boom was the rapid increase in marriages of young adults after the Second World War. Of all brides in England and Wales under thirty, the percentage who were under twenty-one rose from 20.3 in 1938 to 45.0 in 1973. In Australia the proportion of females under twenty-one in the total married population increased from 20 per cent in 1939 to 43 per cent in 1973.[2] In very recent years, however, the popularity of marriage has declined. Figure 1 shows the crude marriage rates (marriages per thousand population) of selected countries. A decline starting in the early 1970s is observable for nearly all of them. That this is not simply a function of changing age structures of the population is shown from Leete's (1979) analysis of the first marriage

Table 1. *England and Wales: first marriage rates per 1000 single population in selected age groups*

Bachelors				Year	Spinsters			
Age 16–19	20–24	25–29	30–34		16–19	20–24	25–29	30–34
18	158	190	91	*1964*	74	258	161	74
19	163	193	93	*1965*	78	265	160	73
22	169	185	91	*1966*	83	264	153	74
22	163	178	90	*1967*	80	254	152	72
24	172	182	94	*1968*	85	265	161	73
22	169	185	89	*1969*	82	260	162	71
27	177	176	91	*1970*	95	262	169	74
26	170	170	86	*1971*	94	250	168	76
26	166	174	93	*1972*	94	247	181	88
25	153	163	88	*1973*	88	226	170	82
23	143	154	85	*1974*	81	209	165	84
21	138	151	86	*1975*	76	208	156	87
18	123	138	83	*1976*	67	191	142	84
17	116	136	83	*1977*	62	181	139	83
16	112	138	86	*1978*	59	178	135	84
15	108	135	86	*1979*	55	171	135	86

Source: Leete (1979) Table 6, supplemented by *Marriage and Divorce Statistics* 1979 (OPCS, Series FM2, No. 6, HMSO, 1981), Table 3.3.

rates in England and Wales per thousand single population aged sixteen and over, which is also standardized for age. Furthermore, the decline has been confined to people under thirty. Table 1 shows a decline in the first marriage rate (the number of marriages per thousand individuals in that category) for both bachelors and spinsters in all age groups under thirty, starting in 1971 and persisting to 1979. In the case of women under twenty, the increase over the period 1964–70 is followed by a falling off of 42 per cent. For women aged between twenty and twenty-four the decrease after 1970 is by 34 per cent and for women aged between twenty-five and twenty-nine it is 20 per cent. However, women aged between thirty and thirty-four show an increase of 16 per cent over the same period.[3] So the reduction in marriage rates may mean only, or mainly, a postpone-ment of marriage, but the extent to which this may be true cannot be known until the relevant age cohorts move into their thirties.

The decline in the marriage rate has been accompanied by a decline in the birth-rate in western countries (see Table 2). What is the explanation of this, and are the two phenomena interconnected? It has been suggested that the explanation may, for a large part, lie in the growing economic opportunities for women (Ermisch [1981]). Subject to availability of prospective partners in the right age groups, there appears to be a correlation between the extent of the disparity between men's and women's incomes (and the availability of housing) and both the propensity to marry and the birth-rate. The greater the disparity, the stronger the propensity to marry. Yet the correlation does not of itself prove a causal relationship. At most it suggests that, where women's earnings are particularly low compared to those of men, couples will have an economic incentive to establish a common household, with the female staying at home and producing children. It does not follow that they should *marry*. Similarly, where female earnings are relatively high, there is no economic reason why they may not maximize their economic potential within a two-earner marriage rather than in unmarried cohabitation. The decision whether or not to set the partnership within the institution of marriage appears to be the result of cultural variables, influenced by, but not necessarily determined by, economic considerations.

It is clear that the decline in marriage has been accompanied by a growth in unmarried cohabitation. In Sweden, Trost (1980) has estimated that, in 1978, some 15–16 per cent of all heterosexual couples living together were not married. However, where the female

Table 2 *Crude birth-rates per 1000 mean population, selected countries*

	1970	1971	1972	1973	1974	1975	1976	1977	1978	1979
Australia	20.5	21.6	20.4	18.8	18.4	16.9	16.4	16.1	15.7	15.3
Canada	17.5	16.8	15.9	15.5	15.4	15.8	15.6	15.5	15.3	15.1
Denmark	14.4	15.2	15.2	14.3	14.1	14.2	12.9	12.2	12.2	11.6
England & Wales	16.1	16.0	14.8	13.7	13.0	12.3	11.9	11.6	12.1	13.0
France	16.7	17.1	16.9	16.4	15.2	14.1	13.6	14.0	13.8	14.1
New Zealand	22.0	22.5	21.6	20.4	19.5	18.2	17.9	17.3	16.3	16.7
Sweden	13.6	14.1	13.8	13.5	13.4	12.6	12.0	11.6	11.2	11.6
United States	18.2	17.3	15.6	15.0	15.0	14.8	14.8	15.3	15.3	15.8
West Germany	13.3	12.7	11.4	10.2	10.1	9.7	9.8	9.5	9.4	9.5

Source: *UN Demographic Yearbooks*, relevant years. Some figures are provisional.

partner was aged between twenty and twenty-four, 57 per cent were not married, and where the male was within those ages, 71 per cent were not married. But between the ages of thirty and thirty-four only 10 per cent of cohabiting women and 14 per cent of cohabiting men were not married. Trost also calculates that 'over 99 per cent' of Swedish couples marrying in 1979 had cohabited in marriage-like conditions before marrying. In England and Wales it is less easy to arrive at precise figures indicating the proportion of people cohabiting without marriage. It has been recorded that some 10 per cent of women first married between 1971 and 1975 had lived with their husband prior to marriage, compared with 3 per cent of those who were first married five years earlier,[4] and that, in 1979, some 10 per cent of all currently non-married women aged between twenty and twenty-nine were cohabiting, the larger proportion of them being already divorced.[5] This must be seen in the context of the decrease in the first marriage rate by as much as 30 per cent for women under twenty-five between 1970 and 1978. While it cannot be concluded that they are cohabiting rather than marrying, it is possible that many are, and, while none of this yields a very clear picture, the signs indicate a tendency towards increasing cohabitation in place of marriage for people under twenty-five.

In the United States it has been observed that 'there have been few developments relating to marriage and family life which have been so dramatic as the rapid increase in unmarried cohabitation'.[6] The increase has been from just over 500,000 such couples in 1970 to over

1.1 million in 1978. One-quarter of the unions had produced children. However, it is important not to draw simple parallels between this situation and that in, for example, Sweden. It seems reasonably clear that, in the United States, cohabitation is to be found among two very different population groups. Both are urban, but one is black (among whom the cohabitation rate is three times that of the white population), poor and suffers high unemployment. The other is white, well-off and frequently enjoys two income-earners.[7] Thus, while unmarried cohabitation may be a growing feature of economically affluent societies, or segments of societies, indicating a new economic and social ordering of sexual relations, it may also continue to be an endemic part of the family life patterns of poorer communities for whom 'traditional' marriage played a comparatively less important role in any case.[8] It may be no accident, therefore, that Figure 1 shows the country with the marriage rate closest to that of Sweden to be Jamaica.[9]

There is one significant respect in which the pattern of cohabitation of unmarried people in Denmark and Sweden differs from that of people in other western countries. In the former countries, the fertility of cohabitants is about one-third that of married people whereas it seems that elsewhere marriage will be entered into prior to child-bearing.[10] Thus the two Scandinavian countries depart from others in so far as it cannot be described as socially deviant to set up a family without marrying. Here may be the cultural variable which might explain the shifting pattern of marriage since the mid-1970s. Sexual activity and procreation of children are increasingly separated. Sexual relationships outside marriage are more tolerated, but (outside Denmark and Sweden) marriage is still seen as the proper context in which to bear and raise children. Hence the movement to later marriage has been accompanied by a tendency for women to concentrate their childbearing between the ages of twenty-five and twenty-nine.[11]

The same implications can be drawn by considering the changing pattern of out-of-wedlock births. In England and Wales, while the total annual number of live births decreased from 811,281 in 1965 to 638,028 in 1979 (a drop of about 25 per cent), the annual number of births out of wedlock over the same period rose from 66,249 to 69,467. But the increase was overwhelmingly concentrated in the under-twenty age group. In 1969, 26.5 per cent of births to mothers under twenty were out of wedlock; in 1979 the proportion had risen to 40.6

per cent. The comparable increase in the age group twenty to twenty-four was from 8.0 per cent to 11.8 per cent, and in the age group twenty-five to twenty-nine from 5.2 per cent to 5.9 per cent.[12] The population seems clearly to fall into two sections. Teenagers, for whom the conception was probably unplanned but are not so likely to be pressured into marriage;[13] and older women who are now relatively rarely likely to bear children out of wedlock. If they do, it is likely that the child's birth will be registered in joint names, suggesting long-term cohabitation (see Table 3). But more significantly, it appears that marriage, followed by childbearing, is becoming increasingly concentrated in a woman's late twenties, reflecting an attitudinal change as found by the Australian Royal Commission on Human Relationships that by the mid-1970s people were placing much greater emphasis on the need for maturity and a period of freedom before marrying.[14] The increase in the proportion of people marrying over thirty is not, however, related to increased fertility at that age; rather, the reverse. It may be that more people in that age group are entering agreed childless marriages or marrying after a child or children have been born at an earlier time.

Table 3 *England and Wales: jointly registered illegitimate births, 1979*

Mother's age	Total	Jointly Registered (Total)	(%)
All ages	69,467	38,349	55.2
Under 20	24,005	10,293	42.8
20–24	22,871	12,744	55.6
25–29	12,306	8,131	66.0
30–34	6,811	4,865	71.1
35–39	2,678	1,854	69.2
40–44	667	431	64.6

Source: *Birth Statistics 1979* (OPCS Series FM1, No. 6, HMSO, 1981), Table 3.10.

Single parent families and unmarried parenthood

It would, of course, be too narrow to confine an examination of families to units of cohabiting adults, within or without marriage, with or without children. The growth of single parent families has been a remarkable feature of recent years. In the United States the

proportion of all children living in such families rose from 9 per cent in
1960 to 19 per cent in 1978. By 1978, female-headed one-parent
families constituted 14 per cent of all American households,[15] and
nearly 11 per cent of British families with dependent children.[16] So
also in Canada, mother–child families increased by 23 per cent
between 1971 and 1976, compared to a 13 per cent increase in *all*
families.[17] The extent of this increase is almost entirely due to the
growth in family breakdown by divorce and the lower remarriage rate
of women than men.[18]

However, a rise in out-of-wedlock births contributes to the number
of mother–child families. In the United States such births rose from
5.3 per cent of all live births in 1960 to 14.2 per cent in 1975.[19] In
England and Wales there has been a steady rise from just below 5 per
cent in the mid-1950s to 10.9 per cent in 1979. As in the case of
cohabitation, however, it is important to caution against viewing
out-of-wedlock maternity as a unitary phenomenon. It has already
been observed that in Denmark and Sweden it is closely linked to
unmarried cohabitation, and this is likely to be true to some extent in
other countries. Its prevalence in the Caribbean countries and among
American blacks suggests that there it is not deviant behaviour but a
reflection of cultural norms.[20] However, in the United Kingdom at
any rate, its rapid growth in the 1960s has been attributed to new
patterns of behaviour 'associated with youth, urban living and
sophistication',[21] and, despite an increase among higher socio-
economic groups, is still predominantly associated with lower social
class, a feature accentuated after the availability of abortion under the
Abortion Act 1967 because resort to abortion is more common among
women of higher social class.[22]

As remarked earlier, the association between out-of-wedlock birth
and youth is particularly striking. Thus, despite the fact that the
number of legitimate maternities to women under twenty nearly
halved between 1969 and 1979, the number of out-of-wedlock births
actually increased. The *proportion* of these births which were out of
wedlock rose from 26.5 per cent in 1969 to 40.6 per cent in 1979. In the
case of many children born out of wedlock, then, a cluster of factors
tend to come together. The mothers are likely to be young, of lower
socio-economic status and to be living singly. The first two factors are
associated with poor obstetric performance and it was these factors,
rather than their single status, which Gill's (1977) study revealed to
be associated with a higher rate of perinatal death among illegitimate

than among legitimate pregnancies. However, he did find that academic performance of children in single parent units was significantly lower than children from complete families 'matched for age, parity and mother social class'.[23] The National Child Development Study (1958 Cohort), looking at children at the age of seven, produced evidence that out-of-wedlock children performed less well, enjoyed less parental support and were even more susceptible to death, injury or illness during childhood than other children.[24]

These problems are attributable to the tendency of non-cohabiting women to prepare themselves inadequately for childbirth and to the severe practical problems of raising children single-handed. But the same study of the 1958 Cohort has shown that at the age of eleven there was no significant difference in school performance, behaviour or adjustment between illegitimate children cared for by their mothers alone and children living in complete families when other factors, such as class, had been excluded. Children of homes broken by divorce or separation seemed to experience greater difficulty. But it must be remembered that the mothers of illegitimate children usually move downward socially and economically, and the findings show simply that the illegitimate children living with their mothers did not do worse than children of complete families in comparable social and economic circumstances. Children living with their fathers alone seemed to do less well, but the numbers were too small to be conclusive.

The divorced and remarried

Between 1901 and 1905, the annual average of divorce decrees made absolute in England and Wales was 546. In 1980 there were 148,302. At first sight this suggests a revolutionary trend to instability of marriage. Yet it is obvious that the real source of family disruption is the fact of separation. Whether or not this is followed by legal dissolution of marriage depends on many variable factors which may have little or nothing to do with the state of the family. At the turn of the century, for example, the sole legal ground for divorce was adultery and even this was an insufficient allegation against a husband, against whom some other matrimonial offence had to be established if a wife was to divorce him. As can be seen from Figure 2, the number of divorces granted increased by nearly 50 per cent between 1936 and 1939. But this was due to the liberalization of the divorce law in 1938, when the offences of cruelty, desertion and the supervening insanity of the other spouse were added to adultery as grounds for divorce.[25] A sharp increase in divorces in 1946 clearly reflects a vastly disturbed social situation in the aftermath of war. Thereafter the number of divorces declined until a steep rise in 1952. This was due, however, to a flood of petitions filed the previous year after the coming into operation in October 1950 of the Legal Aid and Advice Act 1949. Thereafter, and throughout the 1950s, the figure declined. However, from 1960 it began to rise rapidly. In 1960 there were 23,369 divorce decrees absolute. In 1970 the figure stood at 47,421. In January 1971 the more liberal divorce law came into operation and the number of decrees absolute of divorce rose from 58,239 in 1970 to 119,025 in 1972. A further large increase occurred

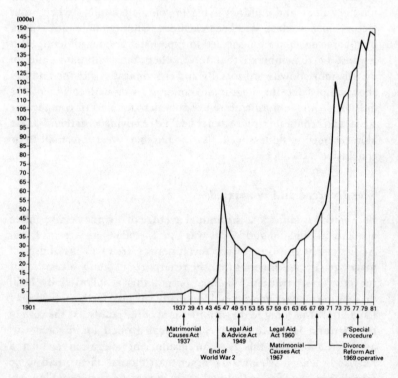

Figure 2 Divorce decrees made absolute: England and Wales, 1901–81

between 1977 (129,053 decrees absolute granted) and 1978 (143,667 decrees absolute granted), reflecting a further change in the divorce procedure in 1977.

There is controversy over the explanation for the rapid rise in divorces, especially after 1960. In particular, it is asked whether legal and administrative changes have simply resulted in the divorce figure now coinciding far more closely with the number of actual marriage breakdowns. The changes include the adjustment of legal aid in 1960 to allow for inflation,[26] the transfer of jurisdiction to grant divorces in undefended cases to the county courts in 1968,[27] the new divorce law of 1971, and the administrative change which, in 1977, introduced divorce without a hearing for undefended cases.[28] The question cannot be adequately answered, if only because it is impossible to know precisely what the actual breakdown rate was before these changes. For example, Gibson (1974) has shown that in 1871 only 17 per cent of petitioners seeking dissolutions under the very restricted divorce laws were manual labourers, although four-fifths of the total population was working class. He demonstrates how lack of means to pursue proceedings for dissolution prevented the legal dissolution of at least 300,000 broken marriages between the wars, and how the proportion of legally-aided petitioners rose on each occasion when important adjustments in the availability of legal aid were made in the period after the Second World War. Other Commonwealth countries also experienced rapid rises in divorce over the same period. In New Zealand the divorces granted rose from 1,755 in 1962 to 4,457 in 1974. The greatest increase was in 1969, when it rose by 38 per cent.[29] This coincides with the liberalization of the divorce law in 1968.[30] Similarly, while the annual average for divorces in Canada was about 11,000 in the period 1966–8, there were 36,704 decrees in 1973, a clear reflection of the reformed divorce law of 1968.[31] The Australian increase has been slower. The relatively minor liberaliz-ation of the divorce law in 1961 introduced by the Matrimonial Causes Act 1959 had no significant effect. But the much more radical reform of January 1976 resulted in an increase in decrees absolute from 24,307 in 1975 to 40,402 in 1976.[32]

While it is now almost certainly true that the divorce rate more faithfully mirrors the actual breakdown rate than it did in the past, it is impossible to attribute these figures entirely, or even mainly, to legal and administrative changes. We have observed earlier the growth in single parent families, mostly female-headed, and its relationship to the growth in divorce. The explosion in divorce has happened in almost all western countries, and it has probably been the growing instability in family life which has led to the changes in divorce law rather than the reverse.[33] As the matter now stands, Leete (1979) has projected that, if the average of the divorce rates experienced in 1974, 1975 and 1976 persist, about 30 per cent of men and women born in 1951, who would have been marrying in the early and mid-1970s, will have divorced by the age of fifty.[34] The prediction in the United States is that some 50 per cent of all current marriages will end in divorce.[35]

Not surprisingly, the growth in divorce has been paralleled by a rise in the number of remarriages, from 16 per cent of all marriages in England and Wales in 1964 to 30 per cent in 1976. The rate is the same in the United States.[36] However, over the period, the *rate of remarriage* (remarriages per thousand divorced persons) has actually fallen, despite a peak in 1972 after the broadening of divorce law in 1971. This is in line with the general decline in marriage rates.[37] A refined study by Leete and Anthony (1979) of persons divorcing in 1973 showed that 55.5 per cent of the men and 48.0 per cent of the women had remarried within four and a half years from the divorce, the proportion falling the older the people were at divorce. Some 60 per cent of those divorcing under thirty had remarried (only a small difference between men and women) but remarriage of women divorcing over the age of thirty reduced more rapidly than in the case of men. Also, about 60 per cent of those who did remarry did so within a year of divorce; after that the rate fell rapidly. Very similar data exist with respect to the United States, where it is estimated that some 80 per cent of divorced persons eventually remarry.[38] The study produced no evidence that the possession of children lessened a woman's chances of remarriage except perhaps for women over forty.

The current population of potential concern for family law would thus seem to be comprised of the following elements. A growing proportion of people in their late teens or early twenties either living singly and experiencing heterosexual relationships or cohabiting without marrying; a large segment of these will marry in their late twenties or early thirties and produce (usually) two children; some will have children without marrying, but whether this will become common outside the Scandinavian countries is as yet unclear; others will continue a childless cohabitation, pursuing separate careers.[39] An important number of women will be living on their own with a child or children, never having married, but they are more likely to be found in the lower socio-economic groups. Similarly prevalent in those groups will be families with children characterized by the informality of the cohabitation between the adults. Moving into the age group above thirty, and under forty, there will be found a significant number of married couples, one or both of whom have experienced prior marriage. Many of them will have been married for the first time before they were twenty-five. They are likely to have children from the previous and present marriage living with them. An (unknown) number of divorcees will be living in a similar manner without having married each other. There will also, however, be a significant number of divorced women living alone with their children, a group which increases in importance in the ages above forty. Predictions are difficult, but it is possible that, if the trend towards the concentration of marriage and childbearing in the late twenties continues, the divorce rate will drop or, at least, be shifted to a later age group.

This, then, is the demographic context in which family law now operates. How the law responds to the needs of the various 'client groups' will be a major theme of this book. But that requires a preliminary consideration of the role of the law in relation to family life.

Purposes of marriage, the family and family law – a functionalist approach

The very formulation of the question 'what are the purposes of marriage and the family?' can be open to the criticism that it accepts the premises of a functionalist approach to social and legal issues. In so far as functionalism accounts for social mechanisms in terms of their relationship to each other and to society as a whole, it has been assailed for distracting attention from questions about individual fulfillment and potentiality and focusing instead on the way social institutions work, thereby giving implicit support to the status quo (how do social mechanisms promote or impede the functioning of the existing social structure?) rather than asking how they may be changed (how do social mechanisms promote or impede individual well-being?).[40] Such criticism of course itself reflects an ideological commitment to explaining social phenomena in terms of (assumed) individual striving rather than of social cohesion. However, a more serious objection to functionalism lies in its tendency to present, or appear to present, social data as if they were quasi-biological truths. The fact that a social institution, such as the family, may be so organized that its female members in fact provide the care of a society's children should not be presented in such a way as to suggest that it is somehow the inherent nature of families (and women) to fulfil that social task, or that it is inevitable that families (and women) perform it. Furthermore, a functionalist account is always prone to attack for selective treatment of alleged functions. Yet, despite these dangers, it is very difficult to avoid reference to goals and purposes when accounting for social phenomena. Indeed, many of the critics of functionalism do this. Observe those Marxists who claim that law is the instrument by which the ruling class maintains power[41] or those feminists who claim that the family is perpetuated to maintain male dominance.[42] Their logic is the same as those who claim that conservative family laws are designed to ensure optimum well-being for society's present and future members. The difference lies only in interpretation of the facts.

Whatever problems there may be in employing a functionalist technique in giving a sociological account of the family and its development, this book is content to adopt a functionalist framework in which to give an account of family law and policy. The potential dangers seem easier to avoid when dealing with law and policy than when describing other social behaviour. The purposes of laws are usually either explicit in their terms, or their formulation preceded or accompanied by extensive discussion. Although the true perception of goals and objectives may be difficult, the attempt to ascertain them cannot be misguided. Where an institution, such as marriage, is heavily overladen with legal rules, it is obvious that the lawmakers, at least, desired the institution to further certain objectives. It is in this sense that I shall talk of the purposes of marriage, of the family, and of family law and policy. They are the purposes held (to greater or lesser degree) by that segment of society in control of its law and policy-making institutions. How far they reflect, or may be reflected by, the population at large is an empirical question the answer to which may or may not be known. However, it is only the framework for the exposition of these matters which is functionally based. It is my intention, in this book, to advance a theory against which the selection and implementation of these functions may be evaluated. The content of the theory will become clear in the course of the exposition. The argument for adopting it will be briefly made at the end of this chapter. Before doing that it is necessary to give a short account of the development of the family, and of attitudes towards it, in recent history.

The changing nature of the family

Glendon (1977) has fully described the revolution in the relationship between law and marriage from the complex and restrictive system developed from the sixteenth to the nineteenth centuries to the relatively simple and open system of today. In pre-industrial societies, political power and economic wealth tend to be regulated through concepts of status. Marriage becomes a crucial link in determining the status both of spouse and children. The concept of legitimacy, therefore, provides a method whereby wealth and political power develop in a relatively orderly fashion.[43]

This system facilitated the accumulation of property and power within recognised groups. It was a combination of marriage alliances and rules of inheritance which enabled the great landed families of England to retain and increase their possessions. Before marriage was entered, a strict settlement might be made which ensured, generally, that the property would pass intact to the eldest son of the marriage. The settlement would provide that, although the real estate would pass to the eldest son on the husband's death, income should be paid to the widow, charged on the property, and capital sums should be paid to the younger sons. Since capital was not always available from which these payments might be made, it might have to be borrowed on the security of the estate. The land, still intact, would become heavily encumbered, so it became desirable, when marrying, to receive capital sums from the wife's family to offset this. These sums were called portions, and were often large enough to enable yet more land to be acquired. The wife's family might have to pay considerably for her marriage into the landed aristocracy and, indeed, it was highly desirable for an heir to marry a woman from a wealthy family. If she happened to be an heiress, this was greatly to her advantage, as land would then be concentrated in still fewer hands. It has been estimated that, in the middle of the eighteenth century, about half the land in England was held on strict settlement.[44] Arranged marriages were therefore frequent and Stone (1960–1) comments that often the parties were practically strangers on their wedding day.

An outstanding feature of family and kinship systems is the subordination of the individual's desires and interests to the requirements of his role. They might not be ignored, but they would not be considered of primary importance. The illegitimate child is clearly a threat to the smooth operation of the system and therefore legal rules would discriminate against him, especially in matters of succession. Wills and instruments referring to 'children' would be presumed to refer only to legitimate children. Strictly, at common law, the illegitimate child was *filius nullius* (son of no one) and had no rights against his parents or they against (or to) him. Social and personal discrimination against illegitimate children is another matter, and need not necessarily accompany legal discrimination. In medieval England, contrary to the contemporary practice in Europe, the illegitimately born did not lose their civil rights. Legal discrimination was mainly confined to matters of succession.[45]

The personal aspirations of adults might equally be subjected to the postulates of a kinship system. Marriage and even divorce, if permitted, might require the agreement of the kin groups, which could be subject to strict terms. But it is on the woman that these systems bore the hardest. Sexual escape from an unhappy marriage, often institutionalized for husbands by a mistress system or prostitution, would be denied to her by reason of her economic dependence and rigorous laws imposing dual standards of marital behaviour. His adultery would be no less distressing than hers, but, since her infidelity might introduce spurious offspring into the family and accordingly upset the smooth operation of the lineage system, it would be regarded with considerably greater abhorrence. When judicial divorce was first introduced in England in 1858,[46] the husband was permitted to divorce his wife on the sole ground of her adultery, whereas a wife would succeed against an adulterous husband only if she could prove additional misbehaviour such as cruelty or desertion. This duality was removed only in 1923.[47]

The relationship between legal regulation of marriage and the ordering of property is so clear that it may be wondered whether family law at that time had any relevance for the impoverished mass of the population. Indeed, it had little. So little, in fact, that Lord Hardwicke's Marriage Act of 1753, which required all marriages (with few exceptions) entered into in England to be contracted in accordance with the rites of the Church of England preceded by notice *in writing* by the parties, and with the parental consent of people under twenty-one, was openly concerned only with protecting propertied classes against the danger that their heirs might secretly marry 'unsuitable' women (thereby jeopardizing the chances of consolidating alliances beneficial to the future of the estate) and showed no regard to the obstacles it created to the marriages of the illiterate poor. Henry Fox commented at the time that the Act would virtually put an end to marriage among the poor 'lest the daughter of a noble or rich family should marry a footman or sharper or the son of a chamber maid or a common strumpet.'[48] Thus the matter stood until the introduction of civil marriage in 1816.[49] Parliamentary divorce always, and judicial divorce when introduced, were beyond the reach of the bulk of society. O'Donovan (1982) has shown that the poor sometimes resorted to wife-sale, which was (wrongly) believed to be legally effective, as a means of terminating their marriages. Their family lives only became relevant for legal purposes when an individual became dependent on public support. The Poor Relief Act of 1601 provided that the father, mother, grandmother and children of any poor person not being able to work should be obliged to maintain such poor person at such rate as a justice should appoint. This 'obligation', perceived to exist among blood relations, was later extended, first to encompass a man's wife[50] and then to include any children she might have when he married her.[51] But it was not an obligation the law provided any means of enforcing unless public funds were threatened.[52]

This brief sketch of pre-twentieth-century family law illustrates how the family can be utilized to further wider social ends. It does not seek to *explain* the conjugal family (and woman's subordinate role within it), as Engels (1884) did, in terms of that policy, namely as the instrument of perpetuating private property and, therefore, capitalism. Rather, it observes simply that the norms, and sometimes the structure, of family life can be influenced and directed to serve the perceived goals of legal and social policy. Donzelot's (1980) description of nineteenth-century French family policy shows this process in action. Again, it was fear of cost to the public purse by a proliferation of illegitimate births which impelled the movement to 'restore marriage' among the working classes. But what would a working man receive in return for his assumption of marital responsibilities? A good housewife and attentive mother for his children. Liberal society sought to achieve these behaviour patterns (which would also keep the children off the street) by philanthropic provision designed to encourage the instillation of the relevant moral and economic virtues. Failure by a family to meet these values justified surveillance projecting deep into the family's life.

The political and economic changes of the late nineteenth and early twentieth centuries have destroyed the kinship network as a means of distributing power and wealth. This has led to a general confusion, at least in western societies, about what the state's attitude to the family should be. This has, perhaps, not been helped by the tendency of some family sociologists to express the matter in terms of changes within the family itself rather than in terms of state policy towards families. Hence, Parsons and Bales (1955) concluded that the modern American family now fulfilled two purposes. One was the 'primary socialization of the children', the other was the 'stabilization of the adult personalities of the population'. Within this context, the woman played the 'expressive' role inside the family, the man, the 'instrumental' role outside it. Much emphasis was placed on the relative isolation of the 'nuclear' family from extended family members. At about the same time, the views of Bowlby (1951) on the crucial significance of the mother's role in the upbringing of children were widely promoted. These functions might be seen as arising, as it were, naturally to replace those of the kinship family and as an 'inevitable' consequence of the new economic organization of society. Hence, Parson's assertion that the restriction of women to the home is society's 'solution' to the *need* to separate family-based relationships from the competitive world of career pursuit and that there is little scope to change this. Americans, he wrote, 'by their commitment to a particular type of general society are automatically committed in broad terms to the appropriate family type. Their dedication must be to making this work if it is at all possible; there is no other course.'[53]

In so far as it purports to be a description of the modern American family, this model is of course open to empirical verification, modification or rejection. It seems to be more an idealized picture of the middle-class family than an accurate account of family life in general in western countries, even at the time.[54] More importantly, it fails to recognize that the picture may represent simply the result of one ideological view of how the family *should* function in the modern world. Seemingly, perhaps oddly, to accept that representation as a true one of the modern family, some critics have concluded that the family is therefore an undesirable social institution. The major critique has come from the radical feminist movement. Heavily

influenced by Marxist theory, it is claimed either that the oppression
of women is intimately related with the capitalist system and will
disappear only with the advent of true socialism,[55] or that women
themselves form an oppressed 'class' whose liberation can be
achieved only by the overthrow of male domination and the
institution of a sexless society.[56] In either case, the family is seen as a
key institution maintaining the perpetuation of the dominant system
(capitalism/patriarchy). 'The causal chain then goes: Maternity,
Family, Absence from Production and Public Life, Sexual Inequality.
The lynch-pin in this line of argument is the idea of the family.'[57] It is
easy to see why the family, at least in the form described by Parsons
and Bales, would be viewed with such hostility. With her major role
confined within this tiny unit, a woman is thereby effectively excluded
from the real sources of political, social or economic power. Since the
family (thus described) and a woman's place within it are often
represented as part of the 'natural' order of things, it is a central
concern of the feminist writers to show that this state of affairs is a part
of social organization and therefore capable of change. One of the
major difficulties facing family law and policy is to know to what
extent such change can be achieved in terms of its implications for
other aspects of social and economic ordering.

The irreducible biological minimum of all human societies is that
women bear children and that young children require an extended
period of nurture and socialization. It has been surmised that the
reason why greater importance is attached to the mother–child
relationship in man than in other primates is the relative weakness of
the human infant at birth. The child's large brain requires its birth
before its body has matured to self-sufficiency.[58] Indeed Fox (1967)
sees the basic family unit as being that of mother and child. But the
mother's commitment to child-rearing in the infant's early days leads
to a tendency to a conjugal link with a male provider of varying
degrees of stability and permanence in different cultures, but usually
for the period necessary for the rearing of the infant. There is,
however, no necessary reason why the child-rearing function should
be provided by the biological mother, or even by women. Among the
Manus of the Admiralty Islands much of it was in fact done by
men.[59] Nevertheless, in most societies this task has been fulfilled by
women. In view of the particularly unique involvement of women in
childbirth and (until recent times) their constant exposure to
pregnancy, this is hardly surprising.

Even societies committed to radical social change have been unable to alter that pattern significantly. In the Soviet Union the hope of the early communists was to weaken family ties and promote equality in sexual roles. The Code of Marriage, Divorce, Family and Guardianship of November 1926 allowed either spouse to escape marriage by single application to a Registrar's Office. There was a reciprocal obligation to support for one year after the dissolution if a divorced spouse was in need and unable to work. Property acquired during cohabitation would be equally divided. Nor was it necessary to enter into formal marriage. These provisions applied to *de facto* cohabitations, a move which was thought necessary to protect women from persons taking advantage of the sexual freedom of the times. There are striking similarities between these laws and the position into which modern western family law is moving. And the difficulties into which they led are reminiscent of some of the most pressing problems faced today. The Soviet reversal of policy in 1936 is well known. Abortion, made free under the initial reforms, was severely restricted. Penalties for avoidance of family maintenance obligations were strengthened and divorce registration fees were increased. The Family Law of July 1944 restored state supervision over entering marriage and put formidable obstacles in the way of divorce.

In a totalitarian state, when policies (and information) are dictated more by demands of party ideology than social realities, it is difficult to discover the true reasons for the abandonment of the policy. But three major factors may be suggested. Firstly, 'the communal housekeeping and creches simply did not materialise'[60] and those that did must have failed to provide adequate child-care facilities, for anxiety seems to have been caused by reports that serious retardation had been discovered in children reared in state institutions.[61] Secondly, the downward turn in the population growth must have caused concern in view of the menace of Nazi Germany.[62] Thirdly, the emphasis upon honouring family maintenance obligations seems to reflect concern that the cost of supporting families was becoming excessive for the state. A very similar progression of events has been recorded in the People's Republic of China,[63] Hungary[64] and Czechoslovakia.[65] The case of the Israeli kibbutzim is a special one. Unlike a nation-state, these are small communities offering unique opportunities for communal child-caring and provision of domestic facilities. However, even then, great care is taken to respect the parent–child relationship and 'familistic' tendencies are reported to be increasing.[66]

These experiences suggest that the resilience of family living *in some form* may be related to its role in the provision of the early care and socialization of children, the promotion of population growth and the mutual economic support of its members. In so far as families may perform inadequately in any of these areas, criticism will always raise problems relating to the proper ambit of state intrusion into private, family life. R. D. Laing's (1971) account of personality development within the family sees the family as a hierarchical structure, founded on fear, by which the older generation indoctrinates the new with its own values and images of reality. A child perceives the world and himself through the eyes of his family. Parents, Laing says, do not so much instruct the child about what to *do*, but 'hypnotize' him into believing what kind of person he *is*. 'One is, say, told one *is* a good or bad boy or girl, not only instructed *to be* a good or bad boy or girl.'[67] This analysis can provide valuable insight into pathological situations (Laing was concerned with understanding schizophrenia), but it is hard to evaluate its force as an overall assessment of family functioning. While it is no doubt true that images of reality are received during primary socialization, it is not clear that this would be any less so if the instrument of socialization were other than the family. The issue would then involve the values of individual liberty inherent in any attempt to replace family autonomy by state-directed alternatives, a question to which we shall return in discussing child abuse and neglect. Since this issue is not confronted by Laing, the critique leads to the extreme position that *any* impositions on the personalities of new members of society cause illegitimate distortions of their free development. Cooper (1971) develops this position, and it is also to be found in Illich's (1971) attack on restraining influences found in institutional systems. The full implications of this fundamentally anarchical position fall outside the scope of this discussion and, although its influence has been quite strong, especially in education theory,[68] it is unlikely to gain wide support in its radical form. More probably it will simply add weight to the side of individualism in the tension that has always existed between the restraints demanded by society and the claims of individual liberty.

On the question of population, it can be argued that, as concern has shifted from under- to over-population, the family structure is unsuitable because the state cannot adequately control fertility within the family.[69] But this issue even more obviously confronts libertarian values. As for the economic role of the family, while it may be argued that support obligations are notoriously difficult to enforce and that therefore the state is coming to view its members solely as individuals as far as economic entitlements are concerned,[70] it remains true that the state also continues to recognize the significance of the diffusion of benefits received by one or more individuals in favour of their family numbers and that the adults can frequently be considered as dealing with the outside world as 'agents' for their children.

It is clearly not difficult to point to other inadequacies, or 'contradictions', in family living in the modern world. Morgan (1975) mentions three: that a child's socialization is meant to prepare him for life *outside* his family, yet it is done within the family leading to an abrupt transition from family to outside world; that marriage is supposed to be based on love, yet is also thought to impose a duty on spouses to remain together to bring up their children; that a woman's expectations may conflict with her role in the home. Yet the problem of child care and women's relationship to it remain. From this, it appears, most other complexities and dilemmas flow. Adults, for their own purposes, may cohabit or marry. How far their relationships, in themselves, should have legal significance is currently a matter of much debate. The growing social and economic emancipation of women has meant that, when adults enter into heterosexual relationships, the woman is less likely than formerly to be undertaking a quasi-servant role towards her husband. The basis of legally controlling such relationships, or intervening after their termination, is problematical. But when a child is born, a whole complex of problems arise which have social, economic and legal implications. These must now be considered the major concern of family law. For, whatever may be its shortcomings, it is likely that the family will remain the major instrument through which society transmits its values, culture and achievements to the next generation. And perhaps, in view of the criticisms that have been made of the family as the means of doing this, it might be speculated that any impetus mankind may have to concern itself with the fate of its future generations, may lie solely in the emotional bonds generated in families between its older and younger members.[71]

The role of the law

The interaction between the law and the various styles of family living prevalent today forms the subject matter of the following chapters. In making the exposition I have assumed a threefold division corresponding to what I perceive to be the major grounds for modern state intervention in family living. The first is to provide mechanisms and rules for *adjusting* the relationships between family members when family units break down. The second is to provide *protection* for individuals from possible harms suffered within the family. The third is to *support* the maintenance of family relationships.

This classification is stated here without full justification. But it is hoped that the evidence which follows will provide sufficient grounds to uphold it. The first two functions require no further explanation. I maintain that it is empirically true that the major thrust of much modern family law is directed at those ends and that this reflects a major shift in the purposive relationship between law and family living from earlier times. There is considerable uncertainty over the extent to which the state should concern itself with the promotion of family ties. Nevertheless, as we shall see, the family remains a unit in both social and economic terms which a state can, in differing degrees and for differing purposes, recognize and exploit. The consideration of this raises a series of complex and interrelated problems.

The preceding account of the development of the family in modern times stressed the centrality of the problem of child care. The evidence presented in the following pages will underscore this. The ideology western societies hold with respect to family living and their economic structure combine to perpetuate the family as the major institution within which children, especially very young children, are reared. But the perceived ideological and economic gains of delegating the task of nurturing the new generation to families must be offset against the inequalities and instability of the family system. Within some families, children may be badly brought up. Other families will disintegrate. The theory to be advanced in this book is that all children have an equal *prima facie* claim against the present adult world for optimal conditions of upbringing compatible with society's fundamental economic and ideological structure. It follows that the major (but not sole) criteria of evaluation of the three functions of modern family law delineated above will be child-centred. This is not to confine the evaluation to the concerns of the child itself, for a child-centred approach will also consider the interests of adults who have themselves contributed to the care of the child. The theory, baldly stated here, will be refined and developed in the course of the exposition.

2
Divorce: Law and Social Change

Divorce and social change

We have seen that, *if the present divorce rate continues*, some 30 per cent of people marrying in England in the mid-1970s and 50 per cent of people marrying in the United States will have been divorced at least once by the time they reach fifty. In these circumstances, the assumption that marriage is a lifelong union clearly cannot hold. However, it is probably true that a majority of people marrying expect, or at least hope, that their marriage will last a lifetime. Roussel and Bourgignon's (1978) study of cohabitees in France showed that a major reason for living together *without marriage* was the wish of one or both parties to retain the option to terminate the union. By implication, then, marriage is seen as involving a commitment to permanency, and a British National Opinion Poll Survey conducted in 1980 showed that 87 per cent of divorcees had indeed expected their marriages to last for ever.[1] Despite the frequency of divorce, when people do divorce, things are still seen to have 'gone wrong'. Apart from the financial consequences (which will be considered in detail later), divorce remains for most adults a severely traumatic experience. It might be considered that this is no or little more than what can occur at the conclusion of any emotional relationship, and clearly in some cases this must be true. But there is reason to believe that, in the case of marriage breakdown, the stresses are usually greater. A number of studies have shown a marked association between marital disruption and physical and emotional disorder.[2]

How far such disorders precede, and therefore cause, marital disruption and how far they are precipitated by the breakdown, is not clearly established.[3] Particular caution should be taken with regard to studies showing a high incidence of divorcees among clinical patients, for this may simply be an artefact of a low incidence of remarriage by those divorcees who experience ill health. Nevertheless a linkage between unusual stress and cessation of marital relationships seems undeniable. The effects on the children are as yet imperfectly known, but cannot be considered minimal. They will be considered in chapter 4. So long as these persist, divorce, despite its frequency, can only be regarded as a pathological event, especially where children are involved.

Why, then, does divorce occur? Demographic data can provide clues, but probably not final explanations. It has been suggested that there may be an association between pre-marital pregnancy and proneness to separation and divorce,[4] but more recently an American study by Moore and Waite (1981) has indicated that the mere fact of pregnancy and childbearing at an early age is not *in itself* associated with increased risk of marital instability. Difficulty arises because the proportion of pregnant brides is much higher for girls marrying under twenty than in other age groups and, since youthful marriages are without doubt particularly vulnerable to disruption, it may be the age factor rather than the fact of pregnancy which disposes towards subsequent instability.

The extent of the association between divorce and youthful marriage is indeed remarkable. The prediction that 30 per cent of persons marrying in England and Wales in the mid-1970s will divorce by the age of fifty, at current rates, expands to 50 per cent when confined to marriages where the bride was under twenty. The divorces granted in 1976 in England and Wales dissolved 2.6 per cent of all marriages taking place from 1965 to 1969 where the bride was under twenty at marriage, compared to 1.5 per cent where she was between twenty and twenty-four, 1.3 per cent where she was between twenty-five and twenty-nine and 0.9 per cent where she was over thirty. The same pattern is repeated with respect to marriages which took place between 1970 and 1974.[5] Thornes and Collard (1979), comparing a large sample of divorced and currently married couples, found a strong association between teenage marriage and the fact of divorce.[6] In the United States, too, it has been shown that women marrying between fourteen and seventeen are twice as likely to divorce than women marrying at eighteen and nineteen and three times as likely as women marrying between twenty and twenty-four.[7] In his Michigan sample of divorced women with children, Chambers (1979) found that 27 per cent of the men and 61 per cent of the women had married under eighteen, compared to percentages of 8 and 29 respectively marrying under that age in the state as a whole.

Yet, decisive though this data is, other factors also appear to play a part in conducing towards marriage breakdown. Both in the United States and in England,[8] higher rates of marital disruption have been found among the lower income-earning sections of the population. But this may partly be a function of the tendency to younger marriages among these groups. Other factors found to be associated with divorce proneness were lower educational attainment[9] and childlessness of the union.[10] In Canada, it has been suggested that divorce is particularly prevalent in areas of high immigrant concentration (suggesting that possible weakening of extended kin ties can destabilize marriages) and where the proportion of women who are university educated and participate in the work-force is highest.[11] As far as remarriage is concerned, statistical data indicate higher instability in these unions than in first marriages,[12] and American research suggests that, in those remarriages which succeed, the parties, especially the women, report a somewhat lower level of happiness than never-divorced people, but that the difference is not great.[13]

It has often been remarked that the emancipation of women from childbearing and their increasing life expectancy as the twentieth century progressed has meant that marriages are now 'at risk' of breakdown for a far longer period than previously.[14] In the United States divorce has replaced death as the predominant mode of termination of first marriages.[15] Yet, it cannot be the increased risk factor alone which accounts for the modern divorce rate, for the significant increases began after the Second World War rather than at the turn of the century. Furthermore, the tendency has been for marriages to break down earlier than formerly, especially if the parties married young. Between 1964 and 1976 the divorce rate per thousand married women under forty-five in England and Wales rose by some 300 per cent after four years of marriage but by some 200 per cent after sixteen years of marriage;[16] and the divorce rate is currently highest (2.1 per cent of married persons) in the age group twenty-five to twenty-nine. Chester (1971a) also found that youthful marriages were particularly highly represented in cases where the marriages broke down within two years of the wedding.

This broad survey reveals a general picture of a peculiar vulner-ability of marriages entered into in the 1960s and 1970s by particularly young people with a heavy concentration in the working class. Is there any connection between the drop in the marriage age and the subsequent explosion in divorce? It has been argued that in the United States the marriage behaviour of the immediate post-war generation had been influenced by their childhood experiences during the depression years where they acquired unusually early exposure to adult problems, disposing them to early marriage. Thereafter, from the 1960s, the more normal pattern of marrying later resumed but was accompanied by a range of social and attitudinal changes (in particular, greater economic independence of women) which have enhanced the incidence of divorce.[17] The picture in Britain may not, however, be completely comparable. While it is true that the age of marriage began dropping throughout the 1950s, the decline extended through to the early 1970s. The young people marrying in this period will have been born in the 1940s and have reached adulthood during the era of social iconoclasm, ethical revisionism and instability of family (and other) authority associated with the 1960s. It can be suggested that, while the growing popularity of marriage during the twentieth century reflected the dominance of affective relationships over the older style of marriage, the emphasis on sexual freedom and the disillusion with conventional morality characteristic of the 1960s had a double effect. On the one hand, we see the escalation of out-of-wedlock births. On the other, for those on whom conventional morality and social pressure retained sufficient hold, the resolution of the conflict by early marriage (frequently following pre-nuptial pregnancy). The instability of this compromise is well captured by Gill:

> Sexual behaviour is seen to be a much more important part of a marital relationship than was previously the case and an ability to perform skilfully and knowledgeably during intercourse has become a prerequisite for sexual compatibility. The essential contradiction in these conflicting objectives is only too apparent. At the marriage ceremony the young people were expected to be virgins, but within twelve hours they are required to perform like trained and conditioned sexual athletes.[18]

It seems unassailable that changed expectations and the improved economic position and social mobility[19] of women have promoted divorce. But it is no less likely that the moral uncertainties following in the wake of the Second World War created a generation of unusually divorce-prone marriages and that this, too, is reflected in the high divorce rates of the 1970s and early 1980s. Behavioural adjustments, in particular the postponement of marriage described above,[20] may, in the longer term, lead to an eventual reduction of marriage breakdown.

The law and social change

The response of legal policy to these changes has been as confusing as the changes themselves. They have brought about radical reviews of the divorce law of almost all European countries, but no clear consensus about what the role of the law and the legal process should be.[21] Should the law simply reflect these social changes? Should it attempt to guide or even arrest their development? How far may the aspirations of individuals be denied for the sake of a perceived social good? What, indeed, is the best outcome for society? At one time, the answer would have been in the unequivocal language of Sir William Scott in an ecclesiastical court:

When people understand that they must live together, except for the very few reasons known to the law, they learn to soften by mutual accommodation that yoke which they know they cannot shake off; they become good husbands and good wives, from the necessity of remaining good husbands and wives; for necessity is a powerful master in teaching the duties which it imposes. If it were once understood, that upon mutual disgust married persons might be legally separated, many couples, who now pass through the world in mutual comfort, with attention to their common offspring and the moral order of civil society, might have been at this moment living in a state of mutual unkindness – and in a state of most licentious and unreserved immorality. In this case, as in many others, the happiness of some individuals must be sacrificed to the more general good.[22]

Nine members of the Royal Commission on Marriage and Divorce, which reported in 1956, took the same view. Divorce should be restricted to cases where one spouse had committed a matrimonial offence against the other since this 'makes for security in marriage because husbands and wives know that they cannot be divorced unless they have committed one of the matrimonial offences which is a ground for divorce'.[23]

Rheinstein's (1972) survey of the post-war development of divorce laws showed how the matrimonial offence basis of western divorce law had become undermined by collusive and interpretative devices leading to what he termed a 'democratic compromise' between conservative majoritarian support for the offence doctrine and liberal pressure for greater freedom of divorce. Indeed, in England these practices had become so widespread that in 1965 Lord Devlin wrote:

> All who desire their freedom from the [marriage] bond must pass out of the hall of judgement. At the main gateway there stand custodians and there is exhibited a schedule of conditions under which permission is granted to leave. But the back door is unlocked and unguarded. Every now and again someone is caught sneaking out and is hustled in again with cries of disapproval.[24]

Rheinstein's conclusion was that restrictive divorce law was an inappropriate method of controlling the upswing of divorce. Instead he advocated the expansion of pre-marital counselling services.[25] More recently the conservative case has been restated by Gorecki (1980), who particularly criticizes the trend in modern divorce laws to abolish the defence of 'recrimination' whereby a party would have a veto to the granting of divorce on the ground that the breakdown of the marriage was substantially caused by the fault of the other person:

> Those who are unilaterally guilty of disrupting their marriages, in particular if the amount of the guilt is great, should be punished, not rewarded for what they did. Their punishment conveys a message to the general society: minimum of responsibility is anyone's family obligation, and so is an effort to avoid inflicting suffering on one's spouse and children, and wrecking their lives. This message, if properly conveyed in the process of instrumental learning, may not but influence general attitudes and may eventually bring about . . . decline of the total sum of suffering and decrease of the broader social problems generated by widespread family disintegration.

This position, however, suffers from weaknesses both in particular detail and general perspective. It is by no means clear how a denial of divorce to the guilty party would (in most cases) benefit the 'deserted' spouse. Such a party would, of course, be disabled from entering another legitimate union, but cannot be prevented from cohabiting and procreating other children. At most, his 'obligations' to his prior family can be enforced against him by property and support orders. But, as we will see, and Gorecki concedes, these are not very effective whether or not he remarries. Furthermore, if he does form a new family, crucial issues concerning the respective economic claims of members of both families remain unresolved. Nor does it seem that to allow the 'defence' of recrimination would affect more than a minute number of cases. Even when divorce laws were firmly rooted in the matrimonial offence doctrine, it was commonplace that the divorce issue (as distinct from custody or financial matters) was rarely contested or, if it was, this was usually to decide in whose favour it should be granted. Even today, when (as will be seen) the economic consequences of divorce strike women harder than men, the majority of petitioners are women.[26] Few people seem to see any reason to resist divorce if the marriage has truly broken down. But even if the defence of recrimination were available, its provision would meet what would be, for some, the insuperable objection that the task of assessing relative innocence and guilt between estranged spouses is not one which a court of law can properly, or should ethically, undertake. The psychological complexity of a marriage relationship can be difficult enough even for psychiatrists, and sometimes the parties themselves, to understand: to expect a judge in a formal court setting to grasp the subtleties of a process of marital breakdown and to assess them against some (unspecifiable) standard is to ask the impossible.

On the broader level, Gorecki's opinion makes certain assumptions about the relationship between law and intimate social behaviour which are difficult to sustain. The undermining of the matrimonial offence doctrine, described by Rheinstein (1972), showed how unstable a legal doctrine can become when faced with profound social change. Duncan (1980) has described how the Republic of Ireland, where divorce is prohibited, also faces the problem of marital disruption and evasion of the civil law. The unfolding of marriage behaviour in England and Wales over the last twenty years may provide a revealing lesson. In 1967 the Latey Committee[27] recommended that the age until which a person needed parental consent to his or her marriage should be reduced from twenty-one to eighteen years because it was thought that it was parental persuasion, not legal sanction, which affected the eventual decision whether or not to marry. In view of the steady increase in teenage marriages at that time, and their recognized instability, this author was among those who regretted the implementation of the recommendation in 1970.[28] As Table 1 (on page 5) shows, the reform was indeed immediately followed by a sharp upturn in these marriages. But thereafter, and throughout the 1970s, the rate declined to well below the figure it was before the reform.

One cannot of course overlook the hardships laws can inflict on some people and the advantages they can bring to others. But care must be taken not to exaggerate the influence individual laws have on social behaviour, especially when the laws are isolated and do not form part of integrated programmes with visible economic impact. The irrelevance of family law to the poor classes in Europe and to much of the black population in the United States, attests to this.[29] The change in marriage patterns suggests that people are in the process of working out for themselves a system of sexual relationships and family living which best corresponds to the social and economic needs of contemporary life. Since it seems that marriage is likely to be increasingly associated with establishing a family, the proportion of divorces involving children is likely to grow. If this is true, we can argue that the divorce process should be *primarily* designed to deal with the breakdown of marriages with children. It has even been suggested that provision should be made for two kinds of marriage, one for couples with and the other for couples without children; the former would be easily terminable, the other a 'much more binding commitment of at least 10 or 15 years'.[30] It is unlikely, however, that the objections to 'strict' divorce outlined above could be overcome, even in cases where there are children. The primary need is for children to be conceived mainly in marriages which are likely to be stable; this, it seems, may slowly be being achieved. The primary purpose of the divorce process therefore should be to provide a mechanism to plan for the best future for the children of those families which break down, once all hope of reconciliation is exhausted. We will look critically at the current divorce process to see how far it is ready to serve this end.

These conclusions are premised upon the likelihood of the survival of marriage as the framework within which most people will wish to procreate and raise children. Apart from Denmark and Sweden, and certain social sub-groups elsewhere, this presently seems a reasonable supposition. But it is important not to tie the benefits of the divorce process to families constituted within the formal marriage framework. A child-centred approach to the problems of family dissolution should be of equal value whether the adult parties live inside or outside marriage. But this point raises issues pertinent to the whole question of legal recognition of unmarried cohabitation, which will be dealt with in a later chapter.

PART TWO: LAW AND ADJUSTMENT

3
Divorce: Law and Process

The law

(a) *Modern evolution*

At the time of divorce, the legal system, and the parties, can use the occasion to survey the history of the marriage, to weigh and evaluate the contributions made to it by each spouse and to arrive at a final balance sheet. They can also look forward, anticipate the needs which the parties and their children are likely to face in the new circumstances in which they find themselves and construct a plan for the future. The first approach may be called the method of justice, the second the manner of welfare. While it is probably not possible to adopt one approach to the exclusion of the other, at many points they will be incompatible and a divorce system may accordingly be seen to incline more to the one than to the other.

The matrimonial offence system, on which the English law of judicial divorce was based, was almost entirely backward-looking. Divorce was granted to give relief when wrong was done. Various doctrines were elaborated to ensure that the successful party was 'innocent' and the other was 'guilty'. They should not have colluded in presenting their case; the offence complained of should have been neither encouraged ('connived') nor forgiven ('condoned') by the petitioner. Nor should the petitioner have been equally to blame for bringing about the collapse of the marriage ('recrimination').[1] In addition, courts retained a discretionary power to refuse relief to a petitioner whose behaviour, in their view, disentitled him or her to the indulgence of a divorce decree. So in a case in 1966 the Court of

Appeal held that a judge had been 'plainly right' to refuse to grant a decree to a man who had shown 'disrespect' for the married state by having sexual relations with a number of women after his wife had left him a second time.[2]

Yet even in the 1930s the exclusive attention paid to past wrongs was modified by concern for a spouse's future when divorce was allowed in England and Wales[3] and in Scotland[4] on the ground of the incurable insanity of the other spouse. This departure was justified in the Morton Report (1956) as being a very exceptional case where the hardship on the petitioner was so great that divorce should be allowed. Yet in the Commonwealth a more significant deviation from the offence principle had occurred. In 1920 it was enacted in New Zealand that 'it shall be lawful for the Court, in its discretion, on the petition of either of the parties to a decree of judicial separation, or a separation order or an agreement of separation or separation by mutual consent, when [that order, decree or agreement] is full force and has so continued for not less than three years, to pronounce a decree of divorce'.[5] Thus consent, far from being a bar to divorce, as taught by the classic doctrines of collusion and desertion, now became an integral part of the ground itself. It was not a *sufficient* condition, however, for the parties must also have remained separate for three years. Furthermore, the court retained a discretion whether or not to grant the decree. But its width was illustrated by a decision of the New Zealand Court of Appeal that a court could grant a divorce under its terms to a husband petitioner against whom maintenance and separation orders had been obtained by the wife. The fact that he may have caused the breakdown of the marriage was not necessarily a bar because 'the policy underlying the legislation is that it is not conducive to the public interest that men and women should remain bound together in permanence by bonds of a marriage the duties of which have long ceased to be observed by either party and the purposes of which have irremediably failed. Such a condition in law which is no marriage in fact leads only to immorality and un-happiness. . . .'[6] Anticipating an argument that was to be developed many years later by Devlin (1965), the Court observed that a divorce decree operated both to dissolve the obligations of the first marriage and also to permit either party to remarry. The discretion to refuse the decree should be exercised only where one party had behaved in such a way that it might not be safe to allow him to remarry. This preference for concern for future welfare over justice was short-lived and in 1922 the New Zealand legislature passed an amending Act stating that, when the ground was used and the respondent opposed the decree, the court must dismiss the petition if it were proved that the separation was due to the wrongful act or conduct of the petitioner.[7] This defence prevented the granting of divorce on the unilateral application of one of the spouses, at any rate, without some kind of inquiry being made into questions of blame if the other spouse desired this. But it left untouched the fundamental principle that parties could agree to terminate their marriage and openly plan for the future and that this in itself, if the position remained unchanged for a period of time, was good reason to allow dissolution.

(b) Dual systems

The attractiveness of the separation ground led to a number of jurisdictions adopting what may be described as a 'dual' system of divorce. On the one hand, the matrimonial offences were retained, sometimes enumerated in great detail. On the other, the parties were free to choose the separation ground. South Australia (1938)[8] and Western Australia (1945)[9] were the first Australian states to introduce a separation ground into their divorce law. When a uniform divorce law was enacted in Australia in 1959, the dual system was adopted. In this case, however, no distinction was drawn between consensual separations, separations sanctioned by court orders and unilateral separations. The parties must simply have 'separated and thereafter lived separately and apart for a continuous period of not less than five years immediately preceding the date of the petition', without any reasonable likelihood of cohabitation being resumed.[10] Since this appeared to open the way to unilateral divorce after the effluxion of the required period, a 'safeguard' was inserted which required the courts to refuse a decree where it was satisfied that, by reason of the conduct of the petitioner, whether before or after the separation commenced or for any other reason, it would be 'harsh and oppressive' to the respondent or 'contrary to the public interest' to grant the decree. Further, where the court felt that the petitioner should make financial provision for the respondent, it should decline to grant the decree until these arrangements had been made.[11]

Canada, too, opted for a dual system when the first federal divorce law was enacted in 1968.[12] So clearly is this conceived of as a dual system that the grounds based on the offence doctrine are set out in one section[13] and those reflecting the breakdown of the marriage in another.[14] Four types of offence are specified: (a) adultery; (b) sodomy, bestiality, rape or the commission of a homosexual act; (c) bigamy; (d) physical or mental cruelty. Section 4 enumerates a number of events all linked to actual separation between the parties for certain time periods, which would be indicative of marriage breakdown but do not necessarily arise out of the respondent's blameworthy conduct. They include alcoholic and narcotic addiction lasting three years, non-consummation of the marriage due to disability or refusal, and separation. They also, however, include situations where the respondent is imprisoned and where he disappears. Separation without any additional factor allows a decree to be granted after the parties have been living 'separate and apart' for three years, but, if the petitioner has been in desertion, the period is to be five years. The court must, however, dismiss the petition if granting the decree would be 'unduly harsh or unjust to either spouse' or would prejudicially affect the making of reasonable arrangements for maintenance as may be necessary for either spouse or the children.[15] New Zealand also operated a dual system until October 1981.

When considering how the English divorce law should be reformed, the Law Commission (1966) leaned in favour of a dual system. It rejected a proposal made in a Report of a group appointed by the Archbishop of Canterbury[16] that the courts should conduct an inquest into marriages to ascertain whether they had in fact broken down. The Law Commission considered this to be impracticable. If breakdown were to be the sole ground, the necessary evidence must be that the parties had in fact separated. But the Law Commission did not think it possible to find an appropriate period. If the time chosen were short, it would not constitute sufficient evidence of the irreparability of the breakdown; if it were long, it would impose an 'intolerable hardship' in those cases of truly outrageous conduct which justified divorce with 'reasonable dispatch'. Therefore they favoured adding a separation ground to the existing offences. Parliament, however, chose to recast the law in a different form. Irretrievable breakdown of marriage was to be the sole ground for divorce. However, its proof was to be limited to the establishment of a number of circumstances which were enumerated in the following manner:

> The court hearing the petition for divorce shall not hold the marriage to have broken down irretrievably unless the petitioner satisfies the court of one or more of the following facts, that is to say
> (a) that the respondent has committed adultery and the petitioner finds it

intolerable to live with the respondent;

(b) that the respondent has behaved in such a way that the petitioner cannot reasonably be expected to live with the respondent;

(c) that the respondent has deserted the petitioner for a continuous period of at least two years immediately preceding the presentation of the petition;

(d) that the parties to the marriage have lived apart for a continuous period of at least two years immediately preceding the presentation of the petition and the respondent consents to the decree being granted;

(e) that the parties to the marriage have lived apart for a continuous period of at least five years immediately preceding the presentation of the petition.[17]

It will be observed that 'facts' previously associated with the matrimonial offences of adultery, cruelty and desertion are retained (in slightly modified form) as conditions, the establishment of which will entitle the court to hold that the marriage has broken down irretrievably.[18] Two separation situations, however, have been added, one based on consensual separation, the other allowing for divorce on the unilateral wish of one party only. Despite their apparently equal treatment with the offences as factual matters providing evidence of irretrievable breakdown, the separation conditions are singled out for special consideration. If either of them is established it remains open to the respondent, after decree nisi, to apply to the court for consideration of his or her financial position after divorce. The court cannot then make the decree absolute unless satisfied either that the petitioner need not make financial provision for the respondent or that the provisions that are made are reasonable and fair or the best that can be made in the circumstances. If the ground is five-year separation without the consent of the respondent and the respondent opposes the decree, the court must consider all the circumstances, including the conduct of the parties and the interests of the children, and must refuse the decree if granting it would result in 'grave financial or other hardship' to the respondent and if it would in all the circumstances be 'wrong' to dissolve the marriage.[19] The limitation of these 'safeguards' to the separation conditions suggests that it was thought that the other situations implied some moral turpitude in the respondent, for why otherwise should not the court be required to be satisfied that the financial arrangements in those cases also are 'fair and reasonable' or the best in the circumstances? Yet, as will be seen,[20] to some extent at least, blameless conduct can be included in the earlier conditions. This is but one of the difficulties inherent in attempting to combine the offence doctrine with the breakdown principle.

(c) *The persistence of fault*

It seems probable that, during the 1980s, the dual system of offences operating alongside breakdown will be seen as a transitional stage in the development of divorce law. Australia and New Zealand have already abandoned it.[21] The Law Reform Commission of Canada has called for a new system for that country.[22] Criticism of the dual system must be seen in the light of statistics showing the way divorcing parties choose to operate it. In Australia in 1974 the separation ground was the basis for only 14.1 per cent of decrees absolute. Desertion was the most popular ground (36.4 per cent), then adultery (34.7 per cent) and cruelty lasting for one year (9.8 per cent).[23] In New Zealand in 1973, 24.4 per cent of decrees absolute were based on adultery, 5 per cent on desertion, 50 per cent on separation by agreement, 6.8 per cent on separation with court order or decree and 15.7 per cent on simple living apart for five years.[24] Hahlo (1975) sets out the use made of the Canadian grounds over the four-year period from 1 January 1969 to 31 December 1972. Three years' separation was the largest single ground (35 per cent), five years' separation only amounting to 5 per cent of the decrees absolute. Adultery was the basis of 28.5 per cent, and 27.3 per cent were based on cruelty. In England and Wales in 1979, 23.8 per cent of petitions filed were based on two years' separation and 7.9 per cent on five years' separation; 27 per cent were based on adultery, 37.3 per cent on unreasonable behaviour and 2.7 per cent on desertion.[25] Since the separation period in Australia was five years, it is not surprising that it was less used than the shorter separation grounds in New Zealand, Canada and England and Wales. Certainly some of the desertion cases (where the waiting period was only three years) would have fallen under the separation ground if the period were shorter. However, the striking feature of these figures is the important role still played by the offence grounds. In each of the jurisdictions except New Zealand, more divorces were based on offence grounds than the separation provisions.

The Law Commission (1966) expressed the objective of a good divorce law as being a means to provide a 'decent burial' for dead marriages and 'above all' to try to 'take the heat out of the disputes between husband and wife and certainly not further embitter the relationships between them or between them and their children'.[26] This view represented a shift from the method of justice to that of welfare, and the Commission recognized that the more often people used the separation ground in preference to the offences, the more the reform would accomplish.[27] On this reckoning the English reform has achieved only about 30 per cent success, and the other systems, except New Zealand, less than 50 per cent.

The major objections to retaining the offence doctrine (whether it is made explicit, as in Canada, or implicit, as in England and Wales) are that it can be capricious in operation and damaging to the parties. Both these results are inherent in its nature. It is capricious because the doctrine seeks to single out forms of conduct which justify one spouse treating the marriage as ended. Hence it represents an *evaluation*, either by society (as where it singles out specific offences, like sodomy), or by a judge (in the case of generalized offences, like cruelty) as to the limits of toleration within the marital partnership. Yet this judgement is bound to vary from spouse to spouse, judge to judge and society to society. Attempts by Canadian judges to evaluate the limits of toleration have led to a proliferation of case law on the subject of cruelty. In one case a judge devoted forty-nine pages of his judgement to analysing the wife's conduct before holding her to have treated the husband with cruelty.[28] Temperamental or sexual incompatibility have been held not to fall within this ground,[29] although persistent refusal to have sexual intercourse has been said to be cruelty.[30] A striking example of the capricious results of this ground is found in Scotland, where it was held in one case that it was not to be considered unendurable to remain married to the defender despite his conviction for murder,[31] and in another that it was beyond endurance to be married to someone convicted of a homosexual act.[32] On one occasion before the English law was reformed a judge referred a petitioner in a cruelty case to a colleague, remarking that the case was more likely to be successful there than before himself.[33] It is not impossible that this could still happen under the reformed law in England and Wales.

The problems inherent in a generalized 'cruelty' ground become overwhelming where the situation faced by the petitioner comes about through misfortune to the respondent rather than 'misconduct'. Before the English divorce law was reformed, the House of Lords held, in effect, that the crucial matter for evaluation in 'cruelty' cases was the effect of the situation on the petitioner, not the blameworthiness of the respondent.[34] This approach has been followed in Canada where drug addiction[35] and schizophrenia[36] have been allowed to form the basis of the allegation. The Scottish courts, however, before Scots law was reformed, refused to allow spouses to complain of the effects of physical disease suffered by their partners.[37] There would be some logic in adopting this approach in a dual system. If 'cruelty' appears among the grounds which are considered to be 'offences', then it seems wrong to include non-fault situations within its scope. It has been seen that in Canada a deliberate attempt was made to separate offence-based divorce from divorce based on breakdown. Alcohol and drug addiction lasting three years were included in the latter category. To hold that drug addiction and other 'blameless' conditions amount to cruelty is to obscure the division. The policy consideration which impelled the House of Lords to remove the necessary requirement of fault from the English law of cruelty in 1964 was that, apart from insanity, divorce in England and Wales at that time was based entirely on the fault principle. By extending the concept of cruelty in this way, limited provision could be made for the operation of the breakdown principle.[38] In dual systems, however, a petitioner who fails to establish an offence can usually succeed at a later date under the separation provisions. The only really relevant question, therefore, in a case based on an offence is whether the circumstances justify an *immediate* decree or whether the parties should wait until the relevant separation period has elapsed. It is, however, seldom stated in this way, not surprisingly because, once a divorce is seen as inevitable, it is hard to find convincing reasons to require such postponement.

The question whether the spouse of a partner afflicted with a misfortune can be reasonably called upon to endure the situation has also faced English courts deciding whether condition (b) (unreasonable behaviour) of the situations indicating irretrievable breakdown has been satisfied. It is clear that the question is not the 'reasonableness' of the respondent's behaviour, but whether it is reasonable to 'expect' the petitioner to live with the respondent.[39] In *Katz* v. *Katz*[40] Sir George Baker P. attempted to draw a distinction between active and passive conditions in the respondent. The latter, being merely a 'state of affairs', could not, he thought, amount to 'behaviour' within the provision. But in *Thurlow* v. *Thurlow*[41] Rees J. held that the passivity of the respondent, who was bedridden and had gradually lost the capacity for self-sustenance, could nevertheless be considered 'behaviour'. There indeed seems to be no point in the attempted distinction between 'active' and 'passive' states, for a petitioner can be as much affected by forms of inactivity as by activity, and the equivalent provision in the new Scottish Act expressly states that behaviour can be both active and passive.[42] But Rees J. doubted whether a spouse who was rendered comatose in a traffic accident and was taken directly to hospital could be said to be 'behaving' within the provision.[43] Would it be different if the accident had occurred in the home? Again, would it be different if the spouse were taken to a mental hospital? There are a multitude of conceivable refinements, all of which add to the chances of arbitrary results. They would be arbitrary because no purpose is served by granting a decree in one case and refusing it in another where the distinction between them is irrelevant to the social purpose of divorce.

The futility of pursuing these distinctions is heightened by the logical incoherence of the structure of the English and Scottish divorce provisions. It is proclaimed, on the one hand, that the breakdown of the marriage is the sole ground of divorce. This is a purely factual matter. On the other hand, the question whether a person can be reasonably 'expected' to live with another is clearly taken in a moral, not predictive, sense. But an ethical judgement about whether something ought to be cannot be relevant to the question whether it is. Yet, by holding that a spouse should endure the behaviour of the respondent in a particular case, a judge can dismiss a petition based, as it must be, on the sole ground of irretrievable breakdown, despite the fact that no one denies that the marriage has actually broken down.[44]

Apart from the unpredictable nature of the application of cruelty and similar grounds and their uneasy coexistence alongside the breakdown principle, there is reason to suppose that the dual system can be both inimical to the proper function of the modern divorce process as conceived by the Law Commission and damaging to the parties concerned. Cretney[45] draws attention to the public discussion of details of the marital history in 'unreasonable behaviour' cases, many of which may appear trivial, but may be painful enough to the parties. He gives examples of very lengthy proceedings in defended cases. In both England[46] and Canada[47] it has been suggested that, where the friction between the parties is a result of the mutual interaction of their personalities, the likelihood of a divorce being granted is diminished because neither of them could be said to be at fault. Judges have remarked on the destructiveness of these cases when they are defended. In one, the judge observed that the husband had suffered a degree of humiliation and distress unique in his experience.[48] In a Canadian case children are reported as giving evidence against their father.[49] But apart from the defended cases, admittedly very few, it is possible that the form of proceedings even in undefended cases based on these grounds does little to promote and may even inhibit opportunities for minimizing the friction between the parties. In order to satisfy the court that he has a substantial case, the petitioner will be encouraged by his legal adviser to set out in the petition the most damaging accusations against the other spouse he can make. This petition must be served on the respondent. It is unlikely to be pleasant reading. Yet the respondent would be ill-advised seriously to contest these allegations for to do so might delay, and even jeopardize, the granting of the divorce, which usually he desires. The price of his co-operation is to place officially on record a version of his marital conduct which may be remote from the truth about the marital relationship.

It is difficult to measure how far this ritualized hostility affects dealings between the parties, during and after divorce proceedings, but there is some evidence that it may be damaging. Eekelaar and Clive (1977) found that respondents in cases based on 'unreasonable behaviour' were far more likely to react to the service of the petition by indicating their intention to defend it than respondents in cases based on any other condition (17.6 per cent in 'unreasonable behaviour' cases against 1.5 per cent in adultery and two-year separation cases and 5.3 per cent in five-year separation cases). Most of these respondents did not persist in that intention, but an atmosphere of increased hostility was likely to have been created. In fact, of the thirteen cases in the whole English sample (of 652 cases) which were defended, six were based on unreasonable behaviour alone and five on unreasonable behaviour in combination with another ground. This partly accounts for the tendency of the unreasonable behaviour cases in general to be much more prolonged than others. Of these, 38 per cent took more than six months from petition to custody settlement, compared to 20 per cent of adultery cases and 18 per cent of two-year separation cases. Furthermore, it was found to be far less likely that the parties to an unreasonable behaviour case would have made voluntary arrangements for the support of the children than parties to adultery or two-year separation cases. It was also less likely that the petitioner would propose that access to the children should continue and more likely that there would be a contest over custody or access respecting the children. The same pattern was found in the

Scottish sample.

Some support for these findings was found in a further study by Eekelaar (1982a) of cases referred to divorce court welfare officers. Cases based on unreasonable behaviour were heavily over-represented in those which were contested over custody or access or where there were other problems. Gibson (1980) records that, prior to the removal of legal aid for undefended divorce petitions in 1977, legal aid was much more likely to be sought by parties where the petition was based on unreasonable behaviour than on other 'grounds'. Davis *et al.* (1982) also comment on the sense of injustice and hostility aroused in respondents to petitions alleging unreasonable behaviour. It is therefore particularly disturbing that Eekelaar and Maclean (1983) found that 'unreasonable behaviour' was a much more common basis for divorce between parties with children than where the divorcing couple were childless.

It might be argued that this apparent uncooperativeness between the parties is not a result of the choice of ground but that the ground was chosen because of the particularly high degree of friction between the parties. This may provide a partial reason for the findings, but it is unlikely to be a complete explanation because Eekelaar and Clive found large variations between regions in the conditions for divorce commonly used. The choice of condition may therefore depend largely on legal and community (or class) practices and is unlikely to be very closely related to the state of the relationship between the parties. That research also found that there was a relatively high level of co-operation between parties to a divorce based on adultery. Voluntary support arrangements were as common in adultery cases (42.9 per cent) as in two-year separation cases (43.1 per cent) and so were proposals that the respondent should continue to see the children (85.7 per cent in adultery cases, 86.1 per cent in two-year separation cases). It is possible that many of these cases are collusive. The English reform, however, abolished the bars of connivance and collusion.[50] It would seem quite open for the parties to 'set up' an adultery specifically in order to obtain a divorce. The only way an English court could refuse a petition if it found this to have happened would be to hold that it was not the respondent's adultery which led the petitioner to find life with the respondent intolerable. This is because the 'adultery' condition is coupled with the requirement that the petitioner must also allege that he finds it intolerable to live with the respondent.[51] However, there is dispute whether a petitioner must allege that it was the adultery which caused the intolerability or whether he need allege only that, for any reason, he finds it intolerable to live with the respondent.[52]

It is submitted that the better view is that the intolerability need not necessarily arise from the adultery. To hold otherwise would be contrary to the fundamental policy of the reform, which was to see adultery as a symptom of the breakdown, not a cause. It would also place a petitioner in an impossible position if he were required to analyse his emotional responses to various actions of the other spouse under cross-examination in a witness box. Furthermore, the Parliamentary history of the enactment shows that it was intended that the adultery and the intolerability were to be considered as independent of each other.[53] Apart from this, however, it is not really necessary for parties to arrange for adultery to make use of the provision. The court will accept evidence from the respondent and the person with whom he is alleged to have committed adultery. The evidence is usually obtained by an inquiry agent, who submits an affidavit testifying that the third party has admitted to having committed adultery with the respondent. Lord Simon has said that it will require 'vigilance' to ascertain whether this reform will involve substantial reintroduction of the rigged divorce which was a feature of the matrimonial offence system.[54] It is obvious that the legal system is unable to provide this vigilance, a point underlined by subsequent changes in procedure to be discussed later.[55] In England, and probably in Canada too, the maintenance of the offence of adultery is almost certainly used, whether genuinely or fraudulently, by thousands of people who wish in effect to terminate their marriage consensually and to avoid having to wait until one of the separation periods has elapsed. As Cretney has put it: 'If . . . the law is to allow immediate divorce by consent, it is not clear why an act of adultery should be required as a condition precedent.'[56]

(d) *Separation grounds*

The rationale for requiring a period of separation before granting a divorce is that cessation of cohabitation over a period is the most visible outward indication that the marriage has not merely broken down, but has done so irretrievably. By using this indicator, courts can infer such breakdown without the need to subject the relationship between the parties to inquisition. This technique has, however, led to three principal difficulties.

The first problem has lain in the choice of the period during which cohabitation must have ceased. In England and Wales it is two years if the parties consent to the divorce, five if one of them objects. Since it can scarcely seriously be thought that reconciliation between the parties is a realistic possibility after two years' separation, the longer period can be justified only as a penalty against a spouse who wishes to divorce an unwilling partner and cannot establish an 'offence' against him or her. It therefore implicitly perpetuates the 'offence' system. The Canadian provisions are even more complex. Separation of one year suffices where the marriage has not been consummated, but three years are needed following breakdown on account of 'gross' addiction to alcohol or narcotics. Three years also are required where the parties have separated consensually and five where the separation was brought about by the desertion of the petitioner.[57] New Zealand abolished the dual system in October 1981. The sole ground of divorce is 'irreconcilable' breakdown of marriage evidenced, in this case, on one condition only, that 'the parties to the marriage are living apart and have been living apart for the period of two years immediately preceding the filing of the application for an order dissolving the marriage'.[58] This follows the lead given in Australia in 1975 when it was provided that irretrievable breakdown of marriage can be held to be established if and only if the parties had been separated for twelve months.[59]

The second difficulty in a separation ground is that it puts parties who are contemplating divorce under pressure to separate, perhaps at an unduly early stage in their differences. Further, it puts at a disadvantage those spouses (generally women) for whom separation may not be easy to arrange without hardship to themselves and their children. Their marital relationship may be deteriorating but may not be sufficiently serious to justify the forcible exclusion of the husband from the home.[60] In any case such drastic intervention may serve only to heighten antagonisms. In Australia, the Attorney-General, who promoted the legislation, sought to meet this difficulty by suggesting that an application might be filed before twelve months' separation had elapsed, but that a decree could not be granted until it had done so.[61] The separation ground was originally framed in this way. The proposal was not, however, pursued. It is now provided that the parties may be held to have separated and to have lived separately and apart 'notwithstanding that they have continued to reside in the same residence or that either party has rendered some household services to the other'.[62] By this provision, the Act allows for immediate divorce in a residual number of cases.

But to conclude that parties have really 'separated' in such circumstances involves the scrutiny of internal domestic arrangements, which partly undermines the advantage of the system, which relies on easily identifiable external appearances. Cases illustrating this difficulty have been reported in Australia[63] and in England.[64] Then, even if the parties have adequately 'separated', what is to be made of occasions when the parties come together for brief periods, perhaps in attempts to save the relationship? Typically, separation provisions contain savings allowing such periods to be disregarded, sometimes depending on the motives of the parties in resuming cohabitation,[65] sometimes not.[66] An element of mathematical arbitrariness inevitably enters into such calculations.[67] However, the extent to which these questions cause real practical difficulties depends on the degree to which courts attempt to investigate facts alleged before them and this, as will be seen, is a very difficult matter.

The final problem relates to the basic purpose of separation grounds: that they are designed to establish irretrievable marriage breakdown. They fail to do this in circumstances where the separation has been forced on the parties, as, for example, where a husband has spent considerable time serving in the army. It has therefore been concluded that, for the ground to operate, at least one of the parties should have regarded the marriage as at an end throughout the length of the stipulated period. This interpretation was grafted on to the separation grounds in Australia[68] and New Zealand[69] when they operated dual systems, and has been followed in Canada[70] and England and Wales, although in the English case the interpretation flies in the face of the express words of the statute and the intention of Parliament.[71] The doctrine still applies in the new Australian law.[72] While logically consistent with the premises of the provision, the requirement opens the way to scrutiny of mental states which is the antithesis of the simplicity which is the major claim to merit of the separation grounds. Of course, much depends on how the courts implement the requirement. In England and Wales a petitioner using a separation ground must state in his petition the time when he considered his marriage to be at an end. If properly advised on the law, he will clearly try to ensure that the date appearing will be early enough to satisfy this requirement. If the petition is uncontested, who can challenge such a statement?

It is probable, then, that practical devices overcome most of the difficulties associated with separation grounds. This in itself is not very satisfactory. But, more importantly, it will be argued below that separation grounds, transformed into 'waiting periods', could be used to achieve positive benefits which their present form loses. First, however, it is necessary to look more closely at the process of divorce.

The divorce process

The first step which most people take on the road to divorce is to obtain legal advice.[73] The ambience of the process set in train at that stage is set partly by the way the lawyer handles the case and partly, of course, by the legal procedures required in order to conclude the case successfully. In England and Wales, prior to 1973, it was necessary in all cases for at least the petitioner to appear in court and answer routine questions from his lawyer and often from the judge. Of course, if the case was defended, the respondent would also attend. In 1973 Elston, Fuller and Murch observed 763 undefended divorce cases in three courts and interviewed the parties of a random sample of those cases where children were involved.[74] In most cases only the petitioner attended the hearing, and in almost all he or she was represented by a solicitor or barrister. In the latter instances, the petitioner had usually met the barrister for the first time a few minutes before the hearing. Eighty-five per cent of the cases took less than ten minutes (in two courts a majority [61 per cent] took less than five minutes). The judge asked no questions about the marriage in 73 per cent of the cases observed. Afterwards the petitioner tended to see the proceedings as a mere formality, a 'farce', where they were only expected to answer 'yes' to questions the answers to which were already known. Yet the petitioners (especially the women) had felt very nervous on going into the witness box and were sometimes worried lest they should show signs of undue co-operation with their spouse which might lead to the court refusing a decree on the ground the marriage had not broken down. In particular many were disappointed that maintenance, property or custody issues, which to them were a major source of worry, were adjourned for subsequent hearing in chambers. The procedure is not fundamentally different in Canada. Hahlo (1975) timed undefended divorce actions in the Montreal divorce court; they averaged slightly over four minutes a case. It is the same in Ontario.[75] Yet in England and Wales, recorders or circuit judges spent 5,115 days in 1973 hearing undefended divorce petitions in this manner.[76] Taking the cost of an undefended petition in England and Wales then at being between £100 and £200 per case, the extravagance of the system was obvious. Worse still, it was an extravagance which served little or no purpose, for the procedure neither enabled a proper investigation to be made into the matters which the theory of the substantive law requires to be investigated, nor did it contribute in any way towards assisting the parties to adjust to their new lives.

In order to alleviate the burden that was falling on divorce courts, the Matrimonial Causes Rules were amended in 1973 to introduce a 'special procedure' in cases based on the two years' separation condition where there were no children of the family. This was extended in 1975 to all undefended cases where there were no children involved, except cases based on unreasonable behaviour. Two years later, the 'special' procedure became the norm, for it was extended to all undefended cases whether or not children were involved.[77] The impetus for this radical reconstruction of the English divorce procedure arose, not from a well-thought-out assessment of the needs of divorcing families, but solely to save money.[78] Under this procedure the divorce file is examined by a registrar and, if he is satisfied that the conditions for divorce are made out, he issues a certificate. The file is thereupon forwarded to the judge who must pronounce decree nisi in open court. Neither party need attend. The function of the judge is reduced to an empty ritual. He may simply say, 'I pronounce decree nisi in cases 1 to 50.' The procedure concedes that the statutory requirement, that 'On a petition for divorce it shall be the duty of the court to inquire, so far as it reasonably can, into the facts alleged by the petitioner and into any facts alleged by the respondent',[79] is incapable of proper application. It is true that the rules require the petitioner to file affidavits stating whether the requirements for divorce have been fulfilled, but how can a registrar who reads these documents be sure that a petitioner finds it intolerable to live with an adulterer, or when one of the parties formed an intention to abandon the marriage, or that the respondent had really behaved in a way that caused it to be unreasonable to expect the petitioner to continue the marriage? Attempts by some courts to supplement the information before them by additional questionnaires or pre-trial hearings have been reported.[80] But these are unlikely to be very efficient. More important, what relevance has that information to the essential problems facing the parties?

If the registrar is not satisfied that the documents disclose the requisite conditions for divorce the case will be removed from the 'special procedure' list and will go before a judge as before. What practices registrars are developing is not yet known, though it is possible that certain variations may be found. But clearly a petitioner should state his case in the appropriate words and, for this, he should receive legal advice. Legal aid, however, is no longer available for the divorce proceeding itself but may be obtained if there is a dispute over other matters, like the children or finance. Essentially divorce has become an administrative process. Sentiment is satisfied by the solemn pronouncement of decree by a judge in a (possibly empty) courtroom. The choice of 'grounds' by the parties is simply part of the ritual. It has not the slightest relevance to the social or legal processes that take place.

Where there are children, the process is a little more elaborate. In such cases, the registrar must usually fix an appointment for the petitioner to discuss the arrangements proposed for the children.[81] This procedure will be examined more closely when special attention is paid to questions concerning children. Here we need only observe the failure of policy makers to give any guidance about how these appointments are to be conducted or even what their purpose is. Davis *et al.* (1983) found wide diversity of practice on such matters, as whether the appointment took place informally, in chambers, or formally, in open court, and whether the judge probed deeply into the issues in question. However, most interviews last less than five minutes and seem to be little more than an empty ritual. There is, however, a procedure whereby a judge, or even the registrar, may refer the case to a divorce court welfare officer, and his remit is to investigate the case and report to the court.[82]

An adversarial, inquisitorial or conciliatory model?

The English divorce procedure, betraying its origin in ecclesiastical law, has always rested on an inquisitorial basis. We have observed how, in relation to the matrimonial offence doctrine, the courts retained a power to refuse decrees despite the wishes of the parties if they discovered facts hidden from them.[83] Indeed, an officer of the court (who still exists), the Queen's Proctor, provided a measure of surveillance which the court itself was unable to exercise. But the changes in substantive law have meant that there is less to hide and the transformation of the procedure has largely deprived the courts of the power to exercise the surveillance. Concern has in any case shifted from the adults to the children and it is here, in the interview in chambers and the investigation by the welfare officer, that the remnants of the inquisitorial process are to be found.[84] But the inquisition had been heavily overlaid with the trappings of the traditional adversarial legal procedure. Divorcing adults frequently, it is true, adopt hostile attitudes to each other, and the guilt v. innocence foundation of the offence system allowed them to flourish. Nevertheless, the breakdown of many marriages could not be characterized in such crude terms and there has always been a tendency for divorcing parties, by collusion, manufactured grounds or abandonment of defences to undermine the adversarial assumptions. Hence it may not be an exaggeration to characterize the English divorce procedure, up to the reform of 1971, as fundamentally adversarial, with an overriding inquisitorial power primarily directed to ensure that the adversarial postures were maintained. Despite the retention of offence-based conditions in the breakdown provision, the advent of the separation grounds has fundamentally undercut the artificially nurtured adversarial element in English divorce procedure. The inquisitorial element has uncertainly moved to the area of children, leaving a profound vacuum of principle regarding the foundation of the whole process. The procedure has been described as 'administrative'[85] and this word probably correctly reflects the emptiness of purpose or design of the present procedures.

We may at this stage turn to the adjustive function posited for modern divorce law. This was clearly the purpose foreseen for it by the Law Commission and, as will be seen in the following chapters, is one which substantive law is accepting. But the procedures have not yet mirrored these changes, perhaps not surprisingly, given the greater difficulty inherent in refashioning institutional structures compared to altering rules of substantive law. The adjustive function, properly applied, demands that the institutional arrangements direct the parties' attentions towards the future and maximize their opportunities to re-align their lives towards new family arrangements which cause the minimum friction to all concerned. It has never been doubted that acceptance by both parties of the arrangements governing their futures in as amicable an atmosphere as possible provides the best chance of achieving those ends.

The divorce process, then, should be directed primarily towards bringing about such agreements. We have already argued that the very retention of the 'offence' grounds, particularly unreasonable behaviour, is antagonistic to this end. But are the institutional arrangements conducive to it either? The answer depends partly on an assessment of the role of lawyers in divorce proceedings, and this, in turn, depends on a range of factors, which either encourage or inhibit the agreed settlement of disputes. They include such matters as the degree of certainty of the outcome of litigation, the degree to which agreements can be re-opened and the parties' own propensities to indulge in legal action.[86] In so far as these issues raise questions of substantive law, such as the rules for distributing matrimonial assets or determining support payments after divorce, they will be discussed later. In the procedural context, two concerns are dominant. We must first ask how far it is appropriate to entrust the handling of the 'bargaining' process to the legal profession alone. Then we must consider what role, if any, is left to the court system.

Although Mnookin and Kornhauser (1979) offer some theoretical reasons why spouses might litigate rather than settle, there is no clear empirical evidence explaining those cases where agreement is not reached. Where the success of negotiation turns on plausible prediction of what a court might do, or the fullest acquisition of financial information or a fine calculation of the balance of advantage between costs of litigation and settlement, it seems likely that lawyers are well suited to undertake or oversee the negotiation process. Where, however, the obstacles lie in emotional antagonisms or deeply held, but conflicting, attitudes over what is best for the children, they might not be. Murch's conclusion from his research was that divorcing adults usually saw their solicitor as being committed to their interests. Interestingly, while most parents approved of this with respect to their own solicitor, when faced with a hypothetical question whether a 'good' divorce lawyer should be partisan or conciliatory, only a small minority preferred the 'fighter'.[87] Davis (1980) asked solicitors whether they ever attempted to conciliate between spouses and the overwhelming response was negative. A large majority, however, said that they would adopt a 'conciliatory approach' and another minority that they might try conciliation through the other spouse's solicitor. Only one solicitor tried seeing both spouses together. However, Davis et al. (1982) have also recorded that some 20 per cent of divorcees interviewed stated that their solicitor made no attempt to ascertain the genuineness of their desire to divorce.

From the research evidence available it is clear that, while the approach may in some cases be 'softened', most solicitors will approach divorce litigation in the traditional adversarial manner. This is approved of by most adult parties, who showed high levels of satisfaction with their solicitor's conduct. The espousal by the solicitor of their (necessarily one-sided) cause provided much needed support during the stress following the breakdown. Yet it is not a person's feelings for a solicitor that matter when the process is over, but his feelings to the former spouse and children and his satisfaction with the arrangements made between them. There is no evidence that the handling of divorce cases by solicitors promotes a favourable outcome in those areas, nor how far agreements actually negotiated by them survive in the long term if the parties retain hostility towards one another.

While most solicitors seem to be conscious of the potential value of conciliation, it is unlikely that the legal profession alone can adequately fulfil that role. A conciliator must work with both parties. As Davis (1980) found, this is a highly unusual event and may even be regarded as unethical, in view of potential conflicts of interests (legally perceived) between the clients. In the United States, it is true, there is an increase in the practice of lawyers offering their services as mediators, a practice now endorsed by Draft New Model Rules of Professional Conduct submitted to the American Bar Association.[88] There are, however, real difficulties in reconciling this function with traditional legal roles,[89] and its popularity in the United States reflects features peculiar to the legal profession in that country. It is unlikely that in England lawyers would at present feel sufficiently threatened by loss of matrimonial work to wish to move into the field of mediation,[90] a role for which their training does not suit them, though some resistance may be expected if conciliation by other occupations became widespread. Indeed, the Law Society (1979) has strongly supported proposals made in the Finer Report[91] for the establishment of a court welfare service geared to conciliation.

Any deficiencies there may be in leaving the pre-divorce process entirely in the hands of lawyers might be mitigated by making available alternative professional services to promote conciliation.[92] An attempt to do this was initiated in Bristol in 1979 under an experimental scheme whereby a conciliation service, staffed by five full-time conciliators, received referrals from local solicitors of clients deemed by the lawyers suitable for referral. The lawyers thus retained strong control over who went to conciliation and over which issues. The scheme has suffered through severe uncertainty over financing. Government scepticism over the process contrasts strongly with the view in New Zealand, where all legal advisers are placed under a duty not only to make their clients aware of mediation facilities but also to take steps they think may assist in promoting reconciliation or, if this is not possible, conciliation. To this end the parties may request the Registrar of the Family Court to arrange for such counselling, the cost of which is borne by the state.[93] In other jurisdictions, provision is frequently made for 'official' mediation services to receive referrals from lawyers,[94] or even, as in Australia,[95] directly from people with marital difficulties.

This leads to the question of the relationship between conciliation and the court system. How far should conciliation machinery be built into the court structure itself? Some American courts have highly developed conciliation procedures. In Los Angeles the mediators will attempt to draft an agreement between the parties which, if achieved, is given a six-week trial period after which modifications may be incorporated prior to the agreement becoming a court order.[96] Under the Australian Family Law Act 1975 a Director of Counselling and Welfare is established, which together with other counsellors and welfare officers, forms part of the court service. The court may advise the parties to use this service if it thinks this may 'assist the parties to a marriage to improve their relationship to each other and for any child of the marriage'.[97] In New Zealand, where the goal of conciliation was enthusiastically embraced by the Beattie Commission in 1978,[98] the Family Proceedings Act 1980 includes a series of provisions for facilitating counselling for the purpose of reconciliation or conciliation. A court may adjourn at any time and refer parties for such mediation by a counsellor. Counsellors may be found outside the court structure, although there is facilitative provision in the Family Courts Act 1980 for the appointment of counsellors who will be officers of the court. But if private counsellors are used, the state will pay.[99] How far these powers will be used to develop a conciliation source as a powerful arm of the family courts in New Zealand will doubtless depend on the availability of financial (and human) resources and the willingness of central government to use them.

Another development is the 'mediation conference' or 'pre-trial review', often referred to as 'in-court' mediation, where the matter comes initially before a registrar[100] or a judge[101] who will sit down informally with the parties (and their lawyers) and try to bring about an agreement. In Australia it is estimated that about 75 per cent of conferences result in agreement.[102] But on matters involving children, the most significant opportunity for mediation in England arises in the referral of a matter to a divorce court welfare officer. This procedure will be considered in detail later in the context of discussion of issues specifically relating to children in divorce. Here it needs to be said only that, although the remit of the officer is to investigate and report his findings to the court, research has shown that, however the officers themselves may characterize their role, it seems clear that mediation frequently forms an important element in their work.[103] It must be remembered, however, that investigation by welfare officers happens in only some 10 per cent of all divorce cases involving children, although, where there is a serious contest, such a reference should invariably be made.

Table 4 *Bristol Conciliation Service: outcome in relation to nature of the dispute*

	No. of issues	% agreed	% partially agreed or inconclusive	% not agreed
Total	153	55.6	17.6	26.8
Reconciliation	10	70.0	10.0	20.0
Divorce	16	63.0	12.0	25.0
Custody	28	61.0	7.0	32.0
Access	59	46.0	36.0	19.0
Finance	18	56.0	6.0	39.0
Matrimonial home	20	70.0	0.0	30.0
Possessions	2	0.0	0.0	100.0

Source: Davis (1980), p. 128.

Attempts to evaluate the impact of conciliation processes face (possibly insuperable) difficulties. Table 4 shows the results of referrals made under the Bristol scheme, described earlier, but it would be wrong, *from these figures*, to draw conclusions about the success of conciliation as a whole, for the clients were pre-selected, both by the lawyers and themselves, for they participated only if willing. Nor is it easy to demonstrate that people who reach agreement after conciliation would not have done so quite apart from the conciliation process. Irving *et al.* (1981) attempted to solve this problem by an experiment in the Toronto Family Court. All willing applicants in that court were randomly assigned either to the established court intake service or to a special conciliation counselling service. The staff of the former were not specially trained, kept normal office hours, seldom offered direct intervention (except in crises) and acted primarily as an onward referral agency. The latter was staffed by professionally trained counsellors working flexible hours who were assigned small caseloads for extensive mediation. Follow-up interviews were conducted twelve weeks after referral. Significantly more of the people referred to the specialized service had reached agreement (21.7 per cent as against 8.2 per cent), and moreover had done so on the more serious issues. A subsequent study concentrated on those conciliation cases seemingly most responsive to counselling (where both spouses agreed to it, where they had been referred by a judge or lawyer and both spouses were reasonably conversant in English) and very high success rates were achieved. Seventy per cent reached agreement (12 per cent being reconciled). The researchers noted that involvement of the children in the process contributed to a successful outcome.

Negotiation and conciliation: problems and solutions

Objection to the promotion of conciliation over adjudication can take at least two forms. It can be argued that leaving the parties to come to their own arrangements, and giving these arrangements binding force, risks both the exploitation of one party by the other and the subordination of the children's (and possibly, the state's) interests to those of the two adults. Additionally, it may be said that the introduction of 'social work' oriented personnel to oversee the arrangements made by the parties promotes excessive regulatory intrusion into private affairs which are better protected by legal and procedural formality.[104] A 'mediation conference' before a strong judge or registrar might also be vulnerable to this criticism. The result would be, as Davis (1983) puts it, that divorcing couples might have 'less, rather than more, control over the outcome of their own case'.

Mnookin (1982) has identified two areas with respect to which the results of bargaining might reflect imbalances between the adult parties. The first concerns their relative capacities to make judgements which fully reflect their interests. The emotional trauma of divorce may disturb the parties unequally. The second relates to their relative bargaining power. This may be unequal due to factors as diverse as the nature of the legal rules which form the backdrop of the bargaining, what the immediate preferences and needs of each party may be and their relative capacities to endure the bargaining process. A solution to these difficulties is seen in permitting *ex post* revision of agreements affected by such factors on grounds of exploitation of the 'transactional incapacity' and unjust enrichment. The problem about this solution, however, is that not only might it be difficult to evolve corrective doctrines of sufficient subtlety to reflect the range of factors which may cause unequal bargaining strength, but that the onus is put on the person alleging such exploitation to challenge it. Apart from the possiblity that that person may already have been ir-redeemably prejudiced, it seems odd to provide as a form of protec-tion to one party the opportunity to challenge an agreement before a court when one of the most significant grounds of challenge envisaged is that the other exploited that person's aversion to legal process in the first instance. Furthermore, any widespread practice of setting aside or modifying agreements reduces the incentive to reach such settlements, which depends precisely upon their likelihood of endurance. Hence Mnookin favours a presumption against the application of any incapacity doctrine where the aggrieved person was legally represented. This certainly seems to be the position taken by the English courts, where it has been decided that, unless there is evidence of exploitation, the mere fact of inequality of bargaining power is not sufficient to permit a party subsequently to disregard an agreement, especially if independently legally advised, even though the resultant settlement may have given that party substantially less than a court would have done.[105]

As in other aspects of divorce, a true assessment of the processes of bargaining and conciliation (or mediation) may depend on whether there are dependent children at the time of the divorce. If the conflict is between lone adults, the scope for successful mediation seems limited. Merry's (1982) assessment of mediation in four traditional societies concluded that mediation was least likely to succeed if the parties had no need for future dealings with each other. Merry also observed that mediated settlements between unequals tended to reflect that inequality. One might add that, if this were not so, the mediator would have imposed an external set of values on the conflict. Thus mediation might not add much to what lawyers can achieve for adult parties as part of the bargaining process. Yet the extent to which lawyers actually protect their clients' interests, or are even capable of perceiving them, is unclear.[106] When an agreement comes before a court it is unlikely to be examined in depth, especially if the parties have been legally advised.[107] Thus it is important to ensure that the parties and their advisers negotiate with knowledge of the ground rules by which the legal system adjudges divorce settlements to be fair. A fortiori, the legal system should provide such rules. What they may be is considered in later chapters.

However, in cases involving children, gains by one party do not solely imply losses by the other, the so-called zero sum game.[108] It has long been recognized in traditional societies that a social group's vital interests in strength and stability can require compromise between hostile individuals.[109] Translating this into the realm of family conflict, we can construct a significant criterion by which to assess the value of compromise. Where the compromise between the adults *enures to the benefit of the children*, it serves a wider purpose. The compromise might benefit them directly, materially, as where an adult relinquishes a proprietal claim to the dwelling in order to maintain a home for the children, or psychologically, as where a monetary claim is not pushed to its fullest so as to encourage relationships with the absent parent.

But who can make the judgement that compromise is desirable in the children's interests? It is difficult to avoid the necessity of reference to some third party, other than the adults' legal representatives. Murch (1980) has proposed an elaborate structure involving the establishment of a full-scale conciliation service, geared primarily to the pre-litigation phase, staffed by suitably qualified married women. An application would come in the first instance before a Family Tribunal, presided over by a lawyer (possibly a registrar), including two specialists in family matters (such as family finances), with the object of 'getting the parties round a table with members of the tribunal with the minimum of formality to see how real the dispute was and to explore the possiblity of settlement'. The tribunal would make only consent orders. Only cases failing to achieve this would come before a conventional court. Both the tribunal and the court would have access to a welfare service but this would be distinct from the conciliation service because its function would be to investigate rather than mediate.

It would be inappropriate to scrutinize the mechanics of such a proposal in this book. What needs to be taken seriously is the importance of this process so that we can discover how it can most effectively be established within the constraints of available re-sources. If one wished to build on existing institutional structures, it might be possible to expand the work of the divorce court welfare service, which would involve its disassociation from the Probation and After-Care Service and more specialized training. This theme is taken up again in the next chapter, in the specific context of the resolution of disputes concerning children. But all significant disputes will *affect* the children even if they are not (on the face of it) specifically *about* them, and this argues for their routine reference to an officer with a specific remit to consider the child's interests. The charge of regulatory intrusion into family life must be met by a direct appeal to the rights of children.[110] Whatever the formal legal provisions may require, children normally lack the institutional means to invoke their protection. Hence this intrusion does not undermine the protection which law offers its citizens, but enhances it for the most vulnerable group. Nor is it supposed that such intervention should replace legal advice and representation. The officer's role would be to attempt an assessment of the children's interests and suggest ways in which compromise might promote them. A parent would, however, be under strong pressure to follow such suggestions because opposition, unless clearly justified, could lead to the charge of preferring his interests to those of the children. But it is suggested that it is right that the issue should be so raised, for that indeed is at the heart of the modern problem of divorce.

In conclusion, we must consider how the law of divorce as a whole might be formulated best to accommodate the policies suggested here. The distinction made by the Law Reform Commission of Canada (1976a) between *justiciable* issues (such as disputes over custody, property or finance) and the *non-justiciable* issue of estab-lishing marriage breakdown is useful for, while all such issues may be open to conciliation, only the true justiciable issues are ultimately susceptible of judicial determination. Hence, to obtain a divorce, it should be necessary only to file in court a notice of intention to seek dissolution of marriage. It should be made clear that, normally, no divorce would be granted unless certain questions, notably the arrangements for the upbringing and support of the children, had been agreed and approved.[111] The requirement of notification would create a point at which reference to the conciliation mechanism could be made in appropriate cases if there were likely to be problems in settling those issues. Such conciliation could commence without necessarily requiring the parties to separate. The procedure would integrate conciliation into an essential stage of the legal unravelling of the marriage, a feature absent from separation-based divorce. If agreement were reached and approved, dissolution of the marriage should follow automatically after a specified period (some six months) after the original notification. Where agreement fails, such matters would require adjudication, followed by formal dissolution of the marriage.

Some modern divorce schemes effectively provide for divorce on demand. The formulae used in those of the United States adopting no-fault divorce[112] such as 'irreconcilable differences' or 'fundamental incapacity' allow immediate divorce if the parties are in agreement and the judge, as is increasingly common,[113] is disinclined to investigate the matter. Sweden openly admits divorce on the unilateral application of one spouse, but requires a 'reconsideration' period of six months if one party opposes the divorce or if children are involved.[114] The scheme outlined above bears some resemblance to the Swedish system and it may be that the logic of modern developments in divorce seems to lead towards recognition of immediate divorce, whether by consent or unilateral application. But this need not be so. In most cases the dissolution of a marriage is fraught with potential for conflict and emotional damage to the parties and their children. Serious problems of adjustment to a new life arise. It is an evolutionary process and the procedure should reflect this. If divorce is to become more child-centred, it is in some framework such as this that the best way to protect the interests of the children can emerge. The next chapter will examine in more detail some of the specific problems which divorce raises in relation to the children.

4
Children and the Divorce Process

What does divorce do to children?

In 1981, 159,000 children under sixteen (or 14 per thousand of such children) experienced divorce in their family. It has been estimated that, on present trends, one in twenty-two children will have this experience by the age of five and one in five by the age of sixteen. In 1981, 60 per cent of divorcing couples had one or more child under sixteen.[1] It has already been observed that children in one-parent families are at special risk of neglect and deprivation, and we have noted the growth of such families.[2] The Finer Committee estimated that, in 1971, there were more than 1,080,000 children living in one-parent families (in England and Wales), and by 1980 this was estimated to have risen to some 1.5 million. Between 1977 and 1979, 1.3 per cent of all families were headed by lone fathers, 1.7 per cent by single mothers, 1.9 per cent by widowed mothers and 7.0 per cent by divorced or separated mothers.[3] The National Child Development Survey (1958 Cohort) showed that, although illegitimate children were at a disadvantage when compared to their legitimate and adopted peers at the age of seven,[4] further analysis of the performance of the children at the age of eleven within different one-parent family contexts indicated that children from homes which have suffered marital disruption encounter hardships considerably more frequently than those who have lost a parent through bereavement and, in some respects, such as progress at school, may be impeded by their family experience more seriously than illegitimate children.[5] This result may be partly due to the unsettling effect which divorce or separation has on the security of a child's accommodation. Eighty-six per cent of the fatherless children in broken marriages had moved, compared to 73 per cent of the illegitimate children.

It is problematic how far the experience of their parents' divorce and separation, accompanied probably by the introduction of a new adult into their family life, is itself damaging to children. Reviewing the evidence in 1972, Rutter found that, while an association existed between delinquency and homes broken by marital failure, there was little or no association between delinquency and homes broken by the death of a parent. He concluded that 'delinquency is thus associated with breaks which follow parental discord, or discord without a break, but not with break-up of the home as such'.[6] It has even been claimed, by Stott (1977), that tension, especially marital discord, experienced by mothers during pregnancy greatly increases the risks of ill health of the child when born. There is also some evidence that a child's difficulties after marriage breakdown may be accentuated if the parent with whom she is staying remarries.[7] On the other hand, Ferri found that the children of the National Child Development Survey had adjusted well to their family situations by the age of eleven and that 'any differences in behaviour and adjustment between children in one and two-parent families were small in magnitude, and our findings have suggested that the absence of a parent had not in itself had the overwhelmingly detrimental effect so often attributed to it'.[8] Nevertheless, the more lasting effects found in that study of divorce on children compared with bereavement provided some support for Rutter's suggestion that 'it may be distortion rather than disruption of family relationships which is detrimental to children's development'.

A major American study by Wallerstein and Kelly (1980) examined the reaction of children of sixty Californian divorcing families at or shortly after divorce, fifty-eight of whom were followed up one and five years later. The findings chronicle the process of marital breakdown through the children's eyes and point vividly to the children's sense of adult indifference to them at this time. Over half the children felt that their father was entirely insensitive to their distress, only 10 per cent having any strong feeling of his sensitivity or understanding. Over one-third felt that their mother was similarly unaware of their feelings and only 15 per cent experienced her to be strongly concerned about them. The perception might have been generated by circumstances forced on the parents. Additionally, one-third of the children suffered extreme anxiety of abandonment by their mother, and two-thirds, especially the younger, expressed intense yearning for the absent parent, a response not affected by the quality of the child's relationship with the absent parent.

The study documents the varying emotional responses of children in different age groups. The youngest (under five) experienced fear, demonstrated regressive behaviour and showed both desire for and fear of close relationships. Many assumed guilt for the separation on themselves. The six-to-eight-year-olds were characterized by a 'pervasive sadness', but those aged between nine and twelve years tended to exhibit intense anger. The adolescents' response centred more around anxiety over the prospects of their own emotional lives, and, while some handled their difficulties with maturity and independence, others regressed and experienced acute difficulty coping with adolescent problems.

The state of the children five years after the divorce depended on such a multitude of factors depending on the complexity of the interplay between developments over that period and the child's initial psychological state, that no clearly identifiable pattern emerged. However, the researchers concluded that 34 per cent of the children appeared to be doing especially well at the five-year mark, but that 37 per cent were 'consciously and intensely unhappy and dissatisfied with their life in the post divorce family' and 'moderately to severely depressed', while the rest demonstrated 'adequate but uneven functioning'.

Another American study, by Hetherington, Cox and Cox (1979) followed a sample of forty-eight white middle-class families for two years after divorce, comparing them with similar married families. The results show a similar picture of emotional disturbance but, unlike the Californian study, indicate this to be more predominant in boys than in girls. There was also evidence of unhelpful responses to the children from outsiders, especially teachers, and particularly towards boys. The situation had improved after two years, though less so for boys. Valuable as these studies are, neither can be considered representative of the effects of divorce on the child population as a whole. The Californian children were drawn from self-referred families in a location notorious for its wealth and high prevalence of divorce. The second study was more randomly chosen and used a control group, but was nevertheless confined to a narrow class and geographical base. The cases referred to divorce court welfare officers in Eekelaar's (1982a) sample are more representative, though not fully so. The officers were asked to record signs of emotional disturbance in one or more children in any of their referrals. They did so in 37 per cent of cases where custody was disputed, 33.3 per cent where access was in issue and a quarter where neither were contested. Tentatively extrapolating these figures to the total number of divorces in England and Wales in 1979, it may be surmised that children suffered observable emotional disturbance in something under 26,400 of the (roughly) 100,000 divorce cases involving children that year.[9]

Such attempts to give some indication of the order of magnitude of the impact of divorce on children remain crude. In particular, it is very difficult to assess its long-term consequences. Alarmist statements[10] on the effects of divorce on national mental health should be treated with reserve. Indeed, Rosen (1979), matching a representative sample of ninety-two middle-class white South Africans aged between nine and twenty-eight whose parents had divorced in the previous ten years with a control group of twenty-five individuals, found no evidence of maladjustment in the divorce sample as a whole compared with the controls, although there was some evidence of poor adjustment where the divorce had been accompanied by a high degree of disharmony. Perhaps all we can say, on the matter of emotional adjustment, is that (as may be expected) children are indeed hurt by divorce and that many will show overt signs of distress, especially where the parents' relationship has been abrasive or where disputes have persisted after separation, at least during the period of the conflict and that this will affect the behaviour of some over a longer period. Perhaps more significant in view of the thesis to be developed later[11] is the American evidence (itself not conclusive) that white individuals who have suffered father absence due to marital disruption during their teenage years were likely to have substantially lower earnings themselves when aged twenty-three than those whose fathers had not been absent.[12] This suggests that the *economic* adversity faced by single parent families after marital disruption, to be considered in detail in chapter 5, may have longer term implications on the economic life-chances of the children. This dimension to divorce will become central to our discussion in later chapters.

The legal process

Apart from the economic question, it cannot be said that the evidence presented above establishes a particularly strong case for extensive state involvement with the children of divorce. This conclusion is fortified when we consider how uncertain we are over the aims and methods of helping them. Even if we knew how to do it, the costs in resources in trying to alleviate the distress of all these children would be prohibitive. As we shall see, the legal system has in fact substantially withdrawn from any such role. But it cannot totally ignore these issues. First, because divorce still requires the state's sanction and compliance with specific procedures. Second, because conflicts raising acute issues for the children's well-being do arise and require resolution. In this chapter, therefore, we examine how far these interests of children are accommodated within the divorce process.

(a) *The 'ordinary' case*

In this context it is important to remember that, at least in England and Wales, it appears that only some 10 per cent of divorce cases involving children lead to courtroom disputes over custody or access.[13] In the vast majority of cases, the parents agree their own arrangements. This invariably takes the form of the child(ren) staying with the mother, with visits from the father, although it seems that in about one-third of cases the father does not visit the children at all, a circumstance which seems more likely the younger the child.[14] Since child support payments are more common and higher where the father maintains his visits, a non-visiting pattern is likely to increase the family's economic burdens,[15] and, although the evidence is ambiguous,[16] may add to the children's emotional trauma. What institutional intervention, if any, is appropriate here?

In England and Wales at present such cases can be probed both by the questions asked by the judge during his private interview with the adult party (or parties) and, if referral is made, by the divorce court welfare officer who files a 'satisfaction' report. Since nearly three-quarters of interviews seem to last less than five minutes and very few exceed ten, it is difficult to see that they can achieve much.[17] Judges are left entirely to their own instincts about what issues to raise and even whether to encourage the attendance of both parents. Some judges routinely refused a decree if the mother was living on social security and the father was not making the appropriate payments to the Supplementary Benefits Commission, but the Court of Appeal has disapproved of that practice unless the judge thinks that a support order significantly in excess of social security could be obtained for the child.[18] No guidance has been offered as to what would be good practice, or even what the interview seeks to achieve. But even if it were, the effectiveness of the interview must be extremely limited. It will be in the interests of each parent to create as favourable an impression of the children's circumstances as they can, for failure to satisfy the judge risks refusal of the divorce decree, which (normally) they both desire. In any case, the sanction of refusal of decree may do no more than drive parents, who have already reached agreement, into serious conflict. It is difficult to resist the conclusion of Davis *et al.* (1983) that little useful purpose is served by these interviews.

Eekelaar and Clive (1977) found that welfare officer investigations are ordered in nearly one in ten divorce cases in England and Wales involving children even where there is no dispute over them, whereas in Scotland further investigation (usually an advocate) happened in only 3 per cent of cases. Courts tended to investigate cases where there were many children involved, or where it had been proposed that a child's residence would change, or where the children were living in different households or with a person other than a parent. However, despite this investigation, the court eventually intervened to change the child's place of residence only in 0.6 per cent of cases in England and Wales and only once in the Scottish sample of 203 cases. An order placing the child under the supervision of a welfare officer was made in 3.5 per cent of the English cases and once in the Scottish sample. The conclusion reached was that, even if the investigation brings to light a less than satisfactory situation, there is little or nothing the court can do about it. A further study (Eekelaar [1982a]), however, revealed another dimension to the welfare officer investigations. Even where the referral was only for a 'satisfaction' report, in 38 per cent of them the officer considered that, as a result of his 'investigation', the adults had made or were thought likely to make voluntary adjustments to their arrangements which would benefit the children and in 27 per cent the officer thought it had resulted in improved attitudes towards the children. This suggests that, despite the officers' brief simply to investigate and report to the court, the intervention can be used to improve attitudes within the family.

It seems that children's interests would be best served by the availability of some such service as this when their parents divorce. The difficulty is to know how to make appropriate referrals to it. They should be made where issues remain unresolved between the adults. Where, however, there appears to be agreement between them, the role of courts and related services must be limited if significant expenditure on resources likely to achieve little effect is to be avoided. The best approach to these cases, it is suggested, is for the legal system to lay down guiding principles which, in its view, form the basis for restructuring the family arrangements in the manner most likely to benefit the children. Failure to agree on these, or agreements falling outside them, would, unless there were good reasons, provide *prima facie* grounds for referral.

What these guidelines might be in financial matters will be considered later. Here we may consider how such an approach could work with regard to the problem of access. Apart from the significant minority of divorced children who appear to lose all contact with their absent parent, regular visits may be infrequent, twice a month possibly being considered a high rate of contact.[19] There is, unfortunately, no reliable evidence about the effects which the exercise or non-exercise of access by the absent parent has on children. This has not prevented dogmatic assertions, on the one hand that

Children have difficulty in relating positively to, profiting from and maintaining contact with two psychological parents [i.e. the person who has day-to-day care of the child] who are not in positive contact with each other. Loyalty conflicts are common and normal under such conditions and may have devastating consequences by destroying the child's positive relationship to both parents.[20]

and on the other that contact with an absent parent should be maintained even if the child is on bad terms with the parent or that parent is 'overtly psychotic or overtly brutal'.[21] The children in Wallerstein and Kelly's sample, however, were notable for the yearning they expressed for the absent parent and their longing for visits. It has even been argued that good relationships may exist between children and both parents despite the perpetuation of inter-parental conflict.[22] Richards and Dyson (1982), reviewing the evidence, conclude that it suggests that it is important for children to maintain good relations with both parents after a separation. Since these children overwhelmingly would have wanted the parents' marriage to continue, it seems reasonable to suppose that, in the absence of evidence to the contrary, children will want to see as much of both parents as possible and that the policy on adjustment after divorce should be to encourage this.

How is this best achieved? Two goals, it is suggested, are necessary. The first is an approach which sees access from the *child's point of view*. The conventional expression that 'the (father) gets (reasonable) access' perpetuates the assumption that access is provided for the benefit of the parent. The Divisional Court opened the way to a child-oriented view of access in *M. v. M.*[23] when it described access as a right of the child, not the parent. But it is not clear that this idea has had much impact on traditional attitudes. The second goal, therefore, is to promote the first through institutional machinery. At one level it might be appropriate for all divorce petitions in which custody and access arrangements are agreed to record the nature of the agreement, the parties being expressly directed to declare that they consider the agreement to be in the best interests of the children. Solicitors would be obliged to consider whether the children's interests were properly promoted in any such agreement. This process could be enhanced by requiring all divorcing parties with children to declare that they have considered the option of joint custody. The significance of joint custody is that it retains in *both* parents the right to participate in important decisions about the child although the day-to-day care of the child remains with only one of them. The Court of Appeal in *Dipper* v. *Dipper*[24] has intimated that this is in any case the result if the court grants custody to one parent only. This position is of dubious legal merit[25] and a joint order in express terms is preferable because it *makes clear* to the parents that, despite the end of the marriage, their role as parents continues. Although the Court of Appeal encouraged the making of joint custody orders where it was thought the parents were likely to use it beneficially,[26] they have been very rarely used.[27] The President of the Family Division noted in 1980 that joint custody orders were now being sought more frequently, but the response has been simply to direct that, where the parents have agreed on joint custody, the judge should 'not make an order which is inconsistent with the agreement if only one parent appears at the chambers interview'.[28] This is far removed from active promotion of the arrangement.

There has been much discussion about joint custody in the United States[29] where some states recognize the practice in legislation, sometimes proclaiming a presumption in its favour. But there is some confusion about what it means, for sometimes it is taken to mean an arrangement whereby children alternate between parents. This idea, it is thought, should be approached with extreme caution. Little enough is known about the effects of disruption to children caused by divorce without experimenting with massive shunting around of children unless it is very clear that this will be to their benefit. Practical circumstances will in any case make this impossible in most cases. The ground for promoting joint custody urged here is simply that it symbolizes the expectation that a parental role will be maintained by the absent parent, impresses the adults that this is necessary from the children's point of view and may help to create an atmosphere conducive to successful visiting arrangements.

Wallerstein and Kelly (1980) and Murch (1980) have described the intense difficulties both parents find in restructuring their parental roles after divorce and it is probable that this is a significant contributory factor to those cases where visits are rare or non-existent. Only one-fifth of the low or non-access cases in Eekelaar's (1982a) welfare officers' sample were attributed by the officer to 'lack of interest' by the absent parent, a proportion certainly lower than it would be nationally because the sample was dominated by disputes over children. But the reasons for this apparent lack of interest may lie deep, perhaps in a feeling that the children are really 'lost' to the absent parent. This category of parent may be greater than it need be. It is not suggested that joint custody be imposed in the face of parental opposition, merely that, in ordinary cases, it be raised early as a desirable objective. If the parents are in disagreement over this question, this might be an appropriate issue to refer to any counselling service, at least where some prospects of success were apparent. Indeed, Pearson (1982) has reported that parents referred routinely to conciliation in a research project in Denver were overwhelmingly more likely to agree to joint custody (in the sense understood here) than were parents not so referred. This alone would not perhaps be enough to justify the establishment of such a service, but we shall see that it would be of importance in other contexts.

(b) *The contested cases: procedures*
Although numerically small in relation to the totality of divorce, contested custody and access cases tend to dominate the concern of lawyers and courts, probably because of their costs in terms of emotion and time. Eekelaar and Clive (1977) found that, in England and Wales, nearly one-third of the contested custody cases took over a year from petition to settlement of the issue; contested access cases

also involved lengthy litigation, often over the course of a year. In Scotland, proceedings were even more protracted, sometimes coming before four or five different judges. Long delays appear in reported cases from other jurisdictions.[30] Goldstein *et al.* (1973) have trenchantly criticized legal delays in determining child custody and argue that the legal process be abbreviated to accommodate the child's sense of time. But the problem requires closer examination. The perils of protracted decision-making seem to be the following: (1) the risk is increased that the final decision might remove a child from an environment in which he has become settled; (2) alternatively to (1), the court might feel compelled to leave the child in an unsatisfactory situation for fear of causing undue disruption; (3) the protracted adversarial legal process adds to the hostility between the adults; (4) the child's security is undermined by the period of uncertainty.

The first problem (and its converse, the second) are real enough. However, the extent to which courts in any event alter a child's residence in contested custody cases is low. Eekelaar and Clive (1977) concluded that this happened, without the parents' agreement, in only 5 per cent of those cases.[31] This is possibly an underestimate,[32] but it remains that the status quo will be retained in probably something like four-fifths of the disputes. Furthermore, it is possible that Goldstein *et al.* have exaggerated the adverse consequences for a child of a change of residence in itself. The view is based largely on Freudian psychoanalytic theory, but also depends heavily on the writings of Bowlby (1951) (1973) and others who regarded disruption of the parent–child relationship as severely damaging to children. In recent years this opinion has been under attack and has undergone modification. The methods of some of the research and the interpretation of the data had been criticized,[33] largely on the ground that mainly extreme cases of deprivation following upon separation were examined and insufficient attention was paid to the chances of overcoming any distress caused by separation in a good environment. Evidence of the successful adjustment of most adopted children relative to the problems experienced by illegitimate children who remain with their mother[34] is suggestive that separation alone does not necessarily lead to permanent psychological damage. Rutter has written that 'the largest differences in anti-social behaviour are associated with the marriage rating and not with separation experiences'; also 'separation experiences of any kind have never been shown to be associated with child neurosis'.[35] Thus it may be that distorted relationships and the failure to develop attachments at all are likely to be causative of psychological maladjustment and not the disruption of 'bonds'.[36]

In this uncertainty of knowledge, courts are wise to avoid taking undue risks by moving children from settled environments where they are happy. However, if a court is of the clear view that a change will be in this child's interests, the probability is that the child will adapt well to the move provided that the new environment is loving and supportive. The situation would be immensely improved if the adults could accept this amicably and the child could maintain a satisfactory relationship with the parent from whom she moved. Hence it is linked to a process creating optimum conditions for achieving common parental perception of the children's interests. The processes of conciliation are best suited to this. There is, therefore, good reason to accept some relaxation in the push towards final settlement if the time is used for an appropriate conciliation process. If this were the case, objection (3) to delay would not apply. The strength of the fourth objection is hard to assess and may indeed be accentuated if the child participates in the conciliation process. But it may be thought that the gains of successful conciliation are substantial enough to outweigh some of the risks inherent in the process, even those inevitably arising on its failure.

It may be thought unsatisfactory that, in litigation concerning her future, a child is rarely a party. English courts have the power to order a child to be separately represented and, if this is done, which is rare,[37] the Official Solicitor will usually be appointed to act as guardian *ad litem* for the child.[38] The Australian Family Law Act has similar provisions.[39] It may be argued in abstract terms that such representation should be a right of all children. But the argument is, in fact, overstated because the child is seldom in dispute with anyone. Furthermore, the position becomes more problematic on close examination. The advocate may confine himself to the role of a channel by which the child's wishes are put before the court. But this task is either simpler or more complex than it looks. If the child is of mature years, it should be possible to present his views to the court in some other way, either by direct statement by the child to the court or through the intermediary of a welfare officer. If the child is younger, it not only becomes difficult to know what weight to put on these opinions, it also requires special expertise, not usually consistent with a lawyer's training or mode of acting, to ascertain them. The very quest may be unreal, for what the child probably wants is for the marriage to continue and the formulation of a preference for one or other parent is impossible for him. Apart from those problems, the lawyer is in any event likely to become involved in courtroom debate with one or both parents, which could lead him into issues beyond those of the child's wishes and (probably) into parental competence. How is he to determine his stance on these matters other than by forming his own judgements or taking instructions from the child?[40]

Of course, the lawyer may see his role either as an investigator, to bring more facts before the court, or as an intermediary between the adults, or both. These may be useful roles, but it can again be questioned whether, institutionally, the performance of such functions should be left to private practice lawyers. The alternative is the appointment of a court officer with the double remit of seeking the children's views and presenting them to the court, and attempting conciliation between the adults. Many welfare officers in England and Wales in fact see themselves in this light: they represent the child's point of view, not only to the disputing adults, but to the court.[41] This function could be appropriately enhanced by re-designating these officers by some such style as 'Friend to the Child'.[42] At present the divorce court welfare service outside London is provided by the Probation and After-Care Service. In the capital it is a specialized agency attached to the courts. While there is some enthusiasm within the Probation Service for developing this aspect of their work, officers are aware of a perceived inappropriateness of the involvement in divorce cases of a service primarily associated with criminal matters.[43] It serves to enhance a view that society is judging the parents' behaviour rather than attempting to promote the children's welfare. But it may be possible to form a separately administered service, under the umbrella of the Probation Service and drawing upon its resources, to perform this work.[44] If all cases in which, at time of filing of the petition, the parents had not agreed on custody or access matters were routinely referred to this service, and cases falling outside the guiding principles were carefully considered for such referral, and a 'Friend to the Child' appointed with the express purpose of elucidating the interests of the child and bringing the adults to a common view on this matter, an adequate and perhaps the optimal institutional response might be achieved without significant strain to the existing structure. It should perhaps be added that the task of making referrals need not be a judicial one.

Contested cases: legal principles

The expression 'custody' in relation to children theoretically encompasses more than care and control. It includes the power to make decisions on important matters of the child's education and upbringing. The English courts have used this distinction to 'split' custody from care and control and grant custody to one parent, care and control to the other.[45] The purpose is to retain in the absent parent some control over the future of the child. In practice it seems that such orders are hardly ever made in England unless custody is awarded to both parties jointly, the merits of which have been considered above. Both parties will then determine the child's upbringing but it is necessary to specify with whom the child should live, and this will be done by granting 'care and control' to one of them. Unless joint custody orders become common, however, an award of custody will, for practical purposes, mean that the custodial parent will not only have daily care of the child but also the responsibility for making important decisions about her upbringing, though, if the decision in *Dipper* v. *Dipper*[46] is followed, this responsibility may be shared with the absent parent.

In making decisions about custody, it is accepted throughout Commonwealth jurisdictions that the court is to treat the welfare of the child as 'paramount'. Sometimes this injunction appears in statutory form and sometimes in judicial doctrine. The fact that the expression constantly used is 'paramount' and not 'sole' or 'exclusive' has suggested to some courts that factors other than those bearing on the welfare of the child may sometimes be relevant to the decision.[47] On the other hand, views have been expressed in the House of Lords that factors not directly related to the child's welfare may be taken into account only so far as they have a bearing on her welfare.[48] The effect of these judgements appears to be pushing the English courts into accepting that the child's welfare is the only consideration.[49] In many cases, however, the distinction may be only a matter of words because courts can incorporate some of those 'other' considerations into their concept of the child's welfare.

There is a danger that the vagueness of the welfare principle can be used in this way to import into a judgement matters that are, on another view, extraneous to it. Mnookin (1975) drew attention to the 'indeterminacy' of the welfare principle, its openness to idiosyncratic application and its susceptibility to conceal the promotion of individual perceptions of the good of society as a whole. In *re L.*,[50] for example, the Court of Appeal refused to award custody to a wife who had left her husband through 'fancy or passion' for another man. There were four possible reasons for denying the wife custody in this case: (a) a wish to discourage other women breaking up their homes; (b) justice between the parties, the husband being 'unimpeachable'; (c) as an attempt to encourage reconciliation between the parties; (d) that the wife had shown herself to be a bad mother. The first two reasons are hard to bring within the welfare principle on any view and have been disapproved in more recent English cases, in one of which Ormrod L.J. said it would be desirable if less was heard of the 'unimpeachable parent' in the future.[51] The third, though possibly justifiable on welfare grounds, involves a dangerous gamble by the court which Laskin J.A. has refused to take.[52] But the last reason opens the way for moral crusades.

Considerations of morality used to deter courts from allowing an adulterous mother custody of or even access to her children.[53] But the welfare principle has displaced that since 1910.[54] Nevertheless, the courts have taken longer to overcome their resistance to allowing a child to stay with a parent who was living in adultery. In *Raldini* v. *Raldini*[55] the Full Court of the Supreme Court of Queensland upheld an order transferring three children, who had been living happily with their mother and the co-respondent, to the father. The court intimated that she might recover them if she married the man. In *D.* v. *D.*[56] the Full Court of Western Australia removed children from the mother because it disapproved of her sexual behaviour, although there was no evidence that this was harming the children. In *re D.* (*minors*)[57] magistrates had awarded custody to a father because, among other things, 'an adulterer should not be allowed to take the place of the husband as father'. Bagnall J., however, effectively reversed this decision by an order under the wardship jurisdiction. Yet in *B.* v. *B.*[58] the Court of Appeal awarded custody to a clergyman father because it would be difficult for him to give his children a proper moral upbringing if they lived with his wife in an adulterous environment. In Canada, parents have been refused custody because they have cohabited with 'immoral' characters[59] or led promiscuous lives,[60] and even where the parent lived on welfare and failed to instil 'a sense of responsibility and constructive participation in society as a whole'.[61]

Other cases, however, have shown courts willing to grant custody to parents of whose practices they disapproved, such as homosexuality.[62] In doing this, the courts were prepared to look primarily to the emotional relationship between the child and the parent. It has been this concern which has, in recent years, led to a reluctance to disturb such relationships. In *re Thain*[63] in 1926 the Court of Appeal upheld a decision returning a child to her father after she had spent the first six years of her life with her aunt. The judges thought that the father's claim should prevail unless it was against the child's interests, and minimized the effect of the removal of the girl. Eve J. said, 'At her tender age one knows from experience how mercifully transient are the effects of partings and other sorrows.' This is not inconsistent with the welfare principle[64] but, with a few exceptions,[65] reported cases in recent years have shown that the courts' perceptions of the dangers of disrupting a child's emotional relationships have changed. In *J.* v. *C.*[66] Lord MacDermott expressly repudiated the words of Eve J., and in later cases Lords Hailsham,[67] Reid and Simon[68] have indicated that the dangers of 'uprooting' a child, even if under two years old, were sufficiently appreciated as not to require explicit medical evidence. Hence, in *P.* v. *P.*,[69] the Court of Appeal allowed four girls to stay with a father who was epileptic and had been convicted of sexual offences. Similar cases have been reported in Australia,[70] Canada[71] and the United States.[72] The judgements delivered in the Supreme Court of Canada in *Talsky* v. *Talsky*[73] are, however, notable for the lack of reference to the attachments the children had formed and the implications of their separation from one or other of their parents. It is impossible to impose rigid rules for the determination of these cases, but the risks engendered by the indeterminacy of the welfare principle demand that the attention of the adjudicator should be more precisely focused. Since the central issue is the quality of the relationship the children have with the adults, legislation should provide that this be the matter of first consideration and that the key determinant should be the maintenance of the relationship which is most important to the child.[74]

It is often alleged that, in determining custody disputes, judges have a bias in favour of mothers, especially where young children (particularly girls) are concerned. It is certainly true that many judicial pronouncements have been made stating that preference, even though it might be conceived of as a rule of 'common sense' rather than a rule of law.[75] Such a criterion for decision may reflect assumptions about what society should be like rather than a true appreciation of the child's emotional ties. It may also reflect assumptions about the nature of parent–child relationships which may be true neither generally nor in the particular case. Sometimes the preference may simply reflect a practical view that, given modern conditions, it is less likely that a father will be able to attend a (young) child's needs as well as a mother can. These points illustrate the hazards of simple reliance on such a standard, especially as courts referring to it seldom articulate which assumption(s) lie behind it.

How far are courts moved by the mother preference? To ascertain this it is not sufficient simply to observe, as Bradbrook (1971) and Prentice (1979) do, that custody awards after divorce are over-whelmingly granted to mothers, for this simply reflects the fact that this is what the vast majority of parents agree.[76] To discern any judicial 'bias' it is necessary to isolate the contested cases. These fall into two kinds, those where the child(ren) is (are) with one parent at the time of hearing and this is challenged by the other, and those where the family is still together at the time. In the first instance any possible judicial bias comes into competition with the general reluctance to disturb the status quo, and it is instructive to see whether one or the other parent is more likely to overcome that reluctance. It is very difficult to obtain an adequate sample of such cases and Eekelaar's (1982a) findings are based on rather small numbers. However, they were consistent with previous findings by Eekelaar and Clive (1977) that mothers are more likely to challenge fathers who have the children than vice versa and indicated that mothers were indeed more likely to 'recover' the children (36.4 per cent success) than fathers (11 per cent success). Furthermore, in the six cases where the parties had not yet separated, the court granted custody in each case to the mother.

These findings do not establish a strong case of *judicial* bias for mothers. Firstly, in all except two cases, the outcome had been recommended by the welfare officer, so, if bias there be, it may not be confined to judges. Secondly, where the father had the children, he was still more likely to keep them than lose them to the mother. However, Maidment (1981) reviewed all reported English appeal court decisions during five years in the 1970s and concluded that 74 per cent of decisions resulting in a return of a child from fathers to mothers could be explained only by judicial preference for the mother. It seems then that, in England at least, while instances of such bias can be found, especially at higher judicial levels, it does not appear to be a pervasive phenomenon, at any rate when it might mean moving a child from an established caretaker. Its significance also is hard to assess in the absence of clear articulation of the assumptions on which it is grounded. Fears that its presence plays any significant part in reinforcing stereotype sex role-playing seem exaggerated on this evidence, especially in view of the massive scale on which parents voluntarily agree to leave children with their mother. Marginal bias towards mothers (whether from judges or welfare officers) in custody determination is surely no more than a reflection of the fundamental structure of our society.[77]

But the possibility of unarticulated bias towards one parent or another can lead to decisions contrary to a child's interest, strengthening the case for legislative guidelines establishing the primacy of existing relationships. Rosen (1979) found no indication that parenting by a father had adverse effects on the children of her sample, and in Eekelaar's (1982a) sample those children in fact showed fewer signs of disturbance than the others. On the other hand, they (especially if a second child) did show greater hostility to their mother than children living with their mother displayed to their absent father. It may be that children harbour deeper resentments against a mother who, in their eyes, 'abandons' them than against a father. If this can be confirmed, it might provide a reason, *from the child's point of view*, to prefer a mother's claim over a father's where the parties are still living together and nothing seems to distinguish their potential as parents. Goldstein *et al.* (1973) suggests that in such cases the 'most rational and least offensive' way of deciding would be by drawing lots, a true counsel of despair.[78] If the parents cannot see it as in their children's interests to agree on a solution, the court, as the children's ultimate guardian, cannot escape the responsibility of endeavouring judgement.

Contested cases: access and name

It has been observed above[79] how the foundation of the right of access as that of the child and not a parent can be used as a tool in the mediation process towards bringing the parents round to agreeing access arrangements between them. Most of the considerations relevant to custody determination are equally applicable to access resolution. However, there are two issues which require special attention.

Sometimes a custodial parent who has remarried seeks to terminate the absent parent's visits by adopting the child jointly with the new spouse. Judges have generally been hostile to such a step. In New Brunswick, Dickson J. went as far as to hold that the consent of a former husband was necessary to the adoption although the relevant legislation specified that only the consent of the divorced parent to whom custody had been granted was necessary. He refused to dispense with the father's consent.[80] In *Penny* v. *Penny*[81] Disbery J. said:

> [The wife] places great stress upon the development of her new 'family unit' and obviously considers it desirable that [the child] accepts [her new husband] as 'Dad' in lieu of, and to the exclusion of, his father. . . . The records of the divorce courts clearly establish that many first marriages were not, as romantics maintain, 'made in heaven', and I have never heard that second marriages have any better prospects for success.

The Divisional Court has expressed similar objections in equally forceful language. Against the argument that the child had a right to a secure home free from interference by the natural father, Sir George Baker P. said:

> It disregards that the father is the natural father and that the child has an equal right and interest not to be deprived of his natural father by other people, be it the mother, the step-father, the social worker, the justices or anybody else, unless it is clearly proved that his welfare requires adoption.[82]

But a number of cases have been reported from Canada where courts have allowed adoption by a parent and stepparent over a natural parent's objections on the ground that the father's interests must give way to the child's welfare.[83] It is the responsibility of legislatures to give the judiciary guidance on the policy to be followed in these cases. Some help has been given in England and Wales, where it has been enacted that where a child's adoption is sought by his parent and stepparent the court must dismiss the application if the judge thinks the matter is better dealt with as a custody issue under the matrimonial jurisdiction.[84] The Act does not state when it is better to deal with the problem as one of custody and access rather than adoption, but the provision at least requires the question to be asked: 'Will adoption safeguard and promote the welfare of the child better than either the existing order or a joint custody order (in favour of the custodial parent and the stepparent).'[85] Essentially the court is weighing the advantages of complete integration into the new family against continuation of some legal relationship with the child's other parent. While adoption may in some cases be desirable, particularly where the absent parent has lost all interest in the child and welcomes the adoption as a means of relieving any support obligation towards her, its disadvantage is that its very completeness and absoluteness prevents separate assessments of different aspects of the problem. The most important aspects are, usually, the child's surname, succession rights, access by the absent parent, the stepparent's status regarding important decisions respecting the child and finality.

Reconstituted families frequently desire any children of a former marriage to bear the name of the new family. It is thought it might be embarrassing for a child to bear a different name from her brother and step-siblings. Whether the embarrassment is felt more by the adults than the child is uncertain. Adoption would achieve the required homogeneity whereas, if a parent has custody only, it is clear that the name cannot formally be changed without the consent of the other parent.[86] Even an informal attempt to change the child's name by, for example, registering her at school in the new name, is strictly contrary to the rights of the other parent[87] and will probably be in breach of the custody order, which prohibits this in the absence of agreement between the parents or the consent of the court.[88] Yet what can be done if the step has been taken? Ought courts to issue orders attempting to control the name conferred on a child by its family? One may agree with Ormrod L.J.'s attempts to diffuse the issue and his observations that it is the child's relationship with the absent parent which matters, not the name she bears,[89] though the Court of Appeal has subsequently re-asserted its view of the importance of the issue.[90] This is eminently a matter which, prior to submission to court adjudication, should be referred to a mediation service.

Adoption is not the only way to resolve concern over a child's succession rights in the reconstituted family. They can more easily (and cheaply) be secured by the making of a will by the stepparent (who should in any case make a new one on remarriage). This has the advantage, lost by adoption, of retaining the child's succession rights against the absent parent. Nor is adoption necessary to solve problems over access. Although it has been held in Canada that an adoption order does not extinguish access rights made under a divorce decree,[91] this is probably not so in England and Wales, although it may be possible to make adoption subject to continuation of access.[92] But if this is done, much of the point of adoption is lost.

The extent, if at all, to which the absent parent should retain contact with the child can, however, be dealt with quite satisfactorily under the matrimonial jurisdiction. If the stepparent is merely seeking recognition of his status *vis-à-vis* the child and the right to be involved in decisions about her upbringing, this could be achieved by appointing him joint custodian with the custodial parent. Whether this would deprive the absent parent of his rights to such involvement is unclear after the decision in *Dipper* v. *Dipper*.[93] Presumably these 'rights' would not be shared between the three adults, so it seems that a joint custody order in favour of a natural parent and the stepparent should give the stepparent the effective status as parent, if that were desired.

Finally, adoption may be thought desirable because, unlike a custody arrangement, it is (generally) unreviewable. Goldstein *et al.* (1973) favour this position for, although they do not advocate adoption, they argue that custody orders, once made, should be irreviewable and that courts should be powerless to impose conditions about access, leaving any such arrangements entirely to the agreement of the parties. Their premises rest on their view of the need of a child for an undisturbed relationship with her psychological parent and the disruptive potential of intrusion by an absent parent. There is no indication, in Britain at any rate, that applications for review of the custody award happen except very rarely (nor, in view of the reluctance to move children, are they likely to be successful), but there certainly is a case for routinely referring any such applications to the (proposed) 'Friend to the Child'. As for the suggestion about access orders, the assumption on which it is based has already been questioned.[94] Further objection to the proposal can be taken on the following grounds:

(a) If maintaining a relationship with the absent parent is viewed as a right of the child rather than the parent, it cannot be right to leave its implementation entirely in the hands of the custodial parent who may have strong personal reasons to deny it. In extreme cases the custodial parent may deceive the child about her origins. It is not clear why the courts should be deprived of all control over these matters, at least if one of the parents wishes to raise them. It may, of course, be desirable if the courts refer such matters initially to a 'Friend to the Child'.

(b) The new family unit might fail through death or subsequent separation. In an extreme case the custodial parent might die leaving the child with a stepparent with whom she had an imperfect relationship. A child might be dragged through a succession of failed marriages without having the opportunity to sustain links with any father figure. In such circumstances even relatively weak links with an absent parent might become strengthened and a source of value.

(c) The knowledge that the custody determination left decisions about access entirely with the custodial parent would inevitably increase the quantity and bitterness of custody disputes. Abduction of children, both before and after custody determination, would be likely to increase.

(d) It is likely that absent parents denied contact with their children through the decision of the custodian would refuse to provide support for the woman and possibly for the child. Problems of enforcement against the aggrieved parent would be particularly difficult and the result may be to throw the woman and child on to state support.

(e) It is possible that too much emphasis is placed on the 'closed' nuclear family unit. In some societies children maintain relationships with numbers of people outside the unit, either in the extended family or community groups. It has been said that 'attempts to reproduce the nuclear family in the step situation are doomed to failure in any case . . . an alternative framework is both available and promising of more heuristic formulation of questions. That is, the step-family can be conceptualized as a structural variation of importance equal to the Kibbutz pattern. . . .'[95]

It cannot be said that the evidence of harm to children generally by visits from absent parents is strong enough to justify these risks. The desirability that access should be agreed between the adult parties is consistent with a general policy favouring voluntary agreements above court-imposed solutions, but, far from allowing private regulation conclusively to determine the matter, Maidment has argued that 'it is totally inadequate to leave the working out of an access order to the parties',[96] and that supervision orders should be made in all cases enabling welfare officers to make periodic visits. This may impose too great a burden on available resources. A more modest suggestion is made by Justice that, on divorce (and, it might be urged, during pre-divorce discussions with their lawyers), the parents should be issued with a 'Visiting Code' which can be framed in such a way as to make parents more aware that access is seen as a child's right.[97] This proposal could be conveniently integrated into the suggestion made here that divorcing parties should be presented with guiding principles within which their arrangements would normally be expected to fall. Indeed, the whole question of possible stepparent adoption might be raised at this stage so as to alert the parents to problems that may lie ahead and to the alternatives available for their resolution. Much might be achieved by simply, and routinely, making available to the parties as soon as an application is made for divorce, a booklet setting out information not only about the legal procedures but guidance as to possible post-divorce problems and a statement of the basic principles with which a desirable divorce settlement should conform. We now turn to consider what, as far as property and financial matters are concerned, these principles might be.

5
The Economics of Family Breakdown: Needs and Resources

Marital separation invariably precipitates an economic crisis for one or both of the adults. Two residences are necessary and the resources which served one establishment must now suffice for two. The man may encounter additional calls on his income from a new partner and other children, although this may sometimes provide a new resource. In this context, the higher remarriage rate of men over women, and the generally low remarriage rate of older women, is significant. If, as is usual, the former wife is left with the children, it is scarcely surprising that they will suffer a serious drop in living standards. This chapter considers the extent of these privations and the resources available for alleviating them.

Needs

At the outset of this discussion of the economics of family breakdown, an important distinction must be made between divorces between childless couples and divorces involving children. Eekelaar and Maclean (1983) have demonstrated that these two categories differ fundamentally with respect to the economic impact of divorce. It is, for example, very rare for long-term support by one former spouse of the other to take place in the former category, while this is normal where there are children. Where the parties are childless, the legal costs of dissolving the union are cheaper. Often the divorce is on the basis of separation and consent, and the only legal transaction apart from the divorce will be the sale of the house (if jointly owned) or the purchase by the husband of the wife's half share. Where there are children it is more likely, as we will see, that the custodial parent will stay on in the house. But most significantly, the economic position of both men and women divorcing after a childless marriage is no different from that of members of the population generally. (70 per cent of the childless divorced men and 73 per cent of the women in the study had incomes above 140 per cent of their supplementary benefit entitlement: 71 per cent of the general population are in this position.) However, where the divorced marriage contained children, only 47 per cent of the men and 40 per cent of the women had incomes above 140 per cent of their supplementary benefit entitlement at time of the interviews. Women living alone with the children were by far the worse off (only 18 per cent above this level). In what follows, therefore, the concentration will be upon divorces involving children.

It has been estimated[1] that, if a man leaves his wife and two children, the remnant family require some 75–80 per cent of the family's former total income if it is to maintain its previous living standard. As we shall see, far from achieving this, these families rapidly descend the socio-economic scale. The main source of income for 350,000 of the 650,000 fatherless families in 1976 was supplementary benefit: 230,000 relied mainly on earnings and some 50,000 on maintenance.[2] Of the children living in a fatherless family at the age of eleven studied in the National Child Development Study, 47 per cent had been dependent on supplementary benefit at some time during the year preceding the investigation. The cause of fatherlessness most likely to lead to this situation was divorce or separation. Sixty-one per cent of children whose parents were in this situation had been dependent on the benefit compared to 48 per cent of illegitimate children and 25 per cent of children of widows. Nearly a quarter of the children living with a divorced or separated mother had been dependent on supplementary benefit for the entire previous year.[3] Table 5 shows the comparison of income in 1981, presented as a percentage of their supplementary benefit entitlement at that time, of a nationally representative sample of people divorced after 1971 who were living with children.

This is not a situation confined to Britain. The Australian Commission of Inquiry into Poverty found that half of fatherless families have an income below or barely above the 'poverty line' as assessed by the Commission, and that separated and deserted wives

Table 5 *Household net disposable income as a percentage of supplementary benefit entitlement for each family, single and remarried parents divorced after 1971*

% SB entitlement	% single (n=52)		% remarried (n=98)	
Above 300	4		9	
250–299	2	8	5	26
200–249	2		12	
National average income for 2-adult, 2-child family				
180–199	0		8	
160–179	2	12	9	37
140–159	10		20	
Poverty line				
110–139	17		13	
90–109	31	79	11	30
Under 90	31		6	

Source: Maclean and Eekelaar (1983). The single parents include five lone fathers and the remarried include unmarried cohabitees. The 'poverty line' follows Layard (1978).

were the most impoverished, largely due to difficulties over housing.[4] Similar evidence exists regarding the United States.[5] The statistics cannot be explained on the ground that women who experience divorce were in poverty before the divorce and that the experience of divorce had no significant effect. Hoffman (1977), using data from a longitudinal study of 5,000 American families, showed that people who remained married over the period 1967–73 achieved a 21.7 per cent increase in real family income over that period whereas women who divorced or separated in that time suffered a 29.3 per cent reduction.[6] Maclean and Eekelaar (1983) have shown that in Britain, too, divorce or separation occasions a significant movement

Table 6 *Parents divorced after 1971 reporting supplementary benefit as their main source of income over time*

Present status of respondent	% at marriage	% at separation	% now
Single parents (n=52)	0	15	54
Remarried parents (n=98)	1	8	13

Source: Maclean and Eekelaar (1983).

into poverty for the remnant mother–child family (see Table 6). In an economy where the number of families in poverty would triple were it not for the fact that *both* parents earn,[7] it is not surprising that the departure of the most significant earner has such dire consequences.

Resources

(a) *Mother's earnings*

Although, at breakdown, it is the segment of the family comprising the mother and the children which has the greatest need, it is precisely this unit which has the lowest capability of generating income. This is so despite the sharp increase in economic activity by women, especially married women, during this century, particularly since the Second World War. Of married women (England and Wales), 9.6 per cent were economically active in 1911, 21.7 per cent in 1959 and 51.3 per cent in 1979,[8] a proportion almost identical to that in the United States.[9] The rate is higher (between 60–70 per cent) where the mother maintains a one-parent family.[10] However, despite a narrowing of the gap between men's and women's earnings about the time of the enactment of the Equal Pay Act 1975, the Law Commission (1980) reported that the average hourly earnings of women are 73 per cent of a man's, and the gap may be widening.[11] Women tend to fill lower-paid positions, to work shorter hours and do less overtime. Seventy per cent of employed mothers with dependent children fill part-time jobs. In large part this is due to attempts to reconcile the demands of employment with family responsibilities that are seen to rest upon women,[12] but the result is not only less daily income but less job security, fewer fringe benefits and no pension prospects. Not surprisingly, then, women are overwhelmingly more vulnerable than men to the effects of economic recession. The number of women who *became* unemployed in Britain grew by 177 per cent between June 1975 and June 1980, compared to 44.6 per cent increase over the same period for men.[13]

These facts in themselves should caution against overly optimistic expectations that the acquisition or resumption of paid employment by mothers is in itself likely significantly to alleviate the economic burden on the mother–child family. Indeed, Maclean and Eekelaar (1983) found that the income of a significant minority (4:10) of single mothers who were in full-time employment was either lower than or virtually indistinguishable from what it would have been if they had worked part-time and relied on supplementary benefit augmented by casual earnings. Only 2:9 were more than £20 a week better off working full-time. And this ignores the costs incurred by full-time employment (travel, eating out, child-minding fees). As for part-time earners, nearly half (7:16) who did not receive supplementary benefit were in fact living at or below their supplementary benefit entitlement although three of them received maintenance payments. Of the 8:16 who received the benefit, five were potential maintenance recipients but the actual beneficiary of these payments was the state. It seems clear that, even when work is available, the earning power of these mothers can normally do little to alleviate the financial adversity of divorce.

(b) *Capital resources of former family*

In 1971 Todd and Jones (1972) carried out interviews with 2,371 married couples and 844 formerly married persons on behalf of the Law Commission in order to discover information about their property arrangements and their views on matrimonial property questions. From the point of view of economic problems on break-down, the following information is relevant. Fifty-two per cent of couples were owner–occupiers of the matrimonial home; 45 per cent rented their accommodation and 3 per cent were not responsible for the place in which they were living. Most renters (62 per cent) lived in local authority houses. The vast majority of the tenancies (82 per cent) were in the husband's name alone; only 3 per cent were in the wife's name and 14 per cent in joint names. Of the owner–occupiers, 52 per cent had the home in their joint names, 42 per cent in the husband's and only 5 per cent in the wife's name. Thus, only one-third of all married couples with a home, either rented or owned, had a joint legal interest in the property. However, there had been a considerable increase in the proportion of jointly owned homes since the Second World War. Only 20 per cent of the owner–occupiers who purchased their home before the war did so in joint names, whereas 74 per cent of those purchasing in the 1970s did so. However, two-thirds of the jointly owned homes were still subject to a mortgage and the extent of the home's value as a capital asset to the spouses is of course reduced by the debt owed to the mortgagee. For nearly half the persons interviewed there was no home which could count as a potential asset. Many had other forms of property, such as current bank accounts (53 per cent, of which 40 per cent had a joint account), savings accounts (87 per cent), life insurance (83 per cent), invest-ments (13 per cent), other property (6 per cent), and businesses (9 per cent: 74 per cent of them owned by the husband, 7 per cent owned by the wife and the rest jointly owned). A more recent survey carried out in Scotland in 1979 found that only 37 per cent of the couples owned their home, a much lower proportion than in England and Wales, but the findings were very similar with respect to the other matters.[14]

A quarter of the English couples said that, excluding the house and current bank account, the total value of their other assets was less than £100 (£426 at 1982 value), and only 19 per cent estimated their assets above £1,000 (£4,260 at 1982 value). Forty-two per cent of the Scottish couples valued their savings and assets at under £500 (£785 at 1982 value). The value of life insurance policies was difficult to assess but, in the English survey at least, was thought to be moderate. Fifty-six per cent of the Scottish couples contributed (through one or both spouses, but mostly the husband) to a private pension scheme, a potentially valuable asset, but whose benefit would only be felt in the future and probably escape the wife altogether after her divorce.[15] It is therefore as true in Britain as it is in the United States[16] that almost always the only significant item of realizable property will be the family home, assuming owner-occupation. And its value as capital is usually much diminished if it is (as is usual) held on unredeemed mortgage.

When it is remembered that divorce is more prevalent among the poor[17] it is abundantly clear that, leaving aside the family residence, if we look to capital resources alone we will rarely find sufficient to contribute significantly to the economic needs of the post-divorce mother–child family. Indeed, for many divorcees with children, the main problem is sorting out debts, not assets.[18] Property distribution schemes on divorce cannot, therefore, realistically be considered to fulfil this purpose. However, it may in some cases be possible to see the house not so much as part of the capital stock of the family but a source of continuing provision. How this may be done will be considered at a later point. However, it seems important at this stage to ask how far divorce (or separation) seems to precipitate insecurity in housing for the remnant mother–child family. Eekelaar and Maclean (1983) found that, where the family has been in public (local authority) housing at the time of the breakdown, on separation the spouse with the children will usually stay in the home. If they were in privately rented accommodation or owner-occupation, their position seems much less secure. In nearly half the cases the house was sold; but where it was not, the custodial parent was just as likely to move out as to stay. In other words, the children moved in about three-quarters of all owner-occupier cases. In about one-eighth they went into the house of their mother's new partner. About half of the women who left were able to re-house themselves in the private sector, thus reducing the disruption to children likely to result from a move from private to public sector housing. Yet, in view of the significant difficulties many of these families had regarding income, it is likely that their position in the private sector remained precarious.

(c) *Former husband's earning capacity*

The Scottish Law Commission (1981) found that periodical allowances *for the wife* were claimed in about one-third of divorce cases, but only in 18 per cent when there were no children. Claims for aliment (child support) were made in two-thirds of cases involving children; in nearly three-quarters of cases the claims succeeded completely, and in the remaining quarter a lesser sum was awarded than that claimed. Thus child support, sometimes coupled with an order for the mother herself, was made in two-thirds of cases involving children.[19] Similarly, in California, Weitzman and Dixon (1980) found that in 1977 alimony for the wife alone was awarded only in some 17 per cent of cases, but child support was awarded in 85 per cent of cases.[20] Combined awards of child support and payments for the mother herself seem less common in California than in Scotland, a point reinforced by the finding that alimony awards to mothers with young children declined sharply after the introduction of no-fault divorce in California. Only 12 per cent received any award in 1977.[21]

So it appears that mothers do commonly seek support for the children from their former husbands, though they less frequently combine this with a claim for their own maintenance. But how much money is, in fact, recovered by this means? An early English study[22] of support orders made in magistrates' courts showed not only that amounts ordered were generally lower than a recipient's entitlement to supplementary benefit, but also that 40 per cent of orders were complied with less than 10 per cent regularity. Chambers (1979) quotes a Wisconsin survey which showed that, in the first year of the order, 42 per cent of payers paid less than 10 per cent of the order, 20 per cent paid a moderate part of it and 38 per cent more than 80 per cent. Four years later, 67 per cent were paying less than 10 per cent and only 22 per cent were paying more than 80 per cent.[23] Yee (1979) has recently shown that, in Denver, 76 per cent of cases where child support was ordered were for an amount that was less than welfare entitlement. It has also been reported that in the United States only about 3 per cent of all eligible mother–child families receive enough in child support and alimony alone to put them above the official poverty level.[24]

This data might suggest that the former husband's earning capacity should be written off as a meaningful source of support for the mother–child family, and, indeed, the Finer Committee virtually did this when it argued for a general guaranteed maintenance allowance for all single parent families payable by the state.[25] However, the low sums specified in support orders and even their apparent low compliance rate should not cause us to underestimate the extent to which fathers do pay over *something* to their former families. Maclean and Eekelaar (1983) showed that in 1981 two-thirds of single mothers with children divorced after 1971 received some regular contribution of this kind and this continued for nearly half of them even after they had remarried. The reason for non-payment seemed largely to be that the fathers were unemployed. American studies suggest a slightly lower rate of income transfer. Only about one-half of divorced, one-quarter of separated and 6 per cent of never married mothers receive any child support payment.[26]

But what impact do these payments have on the receiving household? We have already seen that, in Britain, the full-time or part-time employment of a single mother will generally make little difference to that family's income level relative to official poverty levels, even though the income may be supplemented by maintenance payments. However, as Table 7 shows, maintenance nevertheless constituted 10 per cent of the household income for 20 per cent of the single, divorced, mother's household, 11 to 30 per cent for half of them and over 30 per cent for a quarter. The proportion was greater, the lower the household's total income. However, in a quarter of all cases, all of the lowest income, the maintenance payments in fact benefited only the state because the recipients were in receipt of supplementary benefit and the father's money was either paid direct to the state or simply reduced the amount of benefit. The implications of this will be returned to later. At this point one needs to note merely that, despite the smallness of the total sums in fact paid over, they formed a not insignificant proportion of the receiver family's total income.

Table 7 *Maintenance received as a percentage of household income*

Percentage of h/h income	Single parent families (n=30)		Reconstituted families (n=30)	
	(No.)	(%)	(No.)	(%)
Up to 5	4	20	10	63
6–10	2		9	
11–20	9	50	6	24
21–30	6		1	
31–50	5	24	1	10
Above 50	2		2	
Don't know	2		1	

Source: Maclean and Eekelaar (1983).

Despite the relative importance of support payments, the recipient families, as Table 5 shows, remain significantly worse off than the average family in the population. American studies have suggested that child support awards, as calculated, generally leave a substantial discrepancy between the income of the former husband and his former family. Hampton (1975), using data from the long-term Panel Study in Income Dynamics, found that, after marital disruption, over twice as many husbands remained in the top three income/needs deciles as wives, and only 15 per cent were in the lowest deciles compared to 34 per cent of wives. The situation changed little after adjustment for alimony payments. Weitzman (1981a), drawing on a sample of Los Angeles divorcees, in which more wealthy people were deliberately over-represented, also showed discrepancy in the *per capita* income between men and women, as shown in Table 8.

Table 8 *Post-Divorce* per capita *income as a percentage of the old family* per capita *income*

Pre-divorce yearly family income	Wife	Husband
Under $20,000	129	176
$20–29,000	87	165
$30–39,000	77	176
Above $40,000	48	201

Source: Weitzman (1981a), Table 14.

It is noticeable that the disparity between men and women is weaker for poorer families, which constitute the bulk of the divorcing population. Furthermore, it must be remembered that the data is based on income levels at one year after divorce. The longer time passes after divorce, the more likely it is that the man's *per capita* income will diminish by the calls made upon it by a new spouse (probably with children) and new children born to the new marriage. The position in 1981 in Britain as between mother–child families and reconstituted families of persons divorced over the previous ten years was shown in Table 5. It is there apparent that, while the families of the remarried men are indeed better off than the mother–child families, they are nevertheless less well off than the average family. Unlike the Californian figures, the income of these reconstituted families includes any brought in by the new parent. It would seem, then, that, when the former husband remarries, or, at least, where this introduces new children, he is unlikely to have available any significant amounts to supplement the monies he is already paying to the mother–child family. Maclean and Eekelaar (1983) did, however, find that, where the fathers had no new children in their household, 8:10 did appear to have additional resources which might possibly be called upon and still leave him at a standard of living equivalent to the national average. But of course the financial position of these men might change significantly over time.

Remarriage

Little is known about the effects to a former family which the entry into a new marriage by either or both adults has on their finances. In the case of the recipient, [her] remarriage will in some jurisdictions[27] automatically terminate [her] own maintenance order and in others simply give rise to a circumstance justifying application for variation.[28] But orders for child support will continue in effect. Women, as we have seen, are less likely to remarry than men, but the extent of maintenance payments for the former wife's benefit is so insubstantial that it is unlikely that they form any significant deterrent to remarriage. Remarriage is, in fact, the most reliable way for the mother–child family to approximate its former standard of living.

However, as Table 5 shows, despite the improvement in economic condition which remarriage brings about, reconstituted families are generally less well off than the families of first married people. This may be partly a function of the greater tendency to divorce among the poorer sections of the community. It may also, however, be affected by the larger family size of reconstituted families. It is clear, however, that remarriage is, to a large extent, a mechanism whereby the resources of the main breadwinner are transferred from one mother–child family to another. Child support payments from the former husband may be made into the reconstituted family, but these form an insignificant portion of its income (see Table 7). It is clear that, until the mother remarries, the major resource of divorced and separated mothers and children is the state. However, the extent of their benefit from these resources is presently tied to the level of poverty relief programmes in particular states. How far this could, or should, be altered so as to raise these families off poverty levels is a central issue in any discussion of measures dealing with family economics after divorce.

Needs and rights

Does the evidence present a compelling case for community action to alleviate the adversities of mother–child families? It might be argued that, in over half of these cases, the hardships are temporary only, for the mothers will rapidly remarry. It may also be argued that special provisions for these families will either (1) encourage divorce, (2) discourage remarriage or (3) inhibit the mothers from seeking gainful employment. In so far as divorce has been thought to be associated with the growing economic dependence of women, the possibility that a high degree of economic security after divorce may facilitate family breakdown cannot be excluded. It has not been established whether breakdown is or is not more prevalent in states with more generous welfare programmes,[29] but there is American evidence that welfare systems may affect remarriage patterns.[30] But the British data reviewed above suggests it is unlikely that supplementary benefit payments would deter remarriage in the United Kingdom. Furthermore, it was the purpose of the Finer Committee, in recommending a 'guaranteed maintenance allowance' for all single parent families, that this should be sufficient to offer the parent a genuine choice whether to take employment or care for the children full-time.[31]

A more basic objection might be made to any schemes involving community cost which benefits these families, by appeal to the view that no member of a community owes *any* obligation in justice to less well-off members. This extreme view of Nozick (1975) denies the moral legitimacy of any redistribution of wealth, for, no matter what people's needs may be, they cannot justify the forcible removal from others of their holdings legitimately acquired. Its logic compels a denial of entitlement by the mother–child family to any portion of the resources either of the father or, in his default, of the community. In effect, it denies children any right to beneficent upbringing from their parents, or, in their stead, the community.

Since this position would seem barely tenable, Nozick and adherents to his theory might wish to concede such rights within the family. But this would destroy the major assumption of the theory and make it difficult to resist the transference of the children's rights from their parents to the community if the parents refuse, or are unable, to meet them. It is a weakness of much political and philosophical discussion about redistribution of wealth that it assumes distribution only between adults. Yet poverty largely affects families so that, for the large part, the beneficiaries of, or claimants to, redistribution can be said to be children. Beckerman and Clark (1982) have shown that the major cause of poverty among non-pensioners is large family size. Justification (if any) of redistribution must therefore raise theoretical questions concerning the rights of children.

We can here anticipate a view that will be maintained below,[32] that child protection law can be seen as grounded in a view that children have certain claims to a minimal standard of upbringing; that the child's parents are *prima facie* entrusted with the responsibility to provide this; and that, in their default, the community may override the parents in order to secure the provision of adequate standards. This assumes a direct claim by children on the community. Its foundation may be said to be twofold. First, the obligation on each generation to have regard to the interests of future generations. As Barry (1977) has pointed out, such an obligation is difficult to extract from traditional theories of moral obligation, and might need to rest upon an a priori concept of the custodianship by a given generation of current resources to be handed on to future generations. Such a concept may need to be thought of as a 'self-evident' truth, implicit to a commitment to the well-being of the human race as a community over time.[33] The second basis for the claims of children may be said to rest on a requirement of fairness that individuals should start adult life with the minimum of avoidable disparity between them in their capability of realizing their life-chances.[34] Although it may be true that 'equality of opportunity', as an ultimate goal, is, even theoretically, unattainable,[35] this does not weaken the claim that inequalities visited on children as a result of dealings between adults represent an identifiable species of injustice. Furthermore, removal, or minimization, of such inequalities does not pose the threat to the currently dominant economic and ideological structure of western societies which a theory of equality of result does. Without prejudice to what may additionally be held about the extent to which equality of *result* should be achieved, the theory proposed here is that the obligation in justice to the next generation demands at least the reduction, so far as is compatible with that structure, of such inequalities.

The evidence reviewed in this chapter indicates that parental separation and divorce generate economic inequalities between groups of children which would be avoided if the parents stayed together. How far these inequalities affect the longer term life-chance of the children is unclear. Greenberg and Wolf (1982) claimed that there is a relationship, in the case of white American males, between their experience of father absence in their late teens and their earnings levels at the age of twenty-three. Those who experienced such absence earned nearly one-third less than those from a two-parent home. The association seemed to be with the deficiency of income caused by father absence and the shorter time spent by the mother in the home rather than with father absence in itself. But in the absence of data of the earlier economic profile of the families, no causal connection between these events can be held proved. However, in general terms, it seems that, while an individual's point of origin in the social structure does not necessarily determine his place within it over the course of his life, those originating in the upper brackets are more likely to remain there than those originating outside are likely to enter them.[36]

At least until their mother remarries, if she does so at all, the children of divorce will usually experience not only economic reverse, but its accompaniments: downward social mobility, a degree of insecurity in housing, possibly deterioration in educational and child-care provision and the disruption of affectional ties. While we do not have hard evidence of the consequences of these events, it is plausible to suppose that they have a measureable adverse impact on their life-chances. However, these circumstances do not in themselves establish a *priority* for these children over other disadvantaged groups.

As against the community, all children (for example, those in families of the long-term unemployed) have an equal claim. The unique position of divorce children is that, in their case, there may be additional resources against which they may have a claim. For not only is their position as regards other children in the community relevant, it is also relevant to consider their position as regards the living standards of their former breadwinner and any new dependants he might acquire. The argument here is that, unless and until the state is prepared substantially to improve the lot of all disadvantaged children so as to reduce the inequalities in life-chances between all children, there is an *additional inequity* for divorce children who are thus disadvantaged if this occasions a substantial disparity between their position and that at which their former breadwinner is either potentially able to keep them or at which he in fact maintains other children. It is as if certain children were systematically adversely treated within a family. But the principle of justice used here is founded not on marriage or geographic location but the parental nexus. From the child's point of view, a parent must at least treat all his children so as to minimize as far as possible inequalities between them which may affect their adult lives.

6
Adjustment on Divorce

The family's capital assets

This chapter confronts the question: on what principles should the law adjust the former family's resources on marriage breakdown? It is convenient to start by considering any capital assets included in those resources. Potentially these include any property in which either the adults or any child has a legal or beneficial interest, either alone or jointly (with others or with each other). To understand the present approach to this matter in England, it is necessary to recount, briefly, the evolution of matrimonial property law since the turn of the century.

The traditional law did nothing to assist in the re-adjustment process. The Married Women's Property Act 1882 laid the foundation for the system of separate property between spouses characteristic of Anglo-American law. Each spouse owns and controls his or her own property during the marriage and, on dissolution, each takes out what belongs to him or her. This, of course, is subject to the powers of the court on dissolution, but these were originally very limited. The most a wife could expect on divorce was an income payment, secured or unsecured. There was no power to transfer any property owned by the husband to the wife. An exceptional power to vary ante-nuptial or post-nuptial settlements in favour of either party to the marriage existed, but this depended on the availability of property which fell within the concept of a 'settlement'.

Since, until recent years, most of the capital assets accumulated during a marriage were likely to have been derived from the husband's income, the wife became extremely vulnerable on divorce. Two examples will illustrate this. In *Blackwell* v. *Blackwell*[1] a couple separated after sixteen years of marriage. At that time they had saved some £100 with a co-operative society out of the housekeeping money the husband had been paying the wife. The wife's claim to the money failed. The cash originally belonged to the husband and remained his. *Murcutt* v. *Murcutt*[2] arose in an unusual way. The wife petitioned for divorce on the ground of her husband's cruelty. While this was pending, the husband sought a court order expelling his two daughters (both over twenty-one) from the home, which he owned. His wife in turn sought an order to restrain his application, claiming that, if the daughters were expelled (and they had no legal right to remain in the house), this would oblige her to leave to attend to one of them who was sickly. Willmer J. disallowed her application. Assuming, he said, that she would succeed in her divorce petition, 'the moment is inevitably and inexorably approaching when she will in any case have to leave the matrimonial home'. On divorce, therefore, the wife usually stood to lose both the capital to which she would have had access had she remained and a place in which to live.

The United Kingdom legislature was for many years remarkably unresponsive to these problems. The Royal Commission of 1956 was required to inquire into property rights between married people both during marriage and after its termination. The majority of the Commission rejected a solution through a form of community of property system, common in civil law countries. But they made a number of proposals for the protection of a spouse who owned little or none of the matrimonial property. They suggested that, where a husband deserted his wife, he should not be able to eject her from a house which he owned without obtaining the leave of the court and that she should be able to prevent him from selling the house to another by applying to a court for an order restraining him from doing so. She should be entitled to offer payment of the mortgage instalments, which the building society or other mortgagee would be bound to accept. They also proposed that a court granting a divorce or nullity should be allowed to make an order permitting the applicant to reside in the matrimonial home until further order. It is not clear whether this would have involved the exclusion of the other party. The Commission's proposals fell short of suggesting a power to order the transfer to the wife of any of the husband's property except certain tenancies and the contents of the matrimonial home, of which they suggested the court should be permitted to make an 'equitable division'. With the decision in *Blackwell* v. *Blackwell*[3] in mind, the Commission proposed that 'savings' which a wife made from money contributed by either the husband or the wife for 'housekeeping' expenses (and any investments or purchases from them) should belong to both in equal shares unless they agreed to the contrary.[4] This last recommendation was implemented only in 1964[5] and measures designed to strengthen security of occupation of the matrimonial home were not enacted until 1967.[6] But in 1971 comprehensive new powers were given to the courts to deal with property adjustment on divorce.[7]

During this period of legislative somnolence, the English courts reacted to the deficiencies in the traditional doctrines in a remarkable wave of creativity which was to spread widely throughout the Commonwealth countries. In 1948 the Court of Appeal decided that, where a wife had paid £100 towards the purchase of a £1,000 house, transferred to the husband alone, she had acquired an interest in one-tenth of it because it must be assumed that this was the parties' intention.[8] Thus the courts fashioned a means by which at least some of the assets acquired during the marriage could go to the wife after marriage breakdown without having recourse to the divorce court at all. In theory they were not rearranging property rights[9] but simply declaring what they were. But how does one discover whether a spouse had acquired a share in assets of which the other spouse was sole legal owner? Where there is express evidence of agreement as to what the interest should be, whether in writing[10] or otherwise,[11] that agreement determines the matter. Where, however, no express agreement can be found, one school of thought holds that the courts must always be able to infer from the evidence what the parties' actual intentions were and that the court can require the legal owner of the property to hold it on 'resulting trust' for the benefit of the other if this is what they intended.[12] It follows from this view that, if general monetary contributions to family income are relied on as evidence of intention to acquire an interest in specific property, it will be necessary to adduce further evidence, for example of an 'arrangement', that the parties intended the payments to go towards the property in question.[13] The other view holds that, where property has in fact been acquired by joint efforts, the courts may impose a duty to share equally or otherwise, because it would be inequitable to allow the legal owner to reap the benefits of the efforts by the other. This is called the 'constructive' trust.

The extent to which the constructive trust doctrine can be pressed is illustrated by *Hargrave* v. *Newton*[14] where the wife used her earnings and a reward she obtained for finding some stolen money towards general household expenses such as paying bills and holiday expenses. The Court of Appeal held that she had acquired an interest in the latest of the matrimonial homes because her contributions had relieved her husband of expenses he would otherwise have had to bear. By enabling her husband to save more of his own money, she became entitled to a proportionate share in the home. It was not necessary to infer that the parties intended her contributions to go towards paying for the house. But the line between resulting and constructive trusts may not be as sharp as theory suggests. Under the doctrine of resulting trusts the courts looked substantially to what the parties *did* and, though they might infer an appropriate intention from that, they nevertheless controlled what types of action counted as evidence for these purposes, not surprisingly, because to hold otherwise would have given the courts unrestricted powers to vary property interests on divorce which, at that time, Parliament had not given them. Thus, to give rise to an inference of intention, the contribution had to be substantial, in money or money's worth and *more* than ordinary household work.[15] The constructive trust approach simply removes the (unnecessary) second step of inferring intention. The courts will still require evidence of appropriate factual behaviour, such as that prejudices were incurred or benefits conferred by one party in the reasonable expectation of acquiring an interest in the property and a 'causal connection' existed between those benefits or prejudices and the acquisition of the property in question.[16]

The fundamental principle upon which these doctrines rested remained what it had always been: a spouse took out from the marriage property which belonged to him or her at time of dissolution. The change lay only in the expansion of the mode of acquisition of such property rights. This required a close examination of the economic arrangements between them during the marriage.[17] It bases redistribution on *property entitlements*, but in turn founds property entitlements, at least in part, on *contributions* to the family resources. But can this be a successful approach to asset distribution on dissolution?

There are two separate problems. The first lies in concepts such as 'contributions' and 'reasonable expectation'. If 'household work' is to be excluded, a wife might inevitably be at a disadvantage because her inferior economic status in the labour market will result in less contribution from her than her husband. Legislation therefore has frequently enacted that household services should count as a contribution to acquired property.[18] But if such services are to count, how is a court to assess their extent and value? It is by no means easy to express the value of household work in cash terms.[19] Furthermore, should the extent of property acquisition be scaled down because, instead of staying at home to look after her family and husband, the wife does this 'merely because she considers herself entitled to be supported' or because, on early breakdown of the marriage, she could be said to have left the 'job' unfinished?[20] Similarly, to base the extent of property division on a party's reasonable expectations begs the whole question as to what it is reasonable for a spouse to expect.

The second problem is that a distribution based on contributions may be completely unrelated to the needs of the family members after divorce. In particular, if the major asset is the home, the acquisition of a property interest in it by the mother will usually be insufficient in itself to ensure the continued occupation of the house by the mother–child family.[21] These two problems lie at the heart of modern attempts to deal with the question of asset distribution on marriage breakdown. They can be expressed in this form: (1) is asset distribution to be made on the basis of *entitlement* (adjudged by past behaviour or expectations) or future *requirements*?[22] (2) if entitlement is relevant, how is it to be established?

European systems of community of property primarily follow the principle of entitlement. Those systems themselves have undergone extensive modification in recent years. The preferred approach is to allow each spouse to retain his or her existing property and acquisitions during the marriage, but to impose some form of sharing on termination of the marriage or some prior event. Thus they are described as systems of deferred community of property. They vary, however, in their choice of assets which may be shared. In Holland, for example, property owned before and after the marriage (with some exceptions) and liabilities may be shared.[23] The Scandinavian systems, too, operate in this way, except that debts are deducted from the assets of each and then the surplus is shared.[24] The French system, introduced in 1965, involves sharing only the assets acquired during the marriage, most of which (for example, acquisitions through earnings) remain under the spouses' separate management during the marriage. In West Germany, the spouse with the larger surplus on dissolution of the marriage must pay the other one-half of the difference between the net surpluses. 'The net surplus of each spouse is the difference between what he or she has at the time of the divorce or marriage breakdown and what he or she had when they got married or got afterwards through inheritance, or gift, liabilities in each case being deducted from assets.'[25] Similar systems have been introduced into common law jurisdictions. Forty-eight of the United States have some form of property sharing arrangements on divorce.[26] Most Canadian provinces have enacted legislation providing for equal division of family property on separation or divorce[27] and New Zealand has legislated for the equal division of matrimonial property on divorce.[28] In 1981 the Scottish Law Commission recommended the introduction of an asset sharing system for Scotland.

The common solution to the problem of fixing the extent of the share each is to have is to stipulate for equal division, in the absence of special circumstances. The significance of this choice cannot be overemphasized. If the entitlement rested on economic assessment of contributions alone it is unlikely that a case for equal sharing of assets could often be made out. Support for the equality principle is found in evidence that married people regard this class of assets as 'ours'. Nine out of ten spouses questioned by Todd and Jones (1972) (husbands and wives did not differ) thought that family assets, including savings, should be shared on marriage breakdown and three-quarters thought the division should be equal whether or not the wife had been in employment. In Alberta, three-quarters of couples interviewed also thought that the assets should be equally distributed on marriage dissolution even where the wife had not been employed, at least if no alimony was to be paid.[29] A recent survey in Scotland showed that over 90 per cent of interviewees thought that the house, furniture and savings of £3,000 should be equally shared if both spouses contributed to their acquisition, and 60–70 per cent favoured the solution even if the husband only had made the contribution.[30]

These findings provide strong evidence of the commitment of most married people to the *ideal* of marriage as a partnership. In so far as it becomes reflected in law, it represents the antithesis of the so-called male dominated 'traditional legal marriage'.[31] Its base is ideological, and is not the result of the economic power structure within marriage, for that would, as the traditional law showed, simply reflect the (normally) superior position of the man. Hence it is likely that most instances where the partnership principle is overridden by express agreement (an eventuality for which these schemes commonly provide), or, indeed, in cases where the adults avoid marriage and regulate their relationship according to contract alone, the advantage will fall on the side of the man.

Uncertainty about how far to press the partnership ideology appears in hesitation over the range of property to be brought within it. Is property acquired before marriage, or after marriage by way of gift and inheritance, to be included? What of investments and the ownership of businesses? Kahn-Freund (1971) suggested that the property to be shared should be defined, not in terms of its origin (as in the European systems), but of its purpose. Only property intended for joint family use should be subject to equal division. The distinction made is between investment property and household or 'family' assets. This distinction has been built into the Ontario legislation, where the only assets subject to presumptive equal division are those *actually used* for family purposes, thus excluding savings and investments for future use. Such property can be shared only on satisfaction of the principle of contribution.[32] The English Law Commission (1973) adopted an even narrower approach, recommending that only the matrimonial home should be subject to equal division.

But more usually *all* property acquired *after* the marriage (unless by way of gift or inheritance) is brought within the principle. This might include business property, even goodwill, and investments. The Scottish Law Commission (1981) has suggested that a home and furniture acquired before the marriage but intended to be used as the matrimonial home should be included. The scope of this principle could therefore give rise, in the case of the well-off, to a potentially drastic restructuring of the capital position on divorce. We must remember to see the survey findings showing support for the partnership principle in the context of the paucity of assets most people have, and for whom, therefore, the principle puts relatively little at stake. It is too early to know how far the principle will overcome the economic incentives of the wealthy (primarily men) to evade it by contract or even avoidance of marriage. If this happens, the effectiveness of asset sharing as an indirect means to meet the post-divorce requirements of the mother–child family will be significantly reduced.

For people whose only significant family asset is the home, the principle of equal entitlement comes more sharply against the problem of their future needs. Realization of the home could add overwhelmingly to the hardships of mother and children, but failure to do this, or even significant postponement, conflicts with the father's entitlement. The Scottish Law Commission inclined to resolve this conflict between 'welfare' and 'justice' in favour of the latter. 'There is danger', they said, 'that the supposed needs of children (who, after all, often have to move house and suffer a drop in living standards even in unbroken families) could be used to justify results which would be unfair to one of the spouses.' They therefore suggested that any departure from equal sharing should be kept to a minimum so that, if the house were to be unsold, there should be a compensating payment or transfer to the father, he should pay less in child support or the sale be merely postponed.[33] The Commission appeared to discount the finding that most of the people surveyed considered that, where children were involved, more family property should be allocated to the parent–child family than to the other parent. It is interesting to observe that in California, which operates a system of property-sharing based on entitlement, concern has been expressed over the tendency of courts to apply the equal division rule in the face of the needs of family members.[34]

It is significant that the spouses' earning capacity is not considered property for the purposes of the partnership principle, although logically it might be and in practice it will frequently be their most valuable asset. But so to treat it would perpetuate the much-criticized 'traditional' view of support, for on divorce a former spouse would (logically) be entitled to a perpetual equal share in the other's income. So here again the partnership principle gives way, and different principles of assessment are used to determine the basis of an award (if any) which is made against a former spouse's income. Some of these will be considered below.

Discretion and needs

The principles of asset distribution on divorce in England and Australia give less weight to considerations based on property entitlement.[35] We have described the development of judicially developed principles under the law of trusts and noted the difficulties encountered both in relation to the nature and extent of contributions necessary to establish a property interest and the inability of the doctrines to deal adequately with post-divorce needs. Accordingly, when in 1971 the English courts were given extensive powers to rearrange the divorcing spouses' property between them, they were required by section 25 of the Matrimonial Causes Act 1973 to consider 'all the circumstances' including:

(a) the income, earning capacity, property and other financial resources which each of the parties has or is likely to have in the foreseeable future;

(b) the financial needs, obligations and responsibilities which each of the parties has or is likely to have in the foreseeable future;

(c) the standard of living enjoyed by the family before the breakdown of the marriage;

(d) the age of each party to the marriage and the duration of the marriage;

(e) any physical or mental disability of either of the parties to the marriage;

(f) the contributions made by each of the parties to the welfare of the family including any contribution made by looking after the home or caring for the family;

(g) the value to either of the parties of any benefit (for example, a pension) which, by reason of the dissolution or annulment of the marriage, that party will lose the chance of acquiring.

Having considered these matters, the court was to exercise its powers so as to place the parties, so far as it is practicable and, having regard to their conduct, just to do so, in the financial position in which they would have been if the marriage had not broken down and each party had properly discharged his or her financial obligations and responsibilities.

These considerations were relevant not only to asset redistribution but to the exercise of any power (for example, relating to income maintenance), but the English courts, following the approach taken in Australia, saw their powers as a whole and provision for capital and income as 'interrelated and interdependent'.[36] It will be noticed that paragraphs (a) and (b) expressly refer to future resources and needs and paragraph (f) specifies homemaking as an element in the calculation.

The pervasive weakness of this solution is that it gives no guidance to the courts on the respective weight to be attached to the factors set out in section 25. Furthermore, the overall objective which the provision required the courts to seek to achieve, namely that the *parties* be placed in the position they would have held had the marriage not broken down, was frequently thought to be unrealistic.[37] If it is seldom possible to keep both parties at that standard, should the adjustment nevertheless seek to keep *one* at that level, and, if so, which one? The statute was silent. It was also argued that this principle (called here, for convenience, the 'minimal loss' principle) perpetuated a view of marriage as creating lifelong obligations which survived divorce, which was inconsistent both with the concept of divorce as a right rather than an indulgence[38] and the present economic role of women, which is not, or should not be, one of economic dependence on their husbands.[39] There was reason to believe that, in practice, the minimal loss principle had been largely abandoned, at least in the case of the dissolution of short, childless marriages, and that the appeal courts, at least, were evolving a principle of paramountcy of the children's needs and were qualifying spouses' *prima facie* entitlements by reference to their respective needs.[40] But this left the law in a state of uncertainty[41] which was compounded by the fact that most decisions on financial matters are made by registrars in chambers and are unreported.[42] In addition, a powerful pressure group, the Campaign for Justice in Divorce, argued that orders made on divorce caused excessive hardship to men and their second (or subsequent) families.

In contrast, the provisions of the Australian Family Law Act 1975 offers clarity and decision:

A party to a marriage is liable to maintain the other party, to the extent that the first mentioned party is reasonably able to do so, if, and only if, that other party is unable to support herself or himself adequately, whether by reason of having the care or control of a child of the marriage who has not attained the age of 18 years, or by reason of age or physical or mental incapacity for appropriate gainful employment or for any other adequate reason having regard to any relevant matter referred to in sub-section 75(2).[43]

The criterion of need stands in strong contrast to the principle of minimal loss. Support is overtly based on needs arising from exercise of the child-care function or out of age or misfortune. However, the Act does not stop there but refers to other 'adequate' reasons for lack of self-support. In deciding whether the reason is adequate, the court is referred to 'relevant' matters in a list of fourteen considerations set out in section 75(2) which alone the court can consider in exercising this jurisdiction. It is not easy to be sure which of these matters are 'relevant' to the adequacy of a reason for not earning. Those which coincide with the reasons expressly sanctioned by section 72 (child care, age and health) clearly are. But it is not certain whether the extent to which the party claiming maintenance contributed to the income, earning capacity and resources of the other is relevant to not seeking employment. However, the duration of the marriage and the extent to which that affects the earning capacity of the applicant clearly are. So also is the reference to 'the need to protect the position of a woman who wishes only to continue her role as a wife and mother'. This is a curious provision. After divorce a woman can hardly continue her role as a wife, unless she remarries, in which case a maintenance order will normally terminate. In so far as she wishes to continue her role as a mother, this simply restates the child-care function which section 72(2) itself sanctions as an adequate reason for not earning.[44]

In 1981 New Zealand, too, radically altered its maintenance law. On divorce a maintenance obligation persists only to the extent that it is necessary to meet the 'reasonable needs' of the other party if that party cannot meet those needs due to the effects of (a) the division of functions within the marriage while the parties lived together, (b) any custodial arrangements regarding the children and (c) one party undergoing education or training designed to reduce that party's need for maintenance from the other.[45] These conditions are more precisely drawn than the Australian but equally clearly direct attention to the 'needs' of the recipient.

In 1980 the Law Commission issued a Discussion Paper[46] setting out criticism of the current English law and possible new approaches. The most significant were (1) the principle of 'needs' comparable to that referred to in Australia and Canada, (2) an objective of 'rehabilitation' (to enable the divorced partners to adjust to their new situation and become self-supporting) such as is favoured in California,[47] (3) the clean break, involving little or no continuing provision, but requiring division of assets on a partnership model and (4) a combination of these models. The following year the Commission published its recommendations.[48] Its strategy was to avoid radical reform but to seek evolutionary change by retaining a discretionary decision-base, but structuring it more clearly. The court should be directed to give overriding consideration to the interests of the children. *Subject to this*, legislation should express the desirability of the pursuit of self-sufficiency and require courts specifically to consider whether this should be encouraged by granting limited term support. Similarly, courts should be directed to attempt to achieve a 'clean break' between the parties, although the

Commission concedes that this will seldom, if ever, be possible where there are young children. In 1983 the Government undertook to give legislative effect to these proposals.

The overall effect of these recommendations, if accepted, would be further to accentuate the contrast between divorce involving children and childless divorce. In the former case the principle of needs governs. But in the latter it is unclear what principles will prevail. The Commission paid no further attention to the partnership model mentioned in the Discussion Paper, so any division of property interests would (presumably) continue to rest on the uncertain and unsatisfactory concept of contributions.[49] If the focus is to be shifted to the children, attention now needs to be paid to how this principle can be translated into practice.

Maintenance and children

It is unfortunate that the question of post-divorce maintenance is almost invariably expressed in terms of obligations between spouses, or, more precisely, of a former wife's rights to maintenance. This encourages the view that the issue is solely between two adults or, sometimes, between a claimant former wife and her former husband's new family. The reality is that, unless there have been children, few wives seem to make a claim for maintenance at all or, if they do, they are seldom successful.[50] It seems reasonable, therefore, to separate in our discussion the case where a former wife (or husband) claims only as a former spouse and where she (or he) claims as a mother (or father) who is, or has been, exercising the child-care function. Indeed, the reforms in Australian and New Zealand law discussed above probably do little more than give legislative expression to this distinction. It is evident that the basis for awarding maintenance under those statutes will overwhelmingly relate to the actual or past exercise of child care. Where the claimant parent is presently caring for a child, it is common to consider separately the maintenance payable to that parent and the sum payable with respect to the child. This is a wholly artificial division, for it is the household income as a whole which will determine the child's standard of living. Yet distinctions are (in theory) made. For example, in New Zealand it is enacted that a former spouse shall not be liable to pay the other an amount 'the payment of which would have the effect of depriving the first party, or any dependent person ordinarily residing with the first party, of a reasonable standard of living',[51] whereas no such qualification is found with regard to a parent's duty towards his children. But if in fact both forms of maintenance effectively determine the children's standard of living, the qualification permits the payer to keep his new dependants at a 'reasonable standard' at the expense of the children of his former family. So also if it is thought that a wife's 'conduct' should affect the level of 'her' maintenance. The result will simply be to reduce the standard of living of the children.

On what basis, then, should maintenance awards be made? How are a child's 'needs' to be assessed and how is a fair balance to be struck between those needs and those of the payer and any new dependants? What kind of contribution should be expected from the custodial parent? No clear position emerges from the current practice of the English courts. Attempts to use some kind of 'mathematical' formula, such as the 'one-third' rule, according to which the result between the two families should be that the maintenance ordered to the wife should amount to one-third of the combined income of the two families, have met with limited success. Crucially, and significantly, it fails to incorporate the element in the maintenance attributable to child support and must therefore be irrelevant if the final decision depends on the relativities between the incomes of the two families.[52] The courts have also been ambivalent on the question as to what part the resources of a father's new partner should play in the calculation. It seems to be accepted that, if he benefits from such resources, a larger order may be made than would otherwise have been the case,[53] but it is also held that the order should not effectively be met from the new partner's resources and accordingly that the court should not compare the total income of the new household with that of his former family, for that would (improperly) 'bring into account' the new partner's contributions.[54] Unless the father is making no contribution whatsoever to his new household, the distinction is inevitably artificial and unstable. Nor are there any clear criteria as to what might constitute children's 'needs', or whether the mother should be expected to supplement her income by taking paid employment.[55] Often, the final decision seems to rest on little more than intuition.[56]

We will attempt here to approach these questions from the standpoint of the principles of justice between children proposed at the conclusion of the previous chapter. Injustice arises if divorce subjects children to disadvantages greater than those undergone by the community's children in general. A convenient way of assessing this would be to measure the household income of the mother–child family against some concrete, ascertainable standard, such as the national average[57] income of a two-adult, two-child family. This figure might be expressed as a percentage of the supplementary benefit entitlement of such a family and the actual income of the mother–child family in question expressed as a similar percentage so as to allow comparison between the actual and the 'average' household. This allows adjustments relating to family size to be built automatically into the comparison.[58] If the father has resources which can bring the mother–child family up to the same percentage level above supplementary benefit entitlement as the average family, he should in principle be required to do this. However, the principles of justice expressed here would not require that the father should be legally obligated to go further than that (whatever morality might say), so that, for example, the children of a wealthy man whose pre-divorce household income was greatly above the national average should not expect legal intervention to keep them in that advantaged position. They simply should not go below the norm.

Supplementary benefit entitlement assumes reasonable provision is made for housing costs. Before the objectives set out above can be approached, it is necessary that the children be secured, as far as possible, in accommodation. Where the family were in public housing before the divorce, this is largely achieved through public housing policies,[59] but where they were in the private sector, this must be done in other ways. The English courts have shown themselves sensitive to this issue,[60] using a number of devices, from ordering outright transfer of the home from the husband to the wife[61] to requiring transfer of the home to the parents jointly, to be sold only if the wife died, voluntarily left or became dependent on another man.[62] The Court of Appeal has even preferred the occupation rights of the mother–child family against the interests of the husband's creditors who sought to realize his share of the property.[63] This shows that a simple division of property rights may actually undermine the claims of the mother–child family. But it also shows that, where children are concerned, a settlement of the property issues will seldom be an end to the matter. The children's standard of living thereafter requires consideration.[64] This is surely why Ormrod L.J. has often asserted that it is seldom possible to achieve a 'clean break' between the parties in cases where there are children.[65]

We are concerned here only with the basic principles of adjustment, assuming, as it were, unlimited resources. In practice the issue is greatly complicated by the role of state provision. This will receive special attention in the following chapter. It is also frequently complicated by the reforming of new family units by either or both adults. In the case of the mother, it is clearly accepted that any new resources brought in by her new partner should diminish the sums that need be transferred from her former husband. So strongly is this held that, in some jurisdictions, such as England and Wales, maintenance in her favour ceases on her remarriage.[66] The justification for this is sometimes put in terms of her new partner's obligation to support the mother, whether married to her or not,[67] but the real reason is that the new relationship has probably done more than maintenance payments could ever do to redress the disadvantages of divorce, frequently bringing the household back to the national average standard of living.[68] Yet the maintenance obligation towards the children remains, a further illustration of the unreality of the dichotomy in these cases between a parent's and children's maintenance. Under our principles this new family should be legally entitled to outside support only as far as necessary to bring it to the national average standard of living.

When the claims of the former family come into competition with a father's new household circumstances, it is clear that his new commitments, whether legal or otherwise, to his new dependants are to be taken into account and may reduce his liability.[69] Yet the Law Commission (1981) noted that there was apparently widespread resentment of members of a husband's new family (usually the wife) if their own contribution meant that more was taken from him to support his former family.[70] Yet it hardly seems reasonable to allow the father to *reduce* his liability towards his former family by pleading the new calls on his resources without similarly having regard to new resources from which he benefits in deciding how far to enforce that liability.[71] A woman will lose her entitlement to supplementary benefit if she cohabits with a man, rightly, it will be argued,[72] to the extent that the household can be considered an economic unit. Failure to apply the same principle in the case of a man who is living apart from his dependent children is an unwarranted further institutional bias against the mother–child family.

But to say that the units to be measured should be the two household incomes leaves outstanding the question of the principle by which they should be balanced. A true conflict will arise only if the combined resources are insufficient to keep both families at average income level, for, as was suggested above, the principle proposed in this discussion does not demand a legal obligation to maintain the former family above that level. In case of insufficiency of resources, the same principle demands an equal ranking of children. Its operation may have the result of bringing the payer's family below average income, but this follows as inescapably as it would if the payer had simply expanded his first family without increasing his resources. In fact, it seems that the English courts in practice follow this principle, at least in lower income cases, when they seek to achieve some kind of 'equivalence' between the incomes of the two households.[73]

There must, however, be a floor to the drop in living standards to which the second family is subjected. It would, for example, clearly be fruitless to require payments which would result in the payer's family falling below the poverty level.[74] Should the equality principle apply to any level above that? In the United States, Krause (1981) points out that, despite the argument in favour of equality (which, in the United States, takes on a 'constitutional' flavour) there would seem to be permissible, even 'compelling', state interest to assure a basis for the economic and social survival of the new family, otherwise there is a danger of destroying that unit too.[75] Thus, in Britain, where the supplementary benefit authorities are reclaiming against a 'liable relative' for their support of his family, they will permit him to keep for himself and his dependants sufficient to maintain them at supplementary benefit scale rates (the 'official' poverty level) with an added element for housing costs and *the addition of* one-quarter of his net earnings (or £5), whichever is the greater. His contribution towards his former family is expected to come out of the balance, if any.[76] In Sweden, too, a 'formula' is used. The debtor is permitted to retain a 'reserved' amount of his net income, which is fixed at 120 per cent of a 'basic sum',[77] plus reasonable accommodation costs, and he can additionally retain 60 per cent of that sum if his wife (or cohabitee) is prevented from earning due to illness or caring for their children.[78] In practice, therefore, the principle of equality must be applied within realistic limits. However, in any given case it might be salutary to compare the income levels of the two families by some such measure as was suggested earlier to see how far apart they are after application of any such formulae. It may be that the principle of equality (and, therefore, the interests of the former family) is being compromised more than need be out of solicitude to the new family. But it is more likely that it will be found that it matters not at all to the mother–child family whether the father pays more or less because she will be in receipt of supplementary benefit and the only beneficiary of his payments will be the state. This aspect will be explored in the next chapter.

In comparing the circumstances of the two families, a decision needs to be taken about whether to include the mother's earning capacity as a resource. This problem should be seen as part of the problem of child-care provision. The unsatisfactory nature of child-care arrangements resorted to by many working-class mothers who are forced to work long hours has been documented in England and is discussed later.[79] In such cases it may be unreasonable to consider the mother's earning capacity as a resource.[80] But if suitable child care could be arranged if the mother took full employment, should the father escape support on the grounds that the mother could pay for it from her earnings? The tendency to regard self-sufficiency as a goal might impel judges to expect the mother to meet these costs in this way.[81] Unfortunately neither the Scottish nor English Law Commissions take a clear view about this. Yet it would hardly be fair to cast this burden on the mother, for she would then be forced into the roles of sole breadwinner during 'working hours' and sole homemaker outside them. The right solution, it is suggested, is to permit the mother the choice, within the bounds of reasonableness, whether to discharge her child-care duties herself or through another. Should she choose the former, she would need support to carry them out and her earning potential should be to that extent ignored. Should she choose the latter, a contribution from the father towards the expenses of child care should still be payable.

Where special needs unconnected with the divorce arise, it could be argued that the first call of the disadvantaged child is upon the community, as indeed is increasingly seen to be the case for the sick or handicapped child. But, if the state responds inadequately, the extent to which a child's (possible) moral claim against his father's resources should be legally enforced might be made dependent on the father's commitments (if any) to other children. While it has been argued that these should rank equally with commitments to children of a first marriage so far as the latter are disadvantaged *by the divorce*, claims for disadvantages arising after divorce and unconnected with it should not have the effect of reducing the life-chances of the father's subsequent children. Hence such a claim should (it is submitted) be sustained only if, and to the extent that, the father either has no new commitments to any child or has resources greater than is necessary to sustain them at a standard of a family of average income.

In concluding this discussion of the extent to which a father should be legally compelled to meet the 'needs' of his former family, we turn to the question of the children's education. If a child, on achieving majority, wishes to pursue further education or training, whether at university or other specialist institution, there is no mechanism under present English law whereby either parent can be compelled to contribute to the cost unless they are divorced, because then the child may intervene in the proceedings,[82] or one parent may claim against the other on his behalf.[83] This is in itself an anomaly, which can be compounded by the possibility of the father being required thus to support the child of the first family at the expense of those of the second. Although it might be argued that the state has an interest to compel a father to meet heavy educational expenses of (say) an exceptionally gifted child, it is suggested that the principle proposed earlier should govern and that the obligation should be confined to making such contributions, if any, which would be reasonable to expect from a family of average earnings.

Support for a former spouse alone

The so-called 'traditional' approach,[84] which seemed to be retained in the 'minimal loss' principle of section 25 of the English Matrimonial Causes Act 1973, appeared to derive from entry into marriage alone an obligation for the economically stronger spouse to maintain the other at the standard of the marriage indefinitely after its demise.[85] This approach does not in fact have strong historical antecedents, at least in England, where the approach of the ecclesiastical courts was to base the alimony award on little more than the need to keep the wife from destitution (unless she, or her family, had contributed substantially to the husband's assets). Nevertheless, the practice became, or was *believed* to become, widespread, especially in the United States,[86] and has now been generally rejected[87] to be replaced by conclusions compelled by the emerging philosophy of marriage as a partnership: namely that each spouse has a primary entitlement to an equal share in the family property extant at separation or divorce. But, as we have seen, earning capacity is not property for these purposes, and awards against income cannot be based on the partnership principle.

The clearest case for a further claim is where the wife has borne children and, to a greater or lesser extent, cared for them, but where, at the time of divorce, they are no longer dependent on their parents. Even where, as is likely, she has been in paid employment at some time during the marriage,[88] it is probable that the compromise with her child-care role will have driven her to inferior status employment than she might otherwise have achieved, resulting in irremediable impairment to recover the higher status and a substantial loss of prospects on retirement. She is bearing what Glendon has called a mother's 'triple' burden: child care, employment and irrecoverable loss on family breakdown.[89]

It may be said that this is a risk which a woman who bears children chooses and that she should bear it alone. Yet (apart from the question whether the risk was consciously and intentionally chosen) it results from a function that is central to the well-being, if not the survival, of the community. A strong argument exists for community insurance that a mother in this position is not disadvantaged by the divorce.[90] The basis for attaching a claim against the former husband would be that both adults voluntarily undertook to raise a family and that without such a claim the risk of failure would fall disproportionately on the mother. The Scottish Law Commission, considering that this type of case should attract relief, wished to base it on the principle of fair recognition of contributions to and disadvantages incurred as a result of the marriage.[91] It would be wrong, however, to make the assessment of the contribution the basis of the award. We have earlier observed the difficulties inherent in evaluating contributions.[92] Here they are compounded by the fact that the quantification of loss arising from a woman's sacrifice of possible career prospects must always be highly speculative.[93] The basis of the award should therefore be seen as a corollary to the partnership ideal, and therefore compels the long-term consequences of the breakdown to be, in principle, equally shared between the parents; that is, that the long-term risks of acting as parents should fall on the parents equally.

The practical applications of this solution require either that, if the father is able to maintain his living standard after the breakdown, the mother's standard should remain the same, or, if they must drop, that this should be equal. This principle is implicitly recognized by the realization that property settlement orders requiring the sale of the matrimonial home when the children are no longer dependent can cause injustice to the wife. It also follows that future pension rights should be shared equally. The West German Marriage Law Reform of 1976 allows this, viewing such property as part of the acquests of marriage which are subject to the partnership principle. Hence half of the excess of such benefits which one spouse holds over the other will be transferred to the other.[94] Pension benefits are included in the definition of matrimonial property in New Zealand,[95] and are frequently divided on divorce in the United States[96] and Australia.[97] The Scottish Law Commission recommended that life policy and pension rights should be treated as matrimonial property. It should be noted, however, that, as in West Germany, the wife would acquire only one-half of the pension entitlement accrued at time of divorce and that the benefits become payable only on her husband's retirement. It will remain, therefore, that, unless she receives supplemental payments (or earns additional benefits in her own right), she will still be relatively worse off than her husband on retirement.

This provides a strong incentive for such women to find employment. That she should do so (if she reasonably can) is also demanded by the principle of equal risk, for the husband continues to earn. His obligation should be only to the extent that her earnings fall short of maintaining her sufficiently close to her former position. If, of course, the mother has been able to combine bearing and caring for children with the maintenance of high-paid employment, the risk factor is to that extent diminished, possibly even removed.

The conclusion, then, is that, on divorce, after child care is over, the equal risk principle entitles the former caregiver to minimal loss resulting from the divorce. Where the divorce occurred when children still needed care, a different standard was suggested. The justification for this is that the latter case is founded on the principle of child support obligation. Since the wife is still caring for the children, the effects of this function on her subsequent career chances have not yet been felt. Once the children have left, her claim arises in its own right and she should not be permitted to fall unequally below the standard she and the children enjoyed, but at the same time her actual or potential earnings become relevant to the equation.

What arguments can be made in regard to a childless marriage? Suppose the wife simply chooses to abandon employment prospects and devote herself to 'looking after' her husband. She clearly undergoes the risk of hardship on divorce. Again, suppose the woman impedes her career opportunities while supporting her husband to acquire qualifications for higher earning capacity; or suppose she disadvantages herself on marriage by moving from an area with better employment or training opportunities. The joint risk principle argues that, on breakdown, she should be (so far as possible) no worse off than he is. But, unlike the case of child-rearing, it is unclear that this principle is appropriately applied in these cases. The production of children normally permanently influences personal and economic options over a long period. A fundamental community interest is at stake. The risks inherent in this seem appropriate for joint sharing. But changed life-styles on marriage need not be so permanent. Everyone is aware of the availability of divorce. Hence the basis of a further award would better rest on principles of compensation assessed on an *ad hoc* basis. This is provided for by the Scottish Law Commission as the principle of fair recognition of contributions made and disadvantage suffered.[98] So the wife who suffered hardship by moving to live with her husband would be compensated for the loss only; the wife who supported her husband during his training might acquire some share in his earnings as recognition of her contribution.[99] Division of property acquired during the marriage might be equally shared if the partnership ideology is integrated into marriage, unless the couple chose to exclude it.

Conclusions

We have drawn a distinction between approaching financial provision as a method of entitlement and treating it on the basis of future needs. Yet the dichotomy cannot be pressed too far. Glendon (1981) has described the growing, indeed dominant, significance of the 'new' property (comprising job security, fringe benefits, pension rights) over the 'old'. If matrimonial property is extended to include the new property, as it frequently is regarding pension rights, often payable only in the future, the question at issue is really the allocation of risk between the spouses after marriage breakdown. Division of pension benefits allocates these risks equally. But the concept of property stops short at a party's earning capacity, for this would intrude too obviously into post-divorce life, although the build up of earning capacity is the most significant insurance for the future the couple can have.

The analysis presented here has suggested that a more fundamental distinction should be made, that between marriage in which
children have been reared and childless marriages. The distinction
reflects the growing evidence that, as a practical matter, support
payments are almost entirely confined to payments to mothers with
children. Where there are no children it was thought that the ideology
of partnership, if accepted (except in so far as modified by agreement), might warrant an equal division of assets acquired during
marriage. The court should, however, be enabled to attempt to
quantify, on an *ad hoc* basis, whether one spouse suffered prejudice,
conferred benefits or entertained expectations which were not
adequately compensated by the operation of the partnership
principle. But it is doubtful whether, *in these cases*, the partnership
principle should extend automatically to future pension benefits any
more than to the future earning capacity of the former spouse.
Instead, a short rehabilitation award would ordinarily be more
appropriate. However, access to pension benefits might be justified in
individual cases on the compensatory basis mentioned above.

Where children were reared, a distinction was further drawn
between cases where dependent children remained in the family after
divorce and cases where they did not. The Law Commisson (1981)
had proposed that the needs of the children should be given priority.
To give proper effect to this, it was argued that it is necessary to see
maintenance in these cases as related to the standard of living of the
children's family. Indeed, the division between orders in favour of the
former wife and orders in favour of the children might be abolished
and replaced by a 'family support' order. Either parent's claim to
assets on the partnership principle should be overridden by the
requirements of family support. These should be set by regarding the
claim as one by the children against the whole family's resources in
order to achieve a result (if possible) which would keep them at a
standard equivalent to a similar family at the national average level of
earnings. This figure could be set by administrative order from time
to time on the basis of an agreed formula.[100] Where other children
have calls on the father's resources, all children should rank equally.
The mother's earning capacity should not automatically be treated as
part of her resources. For her part, the mother (if the child's
caretaker) should be entitled to surplus assets (if any) on the
partnership principle and an equal share in accrued pension benefits
on the principle that each spouse should bear the economic risks of

child-raising equally. On the same principle, when child-rearing is finished, the mother should be entitled to be supported from the father's income at the level she and the children enjoyed, although her actual or potential earnings should (where reasonable) contribute to this. Thus, where the marriage breaks down after the children have left home, the principles of partnership and equal risk-taking require (it is suggested) division of family property, including pension benefits, and maintenance at the previous family level, where possible, and, where not, equal sharing of the drop in living standards.

7
The Role of Public Law: Support and Enforcement

State support and family breakdown

A former spouse and children may fail to receive adequate support from private sources either because these are simply insufficient or because the debtor does not meet the obligation to pay. Either situation raises the potential involvement of community resources. But such involvement in turn raises complex issues, not only concerning the interrelationship between state and individual responsibilities, but also concerning equity between competing claims on public expenditure.

The orientation of this book has been to seek solutions primarily in terms of children's rights and to see as a source of these rights the hypothesis that, in principle, all children are entitled to an equal start in life. This is meant, however, only as a guiding principle for matters here under discussion and not an all-embracing political programme, requiring, for example, the abolition of all disparities in family income. The expression of that principle was found in the proposition that a breadwinner with sufficient resources might be compelled to maintain his children at the income equivalent to the national average for a family of that size. If this is not achieved, the question arises whether the obligation should revert to the state.

The Finer Committee's (1974) proposals go some way in attempting to do this. The state was to provide to all one-parent families a guaranteed maintenance allowance pitched at such a level as to offer a lone parent 'a genuine choice whether to work or not'. The

Committee had no wish to reduce work incentives, so the benefit would not be lost if the recipient entered full-time work. Instead, after an initial disregard, the benefit would taper off until the earnings reached the level of average male earnings. Significantly, the benefit was seen as a *benefit for children*, comprising of an allowance to the adult for child care and additions depending on the number of children. It would automatically be payable on the acquisition of single parent status. The state would have the right to reclaim contributions from the other parent.[1] The Committee was anxious that the proposals would not create inequality between different classes of family by, for example, tipping the balance too far in favour of one-parent families over low income two-parent families. Hence the benefit would be means tested. Yet the benefit would be received until the recipient's income reached the average of male earnings, which would inevitably favour some one-parent families over certain two-parent families and this may be why the Australian Poverty Commission recommended a guaranteed maintenance scheme for all families.[2] In this solution, the problem of support for one-parent families becomes interlinked with the general problem of poverty.

This is the major reason why suggestions to provide for the victims of marriage breakdown by insurance based schemes, whether voluntary or compulsory, are almost certainly doomed to failure. The Finer Committee considered such suggestions and rejected them because, to keep payments at a reasonable level, there could be little relationship between contributions and benefits.[3] The association between divorce and low income indicates that the group most likely to be in need of the greatest assistance will be those least able to afford the appropriate level of contribution and least likely to have maintained contributions over any reasonable period of time. Would participation be voluntary or compulsory? If the former, only those whose marriages seemed at risk would be likely to enter, necessitating consequentially heavy premium contributions if the system was to be self-financing. And why deprive children of needed support if their parents failed to participate? If compulsory, when would entry be required (on marriage? or cohabitation?) and how enforced? Any such scheme, even if feasible, would not cover most cases of children born out of wedlock and would thereby create a distinction between types of one-parent family which is inconsistent with seeing the community obligation as being owed to children as a whole.[4]

It would be better, therefore, to look to general revenue to finance any such payments. But to attempt to bring *all* families to the level of the average national earnings by this means would be incompatible with western political and economic systems. To do this only for one-parent families would create inequity between family groups. One solution is to abandon one-parent families to the general poverty programme of the state. Essentially this was the solution adopted in the United Kingdom when the Government rejected the Finer proposals.[5] These families rely on supplementary benefit as their major welfare resource, as any persons within the official 'poverty' limits would do. They also receive 'child benefit', a fixed weekly sum (in 1982/3, £5.75 per child) which is payable to *all* families with children irrespective of means. One-parent families receive marginally favourable treatment in that the rate for a first child is higher than it is for two-parent families. Similarly, the US Aid for Families with Dependent Children (AFDC) is essentially based on poverty levels fixed by individual states[6] and these levels, in 1978, generally fell below the federally defined poverty level for that year. Furthermore, twenty-eight states fixed AFDC payments at levels lower even than their own defined poverty lines.[7]

Alternatively, the desired standard of a one-parent family could be assured with reference to some other group. In Sweden, for example, if a maintenance debtor fails to pay, or pays insufficiently, the state will make a *maintenance advance*. This is calculated by reference to a 'basic sum' which is based on the yearly rate of the (index-linked) national old age pension. The advance is fixed at 40 per cent of that figure *per child*, and this is payable irrespective of the custodial parent's income and continues after he or she remarries. In addition the single parent has special tax benefits and housing allowances,[8] and participates in the child allowance available to all children. This complete disregard of all other sources of income can create undue advantage for these families compared to low-income, first-married couples, although it seems that, for a substantial minority, their economic conditions will remain relatively poor[9] and one-parent families in Sweden still have lower income levels than two-parent families.[10]

It is suggested that the best approach is to fix the community obligation to children of one-parent families by reference to one or more other classes of claimant on the social security system. The proper referent group should be children of families broken by death. There has always been public sympathy for this group of children and this accounts for their relatively generous treatment in social security systems, although implementation may not always have been consistent.[11] Yet, from the children's point of view, it matters not whether economic adversity had been caused by a parent's death or marriage breakdown. In the United Kingdom a widow is entitled to an allowance for twenty-six weeks from widowhood (in 1982 at a rate of £54.95 per week) which is the most generous flat-rate benefit in the social security system. Thereafter she is entitled to further benefit provided she cares for dependent children (widowed mother's allowance) on a less generous scale (£32.85 per week in 1982) but with additions for each child. The benefits are not subject to deduction if the mother earns but cease on remarriage or cohabitation.

This scheme is open to various criticisms even in the context in which it operates. In particular, the lack of deductions for earnings ignores the high level of female participation in the labour force; its confinement to widows reflects sex-role stereotypes, as does its basis in contributions by the husband. As such it could not be transferred to families broken by divorce or separation. In any case, as we have seen, any scheme in that context could not be insurance-based. However, both Australia and New Zealand have been able to introduce benefits to families broken by divorce or separation which are not insurance-based and yet confer benefits related to those given to families broken by death. In 1973 New Zealand introduced Domestic Purposes Benefits payable to all 'solo' parents with the care of one or more children. The rate is identical to that of widows' benefits, and is calculated to give the recipient the choice whether or not to work, but a generous earnings disregard and a 'taper' in the manner suggested by the Finer Committee provides an incentive to employment.[12] In Australia, an amendment to the Social Services Act in 1977 introduced Supporting Parents' Benefits payable either to fathers or to mothers caring for children over six months old once they have been separated by reason of estrangement for a period of six months. The rate of the benefit is equal to the standard Class A widow's pension.[13] A deserted wife may alternatively qualify for a widow's pension, with accompanying fringe entitlements, but the fact that this benefit remains dependent on establishment of fault has meant that many women prefer the slightly less financially attractive Supporting Parents' Benefits.[14] Both benefits are subject to deductions for earnings and terminate on remarriage. These benefits may sometimes put a one-parent family in a better position than a low-income two-parent family. But the deduction for earnings and, above all, the linkage with an already recognized class of beneficiaries, should be sufficient to mitigate any inequity that may occur.

The discussion hitherto has been confined to state support for children of one-parent families, particularly those caused by marriage (or cohabitation) breakdown, but the principles apply equally to children of the unmarried who have not cohabited, and indeed the Australian and New Zealand provisions mentioned extend to that group. But how far does community obligation extend to separated (or divorced) wives who are not caring for children? Where the wife has not borne or cared for children, the arguments for community support are weak. She may indeed have suffered prejudice or conferred benefits by marrying, but, for these, private law remedies against the husband should be available.[15] It is not clear that the community needs to act as ultimate insurers against prejudices a woman may undergo (apart from those related to bearing or caring for children) by marrying. Interestingly, when widows' benefits were first introduced in English social insurance law, childless widows were (controversially) included among the beneficiaries. This was criticized in the Beveridge Report of 1942 and replaced by the present scheme whereby all widows receive the twenty-six-week benefit (to assist in re-adjustment) but only widowed mothers receive the long-term allowance.[16] Even this had been considered possibly too generous to childless widows who may have suffered little, financially, from the bereavement. An argument based on special solicitude for marriage may be made for providing state support to soften the economic impact of bereavement, but it cannot be of high priority against competing claims on the public purse. The same holds true regarding marriage breakdown.

The case is different where children have been involved. Under the New Zealand scheme, for example, an applicant qualifies for the Domestic Purposes Benefit who, even though not presently caring for a child, has done this or cared for an incapacitated relative for fifteen years, or is over fifty and lost the support of her husband (or cohabitee) after a lengthy marriage or cohabitation.[17] In the absence of special provision of this kind, the longer term security of the divorced former child-caregiver is fragile. This vulnerability is seen in the United Kingdom national insurance provisions, where a *former* husband, who had been supporting the mother and children, dies. She becomes entitled to a special benefit while she continues to care for the children (Child's Special Allowance) but, as she is not his widow, the rate is considerably lower than widows' benefits. As regards her security in old age, a married woman may, of course, earn the right to a retirement pension on the basis of her own contributions (Category A pension). But if these are absent, or minimal, in her child-caregiving days, she may nevertheless draw retirement pension on the basis of *her husband's* contributions (Category B pension). If she is divorced when over sixty, she is entitled to the pension she would receive if her husband had then died. But if she divorced under sixty, and did not remarry under that age, she may make use of her former husband's contributions made during the marriage towards her own entitlement to a Category A pension.[18] If, therefore, a woman enters employment immediately after divorce, her ultimate pension position will not be jeopardized. But if her employment is delayed, or sporadic, due to child-caregiving, her position may be more difficult. The United Kingdom provides for delayed re-entry into the labour force by permitting a person (male or female) to satisfy the contribution requirements for a full Category A pension even though payments have been made for twenty years only (instead of the normal forty) if, in each of the other years, 'the contributor was . . . precluded from regular employment by responsibilities at home'.[19] But these provisions are helpful only if the caregiver is able to resume regular employment. If not she will (in Britain) be reliant on supplementary benefit, both then and in old age. The extension of a special benefit, as the New Zealand Domestic Purposes Benefit, to cover such a case would ameliorate her position not only then, but also in old age, for the benefit would operate essentially as an accelerated retirement pension.

The absent parent's contribution

Unlike the widowed family, in marriage breakdown cases the other parent is usually available to contribute his earnings to the former family. We have already argued that, whenever he has sufficient resources, he should be under a legal obligation (enforceable at the instance of the children's caregiver) to maintain them at a level equivalent to the average income family, a standard higher than is likely under state benefits. If he cannot provide at a level higher than those benefits, the unemployed caregiver will prefer to ignore his potential contribution and rely solely on the benefits. In such a case, what steps should be taken against the former spouse?

Both Australia[20] and New Zealand[21] provided for withholding of the state benefits until the applicant instituted proceedings for support against the former spouse. This used to be the practice of the British Supplementary Benefits Commission, even though, by reason of an informal arrangement, any payments made by the debtor would be passed directly by the magistrates' court to the welfare authorities.[22] This practice was strongly criticized by the Finer Committee.[23] Apart from forcing the parties into unwanted antagonism, with potential hazards for their relationships to each other and the children, it is objectionable in principle that the state should require an individual to undergo the pressure of instituting court action as a condition to receipt of a benefit entitlement, especially one for his or her children. As from April 1975 the official practice of the Supplementary Benefits Commission changed[24] and claimants are told that it is their decision whether or not to bring proceedings. The Australian Joint Select Committee on the Family Law Act recommended a similar change for Australia[25] and New Zealand abolished the requirement with the institution of a new collection scheme in 1981.[26]

Where the applicant elects not to pursue the debtor, this right will be assumed by the state. The Finer Committee recommended that the state should be permitted to bypass the court system in seeking contribution from the liable relative and fix his liability by imposition of an 'administrative order' immediately binding on him, appealable (as to quantum) within the tribunal, not the court, system. The analogy would be with a tax assessment.[27] In 1981 New Zealand instituted a collection scheme on this basis.[28] It was observed in the previous chapter[29] that it is usual for the state, when collecting from a 'liable relative', to allow that person a 'margin' below which it will not require his income to fall. This will be some way above the 'official' poverty level for that state. Since, by definition, these are cases where the mother–child family will be living at that level (or only a little above, if, for example, they are allowed a limited right to supplement their welfare income from some other sources), the result will inevitably be that the payer will be officially 'allowed' to live at a higher standard than his former wife and children. This is further institutional bias against the mother–child family, but there may be good reasons for it. To depress the father's family even lower seems to serve no good purpose if the mother and children receive no benefit from it. The state, for its part, is concerned to reduce enforcement costs and to maintain the man's incentive to work. Yet the result seems unsatisfactory. The state forgoes part of its notional entitlement to reimbursement against the father, but jealously refuses to permit the mother–child any added benefits from his payments. All payments made by him must enure to the state's benefit.

It is suggested that the interplay between supplementary benefit (or similar) payments and private maintenance support should be reassessed. If the state is prepared to allow the father's new family to live above official poverty level, why not allow (at least some of) the maintenance paid by the father to raise his former family above that level? This would mean introducing a 'disregard' for maintenance payments.[30] In the United Kingdom, a recipient of supplementary benefit who is in *part-time* employment is allowed to keep earnings from that employment up to a certain limit. If the purpose is to encourage incentive and (possibly) a sense of family responsibility, this argument could apply to maintenance payments too. For why require the absent parent to pay at all in these circumstances? The answer usually lies in a community feeling that his children are a man's responsibility. If this sense is to be encouraged, it is probable (though possibly not provable) that this will be encouraged better by allowing the recipient family visibly to benefit, at least to some degree, by the payments rather than by a levy by the state.

It can be argued even more strongly that the introduction of a disregard, even of small amounts, can nevertheless make a significant difference to the income levels of mother–child families which, in the absence of the introduction of a substantial state benefit to single parent families, can go some way to redressing the inequity suffered by them. Finally, it is probable that the introduction of such a disregard would have a favourable impact on the problem of enforcement, to be considered later in this chapter.

It may be objected that to allow the families of divorced or separated parents to benefit from maintenance income while in receipt of supplementary benefit would be to create inequities within the system, for poor two-parent families would not have that resource. (It should be noted that there would be no imbalance with unmarried single mothers, for any child support they received should be subject to the same disregard.) But welfare provisions are replete with distinctions between categories of beneficiary (compare widowed with divorced mothers, for example) and the potential availability of some support from the former breadwinner is a resource unique to these families, small though it may be. In view of their overall privations and the fact that the inequity in their case arises not only in their position *vis-à-vis* the community at large but also in relation to their former breadwinner's new family, this objection seems unnecessarily dogmatic.

Enforcement

Where the beneficiary of support payments is the state, one might expect the state to pursue its debtors with some vigour. The public nature of this obligation may in part explain the continuance, in a number of jurisdictions (including England), of imprisonment for default, although this remedy is not confined to non-payment only in welfare cases. Despite the presence of imprisonment, or its threat, collection by the state has tended to be very low. The Finer Committee revealed that, in England, only some 16 per cent of payments made by the Supplementary Benefits Commission to lone mothers (whether separated, divorced or unmarried) are recovered from liable relatives.[31] In New Zealand the recovery rate before the institution of the new collection system had fallen to about 10 per cent.[32] In the United States concern over the mounting costs of the AFDC programme and the meagreness of sums collected from debtors led to the passing of an elaborate federal enactment for improving collection of child support debts.[33]

Objections to pursuing a vigorous enforcement policy are strong. Enforcement is conditional on tracing the debtor and this process may involve intrusion into the privacy of the children's caregiver (whose co-operation in identifying and helping to trace the father may be important) and the debtor (if resort is made to social records in the tracing process). Should the debtor be recalcitrant, enforcement by imprisonment might be deemed too severe and disruptive of his present family. Other processes, such as attachment of earnings, may be thought potentially damaging in his employment relations. In any case, it might be argued that an enforcement system, to be effective, is likely to cost more than it would yield in increased debtor contributions.

Such considerations caused the Finer Committee to prevaricate on the matter of enforcement. They avoided the question as to how far a mother should be expected to co-operate (she should merely be 'asked' for information)[34] and objected to the use of public records, arguing that knowledge of their use for extraneous purposes might lead to dishonest returns.[35] Attributing, mistakenly, failure to pay to inability to pay, the Committee were opposed to the sanction of imprisonment for a debt which they considered to arise simply from a 'family obligation'.[36] But evidence from Australia,[37] Canada,[38] the United States[39] and, less reliably, Britain[40] establishes that inability to pay is by no means necessarily the major cause of non- or insufficient payment of child support. Chambers (1979) attributes the abnormally high compliance rate in some Michigan counties to the combination of three factors: (1) the presence of a system of automatic institution of enforcement procedures when the debtor falls into arrears by the issuance of warning notices; (2) a high rate of jailing (indicating that the threat contained in the warning would be acted on); (3) a population size which made the system manageable. Such counties averaged 25 per cent more in collections than others.[41]

The Law Reform Commission of Canada (1976) has claimed a high success rate of enforcement in Ontario when the province's 'automatic enforcement' system is combined with a 'parental support' programme. Under the former, the accounting staff of the family courts observe whether payments have fallen into arrears and will themselves contact the defaulter. Only if these informal procedures fail do the court staff initiate enforcement measures. Under the latter, special workers are assigned to welfare cases to 'trace missing payers, make home visits, assist and give moral support to both husbands and wives in re-hearing situations'.

It cannot therefore be assumed either that the debtors do not have the money or that no enforcement system can be effective. Nor can it be argued that efficient enforcement procedures will not be cost-effective. Chambers calculated that the marginal costs of the arresting, jailing and automatic enforcement policy were heavily outweighed by the income recovered.[42] It is not clear, however, whether this calculation would include the costs of an efficient nation-wide tracing system, such as instituted in the United States in 1975. The difficulties in costing the benefits of such a programme are, however, formidable, especially in view of the expectation that its implementation will eventually lead to a high degree of voluntary payments.[43]

The real issues concern values, rather than simple finances. We return to the question of the community ethic of parental responsibility to their children. Even if we believe that children may have a claim against the community at large for reduction of inequalities in upbringing, we nevertheless believe that the parents are the primary agents to fulfil these claims. This is considered desirable not only in terms of the general social interest, but also for the children. But can a sense of responsibility be imposed by coercive state intervention? We lack the knowledge to answer this question definitively. But an oblique approach may be suggested. We can argue that the approach of the state in this matter should, and could, primarily be *regulatory* rather than coercive. The contribution formulae should provide a framework for settlement, seen within the whole context of post-divorce relationships between the absent parent and the former family. The legal process can assist not only in providing the framework (by mediation) for reaching such settlements, but also by providing its guidelines and, where appropriate, the means for its implementation. Chambers raises the question how far the practice in normal support cases which requires the debtor to make separate payments (either directly or through the court) each week, or month, is not in itself a deterrent to payments. Payment might be easier if made automatically either through attachment of earnings orders, to which the debtor might agree,[44] or through coded adjustments to his net earnings.

We should recall the suggestion made earlier[45] that a payer's contributions to his former family should confer visible advantages on them. It might be possible to relate this to an incentive to voluntary payment. For example, the suggested disregard might operate only if the payments were made under an agreement, or agreed order. The loss to the state would then be compensated by the inducement to voluntary settlement and (less measurably) by improved relationships between families. The objection would be that the former family would suffer if the payer should prove recalcitrant. There may be no way of overcoming this, but it might be justified by arguing that such families would be no worse off than they are at present and that the rationale for permitting a disregard would be its recognition (and therefore encouragement) of a sense of responsibility in fathers for all their children which is manifested by making voluntary contributions to improve the lot of their former family.

Should the threat of imprisonment stand behind it all? Despite its effectiveness, Chambers concludes that the social costs are too great. But his observations relate to a system where arrest and imprisonment were at the forefront of the sanction process. Surprisingly little use was made of wage-attachment.[46] If imprisonment is to be retained at all, it should clearly be a very last resort. Collection through mandatory wage deductions is a preferable option and its feasibility should be explored.[47]

Housing

The argument that stability in the child's residence after divorce is a desirable goal applies to the public law response to family breakdown as much as to the private. Hence the mother–child family's housing needs should be a crucial consideration in assuming the appropriateness of any money payments out of public funds. In Sweden a special, means-tested housing allowance is payable to all families with children to defray (up to a specified maximum) housing costs where these exceed a stated sum. Since the benefit is universal, it serves as a general means of equalizing living standards, but it can clearly be of particular importance to the one-parent family seeking to maintain its residence after breakdown.

Despite the legal machinery for transferring title (and tenancies) on divorce, many mother–child families living in the private housing sector will be forced to move because they cannot undertake the burden of the costs of mortgage or rent repayments and related housing expenses. (They may, however, be assisted by rate rebates and mortgage interest payments by the supplementary benefit authorities.) Families living in public sector housing are more fortunate.[48] The Finer Committee saw as 'fundamental' that the public housing authorities should 'adopt the general principle that the tenancy should follow the children',[49] and it seems as if this advice is being followed. Before the implementation of the Housing Act 1980, local authority tenancies were freely determinable by the authorities, who accordingly adopted the policy that, when a spouse who was the tenant left the home, they should terminate the tenancy and re-grant it to the spouse remaining there with the children. This convenient procedure has now become impossible on the elevation of council tenancies to secured status. So, even if a spouse who is the tenant occupies the home alone, the other having left with the children, legal proceedings now need to be brought to re-instate the children. This may be done under various statutory provisions, such as the Domestic Violence and Matrimonial Proceedings Act 1976 (which can

temporarily exclude the present occupant),[50] but a longer-term
solution will require the institution of divorce or judicial separation
proceedings in order to activate the courts' powers to transfer such
tenancies under either the Matrimonial Causes Act 1973, s.26, or the
Matrimonial Homes Act 1967, s.7, neither of which provisions is
available to former cohabitees who were not married.[51]

It is appropriate to consider, in the context of housing, what means
are available to a spouse to protect his or her security of residence
against possible jeopardy should the relationship break down in the
future. The problem is unlikely to arise in the case of occupants of
public housing, but could be of considerable importance for owner-
occupiers, since a mother might find the house either sold or
effectively disposed of as security to creditors without her knowledge.
The extent of a spouse's (or cohabitee's) protection depends primarily on the nature of his or her proprietary interest in the house. If
the parties are joint legal owners, each must participate in transactions affecting the entire title. Difficulty would only arise if one
disposes his or her share or becomes bankrupt. There is unlikely to be
a market for portions of a matrimonial home, so the occasions when a
co-owner is threatened will usually occur when the other becomes
bankrupt and his or her trustee-in-bankruptcy seeks the sale of the
house and division of proceeds, to which he is technically entitled. But
sale against the joint-owner spouse's (or cohabitee's) wishes requires
a court order, and the court is unlikely so to order if this would put
that person, especially if caring for children, in a position of hardship.
But the postponement may be temporary only.[52] A spouse (or
cohabitee) in occupation of the home who is not a joint legal owner
but who has acquired an interest in it under the trust doctrines
mentioned earlier,[53] itself not always an easy matter to determine,
was given somewhat similar protection by the House of Lords in
Williams and Glyn's Bank v. *Boland*.[54] The Law Commission (1982a)
criticized this decision, largely on the ground that third parties might
have no reasonable means of knowing whether such an interest might
exist, and preferred a scheme whereby such rights would be protected
only if registered.[55] It should be stated that, under the present law, a
spouse (whether the holder of an interest in the home or not) is given
'occupation rights' which can be protected against third parties by
registration under the Matrimonial Homes Act 1967, but that this
protection does not extend against the other spouse's creditors.

Apart from the technical problems, the difficulty of policy lies in determining priorities between a family's need for adequate housing and a system of free disposability of an individual's property. A system which, for example, exempted a matrimonial home from attachment by creditors does, to that extent, remove family homes from the private property market and treats them as if partially in the public domain. This is done in those systems (some American states and Canadian provinces)[56] which have enacted 'homestead' legislation, under which, typically, a matrimonial dwelling house may not be disposed of without the consent of each spouse (often, without a registration requirement) and the home is exempt from creditors, at least up to certain values. Similar protection might be given to household effects. It has been urged that 'the claims of the family should be preferred to those of creditors to the minimum extent necessary to preserve the family in the home judging by modest standards'[57] but the present protection in England is very inadequate, even derisory.[58] These issues cannot be entirely severed from those of support of the mother–child family, for loss of the house, or its contents, may push them into dependence on state support. It certainly should be possible for a spouse, at least if caring for children, to obtain an order restraining the other from disposing of household effects without his or her consent as recommended by the Law Commission in 1978.[59] Protection of the home by registration is likely to be effective only if homes, which are not jointly owned, are routinely registered and some mechanism enabling this, or incentive encouraging it, perhaps by conferring a degree of protection against creditors, or by exempting 'registered' homes from estate and stamp duty, would need to be found.[60] Unless linked to advantages unconnected with the prospects of potential marital discord, registration alone would seem to be a less than whole-hearted commitment to family protection.

The issue is one of balance between family needs (and children's rights) and individual property rights. It arises in another form when the courts respond to a short-term crisis which might arise where, as a marriage breaks up but the issues have yet to be finally determined, the adults find it impossible to live together. Here the English courts have until recently taken a significantly child-oriented view. If it is clear that the circumstances in the home have created an intolerable situation for the children,[61] or that they will be (or have been) moved by one of the parents to unsatisfactory surroundings, they have used their powers (originally conferred to protect family members against violence)[62] to sort the issue out. They have followed a policy that occupation of the home should follow custody so that where, either through understanding between the parents or provisional determination by the courts, the children will remain with one parent rather than the other, the custodial parent will be granted exclusive occupation pending final resolution of the matter whatever the position is regarding legal title to the home and whatever the merits of his or her attitude to the other spouse. However, in *Richards* v. *Richards*[63] the House of Lords ruled that in determining a dispute over housing prior to divorce, the reasonableness of the conduct of the spouses towards each other should be weighed equally with the needs of the children. Since 'fairness' to a spouse and the welfare of the children may sometimes conflict, it is important to know which should prevail in such an event. The decision gives no guidance on this matter, which accordingly falls to the subjective discretion of judges. The failure to accord priority to the children's needs, welcomed though it was by some,[64] is a striking example of the hollowness of much rhetoric supporting the cause of children in divorce. For it is only when their interests conflict with those of the adults that the genuineness of a commitment to child-centred divorce is revealed.

8
Unmarried Parenthood and Cohabitation

The estimated extent of and possible motivation for unmarried cohabitation were discussed in chapter 1. The problem of legal response in these cases is related to the issue of unmarried parenthood in general, though it goes wider for it includes the situation of childless cohabitees.

The issue of cohabitation has caused a good deal of controversy in recent years. Blanket questions as to whether unmarried cohabitation should be 'legally recognized' or not conceal the multitude of differing contexts in which that question can arise. For example, is the entry into cohabitation to be a reason for loss of support entitlements (whether from the state or a former spouse)? Is a cohabitation relationship to be sufficient to qualify for benefits arising on the death of the partners? Is the relationship sufficient to justify special protective remedies against the other partner or to generate support claims? Of what relevance is the introduction of a child into the union? These and other questions do not necessarily demand uniform answers, and they will be distinguished. However, in line with the basic orientation of this book, a fundamental distinction will be drawn between those cases where a child is and is not present.

Children and the unmarried[1]

Until recently, the support rights of a child in private law were significantly affected by his status at birth. If legitimate (born within marriage) they were stronger than if illegitimate, because in the former case the parent claiming support from which the child would benefit had more powerful legal machinery available to pursue these claims. Indeed, this is still to some extent the case in English law. Maintenance on behalf of an illegitimate child can be sought only by his mother against the father (never by the father against the mother, which would be possible if the parents were married) and this only in 'affiliation proceedings' in magistrates' courts. The procedural consequences of this are that no property orders may be made to secure the child a home even in public sector housing,[2] that orders for capital payments are subject to a limit of £500,[3] that security cannot be ordered for maintenance payments and that proceedings must normally be brought within three years of the child's birth.[4] Nor can the mother claim support for herself, but the amount ordered for the child may include an element for her support while caring for the child.[5]

The legal position of the father *vis-à-vis* the child is correspondingly deficient. He has no standing to be consulted by the mother concerning the child's upbringing nor against welfare authorities should they seek to assume rights over the child (though he may institute proceedings to be granted custody of the child);[6] he has no right to have his name recorded as the child's father unless the mother agrees,[7] and he has no claims to any contribution from the mother, whatever her means, if he is caring for the child. Such are the distinctions which presently still flow from the perpetuation of the status of illegitimacy. Status discrimination falls foul of anti-discrimination and egalitarian ideals in modern societies. The Supreme Court of the United States has held that legislative discrimination against children in succession matters violates the Equal Protection Clause of the Fourteenth Amendment[8] and European countries have signed a European Convention seeking equality of treatment for children born out of wedlock.[9]

An apparently simple way to equalize the position of marital and extra-marital children is to enact a general equality provision. This was done, for the first time in the Commonwealth, by New Zealand in the Status of Children Act 1969, section 3(1) of which provides: 'For all purposes in the law of New Zealand the relationship between every person and his father and mother shall be determined irrespective of whether the father and mother are or have been married to each other, and all other relationships shall be determined accordingly.' This enactment and its related provisions have served as a model for later legislation in Australia[10] and Canada.[11]

The Law Commission at one time favoured making a similarly complete abolition of the status of illegitimacy in England and Wales,[12] but later recommended that it should be retained (though renamed 'non-marital') without, however, any of its disadvantageous consequences to children.[13] The problem is that a general abolition of the status throws up further specific difficulties, for the child's legal relationship with his father cannot be seen in isolation from the relationship between the parents. The newly recognized relationship would require the involvement of the father in the child's upbringing, at least if he desired it and unless barred by court decision. It might also entitle him to public recognition of the relationship by the appearance of his name on the registration of the child's birth, and equally it might subject him to greater potential liability to support the child. Are these matters to be decided purely on the basis of biological connection, or has the social context, evidenced by cohabitation or otherwise with the mother, any relevance?

On the question of support, there is little doubt that an inexorable consequence of equality would be that a range of enforcement measures, equivalent to those available for marital children, would now be at the disposal of the extra-marital child. But would the child's caregiver be similarly entitled to support for caregiving and given a right to seek a property order to secure the child's residence? We have observed that a child-care element may be included in any award made for the child, but some jurisdictions have gone further and permitted the caregiver to claim on her own account. Thus, in New Zealand, a parent 'who has *or has had*' custody of the child may be awarded support from the other if the court deems this desirable 'in the interests of providing, or of reimbursing the applicant for having provided, adequate care for the child . . .' and if it would be reasonable (having regard to earning capacity, means, needs and other responsibilities) to make the order.[14] Sometimes that additional right arises only after the parents have cohabited, usually for a specified time,[15] or simply for an indeterminate period provided that the cohabitation was in a 'conjugal relationship of some permanence'.[16] But these entitlements are for support only and do not extend to property matters.

It would be hard to resist the argument that a father should be liable to provide for his extra-marital children on the same principles as for his marital family. A possible ground for modifying the obligation might be that, on marrying, a man consciously undertakes this commitment and must be taken to bear the risk of conception by his wife, even if unintended, whereas a man does not necessarily have this commitment in the case of births resulting from non-marital liaisons. The argument might be given added force if, for example, the man (reasonably) relied on the woman having taken contraceptive precautions. Policy might conceivably draw this distinction and confine the obligation to procreation resulting from intercourse within marriage, which might, on the rationale of the argument, be extended to include quasi-marital cohabitation. Yet it is suggested that the current position, which disallows such exoneration, is correct. Adults know the essentially procreative nature of sexual intercourse. The risk of unintended consequences must assuredly lie on them, not the child. However this undermines the rationale for making cohabitation a condition for extended obligations. Support for the caregiver is support for the child. There is also no logical place to stop short of giving all extra-marital children the same entitlements against their fathers as marital children. Security of residence (a concept distinct from property sharing, on the partnership principle) could be an important element in this, and Canadian legislation[17] makes provision for possessory orders to be made in favour of cohabitees who fulfil the statutory conditions entitling them to support rights. But here practical differences are likely to be found between cohabitation and other cases. Suppose a child is born to a woman cohabiting in a residence owned or rented by the man. On breakdown of that union, the child's security may be protected by giving the mother a right to continue occupation. Where the adults are not cohabiting and the mother and child are not residing in property belonging to the man, there may be no practicable way (other than through income support) of achieving stability of residence for the child through private law means.[18] The conclusion, therefore, is that a child-based family support law cannot, in principle, distinguish between marital and extra-marital children, although the range of options available is in practice likely to differ according to whether the parents were cohabiting (married or otherwise) or not at the time of their estrangement. All measures that may benefit marital children should in principle be available to non-marital children, irrespective of the relationship (determined by cohabitation or otherwise) between their parents.[19]

A child-centred approach has further consequences. It can be maintained that the extra-marital child is as entitled to the contribution of his father to decisions about his upbringing (if he is willing to be involved) as is the marital child. The father, then, should have the right to such consultation and, consequently, the right to recognition as the father. Two related concerns may oppose this. The mother herself may resist further involvement with the father, claiming that it jeopardizes her chance of marriage.[20] It may also be thought better for the child to develop relationships only with the mother and any man with whom she may subsequently enter a stable union. The arguments are reinforced if it is supposed that the child was conceived as a result of rape or incest. These questions raise genuine issues concerning the child's welfare. It is important (as in the case of the analogous area of post-divorce access) not to fall into extreme postures. It would be wrong to give the mother alone the absolute right to determine whether or not the father should be involved with his children and even whether his identity should be revealed to them. This, as we noted, is the present situation in England, and the Law Commission (1982) thought this should continue, but qualified it in cases where there was a maintenance order against the father, a custody order respecting the child in his favour or an order giving him any parental rights. In such circumstances the father's name could be recorded, should he so wish, despite the mother's objection. If a court had made a finding of paternity with respect to a man, the births' register should automatically be amended to refer to that fact.[21] Thus, even if the mother knows who the father is and (to make the case vivid) he is *voluntarily* contributing to the child's support, the father would have no right to have his identity recorded unless the mother agreed. It seems as if this might be the case even if he was making a compulsory contribution towards the child but this was done at the behest of the supplementary benefit authorities rather than the mother. He would need to initiate proceedings for custody or 'parental rights', or (by withholding support) provoke proceedings on the mother's part, to acquire this right.

Even if the man's name is recorded as the child's father, this in itself would not, on the Law Commission's proposals, be sufficient to establish a legal relationship with the child. For this to be achieved, the father would need to have successfully taken proceedings granting him legal custody or some or all of the 'parental rights and duties'.[22] A full parental rights order in favour of a father who was living, unmarried, with the mother, would have the same effect as a joint custody order. It might be thought that a father should acquire this position simply by the fact that his name had been registered as the child's father at the joint request of himself and the mother. The delay and expense of a court application seem unreasonable preconditions. However, the Law Commission (1982) rejected this solution, largely out of fear that 'unscrupulous' natural fathers might put mothers under severe pressure to consent to joint registration, thus obtaining important leverage in any further involvement with her. The requirement of legal proceedings would interpose judicial assessment of the child's interests before facilitating that involvement.[23] It may be unfortunate that the Commission were influenced more by the spectres of the unscrupulous than the position the more reasonable man is likely to find himself in, unsure how he should exercise his parental role in the face of the (possible) desire on the part of the mother to terminate *her* relationship with *him*. It may be understandable that such mothers see *their* interests threatened by the recognition of the relationship between the children and their fathers, but it need not be assumed that their interests are coincidental with those of their children, any more than are the interests of divorced women wishing to construct a new life free from their former husband.

A final issue concerning the support of the lone unmarried mother and child must be mentioned. She may be reluctant to reveal the father's name and he, too, may wish his identity to remain undetected. We must here distinguish cases where a man claims to be the father and the mother refuses to co-operate in an inquiry establishing whether he is the father or not. In such a case the father might bring proceedings for custody or parental rights and obtain an order requiring the mother and child to submit to blood tests in case these will assist his claim. This must be provided for in any system making paternity in itself the basis for according legal recognition to a relationship. Where, however, no one claims paternity and the mother herself makes no allegations, what case exists for legal intervention?

The case can rest on two grounds. First, it may be argued that it is always in the child's interests to have the name of his father recorded. On this view, apart from exceptional cases, the mother would be required, on pain of court action, to name the father for record when the child is born. Second, where the mother claims support from public funds, it could be thought in the community interest to require her to reveal the father's identity to enable recourse to him for contribution. Acceptance of these arguments calls for strict measures, perhaps even automatic paternity proceedings, when a child is born to an unmarried mother and no father is acknowledged.[24] The Law Commission (1982) rejected such an approach on the grounds that they would be expensive, achieve little and put unreasonable pressure on the mother.[25] In the United States, welfare authorities supporting the children of unmarried mothers can *require* her co-operation in locating the father, but her refusal is visited with denial only of her own benefits, not those of her children. Furthermore, she is permitted to withhold co-operation for 'good cause' (which is left to interpretation by welfare agencies and is done so quite narrowly).[26] There seems little point in trying to *impose* a relationship between father and child if neither the father nor the mother wish it. But the argument from community interest is another matter. A mother may indeed be reluctant to participate in proceedings if they yield no benefits for her or her child and simply put the father under liability towards the state. Yet to abandon the state's right to contributions to the mother's veto would undermine the rationale of collecting such contributions at all. This reinforces the argument made earlier[27] that a proportion of the contributions collected from the debtor should go directly to the mother, especially if they are forthcoming as a result of voluntary agreement. In other words, if the state is unwilling to coerce mothers, it could encourage their co-operation by allowing them some of its fruits.

Cohabitation without children

In the absence of children, how far should the fact that a (sexual?) relationship between unmarried adults (of opposite sexes?) is accompanied by a (greater or lesser) degree of cohabitation deserve special legal consideration? The law was initially drawn into this area for negative reasons. Any attempt by parties to regulate their financial affairs in such a context might be struck down as being made for an immoral purpose.[28] If an agreement purported to put one party under an obligation to the other after cohabitation ended, it was hard to see what consideration the beneficiary party was offering:[29] the promise would be gratuitous and thus unenforceable unless under seal. Yet, in the absence of any alternative mechanism for regulating their economic relationship, cohabitees can do no other than to rely on the law giving force to their agreements.

Despite those difficulties, English courts have in recent years found it possible to give effect to actual or assumed agreements between cohabiting or formerly cohabiting adults. This has been especially evident in cases where the parties have built up assets by their joint efforts during their cohabitation. In such cases the courts will now[30] be ready to use the trust doctrines referred to earlier[31] and, through them, give effect to their intentions.[32] The result is that, where assets have been built up, a distribution grounded on property entitlement related to the proportionate *contributions* of the parties can be made. The ideology of partnership does not apply and indeed there seems to be no reason why it should. While we may, with certain justification, assume such an ideology between married people, there is no reason to do so for the unmarried. Nor, indeed, is cohabitation strictly necessary. It matters not whether the parties lived together or, if so, on what basis, or even if they are of the opposite sex.

If courts are prepared to give covert recognition to agreements between cohabitees within the trust doctrines, should they not openly do so, thus encouraging express agreements? Apart from allowing the parties to regulate property matters more openly, such agreements could extend more widely to include, for example, such matters as support obligations after breakdown. This would require a direct confrontation with the traditional public policy prohibition on such contracts. Courts in Australia[33] and the United States[34] have done *Marvin v. Marvin* this and attempted to remove the 'immorality' stigma from such arrangements provided that the agreement was not solely for sexual purposes. Where the agreement related *solely* to future support, an English court may still have difficulty in finding sufficient consideration. Some legislatures have attempted a solution by express enactment. The Ontario Family Law Reform Act 1978, for example, permits a 'man and woman who are cohabiting and not married to one another' to enter a written agreement on their respective rights and obligations both during and after cohabitation; these may include ownership and division of property, support obligations (during or after cohabitation), rights over their children's upbringing (but *not* custody or access) and 'any other matter in the settlement of their affairs'.[35] Legislation of this kind, which makes the fact (not intent) of cohabitation a condition precedent to validating such contracts, might be too narrow. It requires the adoption of a conceptual model of cohabitation. The Ontario Act states that this implies a 'conjugal relationship'[36] and courts may easily be led to superimposing a model derived from an ideal of marriage (commitment, exclusivity, heterosexuality) on a very different relationship. All that seems necessary is to provide, simply, that agreement concerning property division and future support should be enforceable notwithstanding that the parties are cohabiting (or engaged in any other sexual relationship) at the time and notwithstanding that any obligations are stipulated to arise after the termination of the relationship. In this way it becomes unnecessary to conceptualize the idea of 'cohabitation' as a condition justifying legal protection. All that is done is that a possible impediment to contractual enforcement is removed.

But, assuming the expansion of contract law in this way, will this be adequate to deal with childless, unmarried cohabitation? To be sure, novel problems of contract law could arise. How far are the terms of such contracts to be legally recognized or enforced? Some suggestions for the content of contracts for intimate relationships seek to govern many details of domestic life, such as who is to perform which household function, from where the couples may select their friends, how they shall behave in public before one another, what days they may spend as 'private' days when their activities go unquestioned by the other and how they shall arrange their contraceptive practices.[37] How breach of such terms can be determined and what the consequences shall be (if not specified in the contract) could lead courts into the most unseemly areas. Furthermore, any development of notions such as whether a breach by one party was fundamental could reintroduce normative judgements not unlike those made in divorce cases in the past. There may be no harm in people inserting such terms in contracts should they desire to do so, but there is much to be said for confining legal recognition to matters of finance and property.

Contract law has other limitations. The economically more powerful partner is likely to wish to protect his or her interests, at least if significant amounts are at stake. Circumstances may change, radically altering the balance of economic power between the couple. Suppose (to take a strong case) the contract imposes no post-breakdown support obligations. Unexpectedly the woman becomes pregnant, and, without thought of modifying the contract, she decides to have the child, which dies in childbirth, leaving her physically impaired, and the man leaves her. Can a court effectively re-write the contract to cover the new circumstances? It has been argued that contract law is sufficiently flexible to respond to these difficulties.[38] It may turn out so, though the kind of principles that may develop under the rubric of contract law *in this area* may be very similar to familiar family law principles. It is significant that the 1978 Ontario Act permits courts to set aside a provision for support in a contract between cohabitees 'where the provision for support or the waiver of the right of support results in circumstances that are unconscionable' or where the former partner qualifies for public support payments.[39] Presumably this permits a court to insert such a provision if it is totally lacking in the contract.

Apart from these conditions, cohabitees may not have entered into a contract at all. This does not mean such parties have no alternative remedies under private law. We have seen that trust doctrines may establish their entitlement to a share in assets related to their contributions, although there may be difficulties in determining their scope.[40] In certain circumstances the courts might look to the expectations entertained by one party and, if these were induced by the other, provide a remedy sufficient to fulfil those expectations. In one case (possibly extreme), a widow moved into a man's house, initially as his housekeeper, but subsequently they cohabited as man and wife. Later he began a relationship with another woman, but told the widow that the house was 'hers'. Relying on this, she remained in it, doing some repairs and redecoration. When the man sought to renege, the court responded by transferring the house to her.[41] Such doctrines, if developed, could be used to supplement defective contracts and provide remedies where contracts are lacking. They may go some way in providing recompense for cohabitees on similar principles as for married people who have conferred benefits on the other party or undergone disadvantages.[42] But at present they are juristically unclear and uncertain in scope. In particular, it is unlikely that any right to compensation arises simply on the basis that one party has conferred benefits on the other. There must at least have been expectation of reward, possibly induced by the other.[43]

The apparent inadequacy of existing private law has led some legislatures to subject cohabitees to liability for support obligations. Normally such liability will arise only after the parties have cohabited for a stated time-period.[44] Despite arguments against such developments,[45] it is suggested that they are justifiable. If it is right that a married person should receive some compensation on the basis of benefits conferred and disadvantages suffered during marriage, why should such compensation be denied a cohabitee? Indeed, the private law doctrines discussed above do seek to give them some measure of compensation. The extension is warranted only in so far as it *improves the remedies* for compensation but maintains the same principles. An analogy can be drawn with Swedish legislation of 1973,[46] which gives a cohabitee who has the greater need the right to take over a tenancy held by the other party. This applies mainly to cases where children have been born (reflecting the importance of the distinction between those cases and childless cohabitation), but may apply to childless cohabitation where there are 'urgent' reasons, for example, if the woman is pregnant or the cohabitation has been for a very long period.

If the rationale for such remedies rests on the notion of compensation for benefits and disadvantages, it is these matters rather than the character of the cohabitation which justify the claim. Hence it is unnecessary to conceptualize the concept or even to fix a time limit for its application. It should be sufficient if benefits or disadvantages occurred as a result of entering communal dwelling and that these have not been adequately compensated. And since the basis lies in 'neutral' principles of justice, there seems no reason to confine the remedies to heterosexual relationships.

But in some cases conceptualization is difficult to avoid. For example, under the Rent Act 1977, 'a member of the original tenant's family' who was resident with him at his death, is entitled to succeed to a protected tenancy held by the tenant. In 1950 the Court of Appeal decisively rejected the claim of a cohabitee to be regarded as a member of the tenant's family,[47] but in 1975 it equally determinedly included a cohabitee within the expression.[48] The question is, of course, one of ascertaining the true purpose of the legislation, and this includes seeing the matter from the landlord's perspective. A resident spouse is clearly a family member and, while he may not be too concerned as to the validity or otherwise of the marriage (and hence, conceivably, even its existence), the landlord may reasonably be expected to be bound only if the relationship has the *outward appearance* of a marriage.[49] But it may further be asked why this protection should be granted, and confined, to family members. The answer must lie in some conception of the unity of the family, on behalf of which one or other of the adults routinely deals with the outside world. Benefits so acquired are seen as the family's benefits, not just his or her own, and hence can reasonably remain in the family on his death (or other departure).[50] If a group has the outward appearance of operating in this way, then it may not matter whether or not the adults are married to each other.

This concept underlines moves to confer other benefits on cohabitees. Thus, in the United Kingdom, rent rebates in favour of married people extend to unmarried cohabitees[51] and local authorities are under a duty to house a qualified applicant 'and any other person who normally resides with him as a member of his family'.[52] The same argument applies with respect to benefits that arise only on the death of one of the adults. These, *a fortiori*, can be seen as 'family' benefits, whose rationale depends on the economic unity of the family. This is obvious where there are children, but, even where there are not, certain social security and insurance benefits (such as widows' benefits and life insurance provisions) may be 'earned' by one family member for the benefit of the remaining members after his or her death. The important feature of these benefits is that they recognize the economic advantages which the family unit as a whole acquires through certain individual members. Even non-insurance based benefits sometimes have this character, as in the case of the New Zealand Domestic Purposes Benefit. This is payable to a woman alone who lost the support of her husband after she reached fifty and had been married to him at least five years[53] and is payable even if she was not married to the man but the relationship was one 'in the nature of marriage'.[54] Recognition of such future family entitlements in this way is not found in England. Even in Sweden, a cohabitee living with the deceased at his death is entitled to a basic widow's pension only if she has had children by him.[55] English public sector occupational pension schemes, too, generally allow cohabitees to benefit only if specifically so nominated by the insured after retirement, and then only in the character of a dependant, which restricts benefits to provision for necessaries.[56]

Yet it would seem right that acquisition of benefits that might loosely be described as 'family benefits', in so far as one family member's entitlement to them is intended to benefit all members of his family unit, whether during his lifetime or afterwards, should depend on the existence of the economic *de facto* family than on the presence of legal marriage. The point is certainly taken in the converse case where benefits may be lost where the beneficiary (invariably the woman) cohabits with a man as his wife. In such a case the parties' resources are aggregated and only the man has the right, if any, to claim benefit. This has been criticized on the ground that the cohabiting woman has no right to support against the man with whom she lives.[57] The relevance of this is unclear, for even a married woman has very imperfect rights to enforce support against her husband while she is living with him.[58] Mere sexual relationship, or even common residence, should not, of course, be sufficient to disentitle a claimant. The test should be whether the income of either benefits the other in the way family income does. In such a case, it is surely right to deal with that family in the same way as all families, whether married or not.

Finally, we should consider claims a cohabitee might have on the death of his or her partner. This is different from the pensions and social security position because there the question is essentially whether *the benefit in question* can be seen as enuring to a cohabitee's 'family'. This is not necessarily true with regard to the estate of a deceased cohabitee any more than it is necessarily true respecting the assets of each cohabitee on breakdown of the relationship. The former partner stands in competition with other family members. If the parties were married, the surviving spouse would be in a strong position, taking all personal effects (excluding business property), whatever is left of the estate up to the value of £15,000 (if there are children), or £40,000 (if there are no children but other relatives), or all of it (if there are no children or relatives).[59] A cohabitee, however, has to make an application to a court and, provided (she) can show (she) was being supported, wholly or in part, by the deceased immediately before his death, (she) may be awarded a sum for her 'maintenance'.[60] Glendon attributes the remarkable improvement of the position of the surviving spouse *vis-à-vis* other family members during the course of this century to the ascendancy of the value of companionate marriage over the claims of next-of-kin.[61] Indeed, she cites a 1978 study by the American Bar Foundation which showed general willingness that the entire estate, no matter how large, should go to the surviving spouse when in competition with the deceased's relatives.[62]

Should the situation be different for a cohabitee? It is suggested that it should. The ideology behind the preference for the surviving spouse is analogous to the willingness of married people to regard their assets as jointly owned,[63] that is, the ideology of partnership. We have argued that this assumption cannot be taken for granted in the case of the unmarried. Should they wish it to apply, they may do so by contract (assuming enforceability problems can be overcome) or by will. In the absence of that, the cohabitee's claim rests on general principles of compensation for benefits conferred or disadvantages suffered. Some claim against the estate is supportable for these reasons, but there seems no good ground to confine such claims to maintenance support, or even to make *de facto* dependency a condition precedent. Least of all is it relevant to erect a requirement that the deceased should have 'assumed responsibility' for the claimant cohabitee's maintenance, as currently required in English law,[64] for this is to import into cohabitation a conceptualization taken from marriage. It may be precisely to avoid such responsibility that the parties did not marry. Is this to mean that no principles can be found to justify *some* distribution to the survivor?

PART THREE: LAW AND PROTECTION

9
The Origins of Modern Protective Legislation

The historical roots of family violence

For centuries our society has accepted the family as the natural unit for the incubation of the future adult. How families arranged the upbringing of their children was not the concern of the wider community. Families, therefore, tended to seek to ensure that their children would bring the maximum advantages to themselves or the class to which the family belonged. We have noted[1] how the landed classes forged marriage alliances for their children in order to consolidate their economic position. It was common practice in England before the Restoration for children of the upper classes, and later also of the middle classes, to be sent away from home, sometimes to friends or relatives, often to strangers, so that they could both provide services and at the same time be trained to fulfil the tasks that awaited them in their station in adult life. Girls, for example, would in this way learn the arts of managing a large domestic household which was the task expected of them once entering a wealthy marriage.[2] But the self-interest of adults stretched far beyond these commercial arrangements. Discipline in the home would often be imposed with extreme brutality. The expression of natural aspirations was frequently cruelly suppressed so that the children would conform to the adults' conceptions of what they should be.[3] Among the poorer sections of the community, especially in times of economic hardship, children were ruthlessly exploited by their parents and others for economic gain. The deliberate maiming of children to increase their appeal as beggars, or the deliberate training of boys as thieves and girls in prostitution, with the consequential risks of capital punishment and disease, continued until well into the nineteenth century.

The absolute power of parents over their children was integral to the social structure. The normal protective reach of the criminal law would stop at the family's threshold. No compelling social interest existed to justify, let alone compel, its intrusion. Violence towards children within the home, if visible at all, simply did not register in the social consciousness as worth remarking. Indeed, it may not even be considered *violence* at all, but looked on as necessary discipline and correction; as natural a part of childhood as illness, learning and labour and, in some societies, ritual mutilation.[4]

The same held true with respect to a husband's power over his wife. There appears to be no detailed account of the extent or severity of altercations between married couples in past ages. The accounts of the poverty, drudgery and affectionless lives of spouses from the middle ages to modern times seldom refer specifically to the violence suffered by one spouse (usually the wife) at the hands of the other. Stone (1977) considers that, prior to the eighteenth century, violence tended to occur more often between families than within them. But modern experience has shown how difficult it is to detect intrafamilial violence or even perceive it as such, and the historical experience is unlikely to be very different. Such violence, when mentioned, appears to be considered as a usual component of a woman's subjugation to her husband. In 1765 William Blackstone, in his Commentaries on the Laws of England, described how husband and wife were treated as one person by the common law so that neither could sue the other for redress nor give evidence for or against the other in criminal prosecutions. He added that by the old law a husband might give his wife 'moderate correction' and that, although 'in the politer reign of Charles II, this power of correction began to be doubted: and a wife may have security of the peace against her husband', nevertheless, 'the lower rank of people, who were always fond of the old common law, still claim and exert their ancient privilege: and the courts will still permit a husband to restrain a wife of her liberty, in case of any gross misbehaviour'. Shorter (1976) describes a Bavarian case of 1750 where the fact that 'men whack their wives about' was considered normal by a court, and a similar attitude appears in an English case reported in 1755.[5]

The discovery and re-discovery of domestic violence

From about the middle of the nineteenth century, voices of concern about the brutality to which many women were subjected could be heard. The principles of political liberalism, which demanded equal protection for individual adults regardless of sex,[6] the growth of women's political consciousness and the moral concerns of evangelical Christianity[7] combined to raise consciousness that wives should not be so treated. In 1853 an Act was passed increasing penalties which could be imposed on men who assaulted their wives and children.[8] But, although the common law recognized criminal cases where the accused was charged with committing a crime of violence against his or her spouse as an exception to the rule that a spouse could not give evidence against the other,[9] it was clear that the criminal law had little or no impact. Some judges argued that flogging should be imposed as a deterrent, but it was replied that this would only further brutalize the men.[10]

The ecclesiastical courts gave a form of protection in the divorce *a mensa et toro*, which was no true divorce at all but merely a decree which removed the complainant spouse's obligation to live with the other. This could be granted in cases of cruel conduct where cohabitation had become a 'danger' to the complainant. When the power to dissolve marriages was conferred on the civil courts by the Matrimonial Causes Act 1857, a wife could obtain a divorce decree against her husband for his cruelty if, additionally, he had committed adultery. The divorce *a mensa et toro* lived on in the form of judicial separation and this would entitle her to live apart from him if he maltreated her.

The law of cruelty in the context of divorce and judicial separation was initially designed to protect one spouse against the other. Lord Merriman said of it that 'protection lay at the root of the matter'.[11] Therefore the complainant had to show actual or apprehended injury to his or her health.[12] Yet it provided only a very imperfect form of protection. Its main effect was rather to keep intact the woman's right to receive support from her husband although she was living apart from him. Even then she must be careful not to commit adultery or to excuse her husband's misconduct, for she would then lose her remedy. For four years the courts took the view that a lower award should be made to a wife who sought divorce rather than judicial separation, for there should be some inducement to keep alive the marriage bond.[13] If the court felt that she had contributed to the state of affairs, no matter how violent, it would refuse the decree.[14] Certainly these remedies provided no immediate succour to the threatened wife. In any case, as has been seen, the existence of these remedies in the higher courts was remote from the generality of the population. In conditions of overcrowding, economic dependence and the constant bearing of children, there was little the beaten wife could do but endure her lot. If the wife had been deserted and left destitute, an Act of 1868[15] empowered the Poor Law guardians to bring proceedings against the husband before justices and obtain a maintenance order against him; but not until the Matrimonial Causes Act 1878 was passed, after a campaign against 'wife torture' by Frances Power Cobbe,[16] could a wife in her own right bring a complaint before justices that she might be formally released from her obligation to live with her husband and that he support her. To succeed, she had to prove that he had committed an aggravated assault upon her. This 'poor person's divorce' (though still no true divorce) was the foundation upon which the modern English law of matrimonial proceedings in magistrates' courts is based. Although the grounds upon which a separation and maintenance order could be obtained were extended in subsequent Acts,[17] the grounding of the jurisdiction in offences committed by the husband permeated maintenance law until well into the 1970s. Furthermore, to obtain this remedy, as well as those in the higher courts, the wife, although entitled to live apart from her husband, must not herself enter a sexual relationship with another man, even (until 1925) if she had been led to this by reason of her husband's failure to support her. When it is considered that, until the last quarter of the nineteenth century, whatever money and movable goods the wife had owned had become her husband's on marriage, the inadequacy of these techniques in providing any real protection for a beaten wife is obvious.

Yet the problem dropped from public view during the larger part of the twentieth century. Two World Wars, severe economic recession and the institution of (intended) radical social reform were probably sufficient to mask it. It is not clear that the resurgence of the women's liberation movement in the 1960s played any significant role in raising wife-battering once more to public consciousness, for its original concerns were more centred on the restrictions which the family and wider social system placed on a woman's life-opportunities. Rather, two other factors may have been more instrumental. Probably the most important was the crusading work of Erin Pizzey, who set up the first Women's Aid shelter in Britain in Chiswick in 1971 and published an account of its history in 1974 (Pizzey [1974]). The other factor has been the gradual realization of the emotional harm that can be caused to children by severe friction between their parents. Thus the concern about violence between adults is linked to the problem of child abuse. This potent mixture provided the ingredients to lift the level of concern to one about the health of society as a whole. Spousal abuse could become symbolic of a society arranged by men for the oppression of women,[18] or permeated by social and economic inequalities leading to stress and frustration,[19] which, once perpetrated, tended to institute a cycle of violence.

The discovery and re-discovery of child abuse and neglect

Public concern about child abuse and neglect has followed a very similar course. Perhaps not surprisingly, the plight of children in recent history claimed public attention only when the consequences of child neglect appeared to threaten social stability. The increase in urban crime following industrialization in the early nineteenth century was the original impetus of movements to improve the conditions of children. Their delinquency was seen to be socially caused and therefore susceptible to rehabilitation and prevention by modifying their social environment. The reformatory and industrial schools set up in this period to deal with delinquent and vagrant children provided the basis of the welfare orientation which informs juvenile justice law to this day. Yet it was the perception of these children as visible threats to society which provided both the impulse and justification for welfarist intervention.[20]

The problem of juvenile crime was, then, inextricably linked to the problem of poverty. It is therefore in these two contexts that children first became the objects of community concern and wherein the origins of modern English child welfare legislation is to be found. The original solution to the problem of family poverty was to attempt to provide families with facilities for profitable employment within locally established workhouses. But such institutions could never become self-supporting and the policy introduced by the Poor Law Amendment Act 1834 saw the workhouse as a deterrent against poverty. In order to encourage persons to seek employment, the 'principle of less eligibility' maintained that conditions in the workhouse should always be worse than those which could be obtained at the lowest level in independent employment.

Although it was not the original intention that the aged and the sick should be taken into workhouses as a condition for the receipt of relief under the Poor Law, this became common as it was thought to be much cheaper to maintain the poor in these institutions than outside them. One contemporary observer wrote:

> Each of the buildings we so absurdly call a workhouse is, in truth, (1) a general hospital; (2) an almshouse; (3) a foundling house; (4) a lying-in hospital; (5) a school house; (6) a lunatic asylum; (7) an idiot home; (8) a blind asylum; (9) a deaf and dumb asylum; (10) a workhouse; but this part of the establishment is in general a lucus a non lucendo, omitting to find work even for able-bodied paupers. . . . It is once equally shocking to every principle of reason and every feeling of humanity that all these various forms of wretchedness should be thus crowded together into one common abode, that no attempt should be made by law to classify them and to provide appropriate places for the relief of each.[21]

Another observer wrote that 'the space assigned to 300 persons by the Poor Law Commissioners would not accommodate 45 on the scale of the London hospitals and not above 65 on the scale of the military hospitals'.[22]

Yet in 1840 there were estimated to be 64,570 children in English workhouses.[23] The conditions were hardly better than on the streets or in the factories. In the 1780s, when the normal death-rate for children under fifteen was estimated at about 1 in 40, that of children in workhouses was estimated at between 1 in 8 and 1 in 14. For infants, it was discovered that only 7 per cent of those born in workhouses in 1763 were still alive in 1765.[24] Already in the late eighteenth century a statute[25] permitted London workhouses, as an experiment, to board their children under six in lodgings three miles outside the city. Although this was thought to save the lives of some 1,500 children per year, another century was to pass before boarding-out became a serious means of child care. The Poor Law Amendment Act 1834, s.15, recognized that children in workhouses should be housed separately from adults, but breaches of this principle were found as late as 1946.[26] It was through very gradual attempts to provide education for these children that an institutional and legal structure was fashioned to meet their needs. The 1834 Act recognized the desirability of providing them with a basic education, but its implementation was haphazard and even resisted on the ground that it breached the principle of 'less eligibility'. In London, however, the Poor Law authorities adopted the expedient of allowing the children to be educated in residence by entrepreneurs, who were paid by the Poor Law guardians and looked forward to eventual profits from the labours of the children. The conditions in these establishments often fell below elementary standards of hygiene and in 1849 an incident occurred in which the Poor Law guardians refused to remove their children from a residence where between fourteen and twenty of them were dying daily in a cholera outbreak.[27]

Some Poor Law unions responded to this by combining to establish and manage their own district schools. These large 'barrack' establishments, mainly in London, may have been an improvement over the contractors' schools, but provided little for a child's emotional, intellectual or physical well-being. Although the Education Act 1870 imposed a general duty upon local education authorities to make schooling available for everybody, and the Poor Law authorities could make use of those facilities, the duty to provide education for workhouse children lay primarily with the Poor Law authorities until 1929.[28] Eventually, the growth of public education shifted the emphasis of the responsibilities of the Poor Law authorities to the provision of accommodation for workhouse children. This duty was met partly by the replacement of 'barrack' homes by smaller, 'cottage-style' establishments of small units grouped together, often separate from the rest of the community. Towards the end of the nineteenth century the use of individual houses within the community was preferred, for the children would attend the local school and would not be isolated from their peers after school hours. Alternatively, the Poor Law authorities encouraged boarding-out. Only in 1868 was boarding-out of children permitted beyond the boundaries of the Poor Law union, although the practice had long been common in Scotland. Since it was necessary to make relatively generous allowances to foster-parents, it was felt that the system breached the principle of 'less eligibility' and hence it proceeded with caution. Indeed, in its earlier stages, illegitimate children were not entitled to its benefits. In 1906, of the 69,288 children supposedly on 'indoor relief' under the Poor Law, 26,983 were in homes and schools, 21,526 in workhouses and 8,781 (12.6 per cent of the total) were boarded out.[29] In 1977, one-third of the 96.2 thousand children in care in England and Wales were boarded out.[30] Workhouses were abolished by the National Assistance Act 1948, but in 1946 there were still nearly three thousand children in workhouses in England and Wales.[31]

But what of the neglect and ill-treatment of children living outside the workhouses? Within the great English cities in the nineteenth century the conditions of thousands of children outside the workhouse were scarcely better than for those within it. Leaving aside the frequent brutality of the labour and apprenticeship system, it was estimated that there were some ten thousand child beggars on the streets of London at the turn of the nineteenth century. If these were the children of adults on outdoor relief, Poor Law policy originally forbade contributions from the poor rate towards their education. The Education of Poor Children Act 1855, however, permitted such contributions to be made, but they could not be made conditional upon the parents' sending the children to school. Not until the Education Act 1870 laid the first tentative foundations of a comprehensive state education system was a serious attempt made to remove these children from the streets. And only in 1880 were school boards put under a duty to pass by-laws establishing compulsory school attendance up to the age of thirteen (raised to fourteen in 1900); moreover, although the boards had power to remit fees, elementary school education in fact became free only in 1891 on the introduction of a system of *per capita* grants to education authorities.

Many infants, however, simply perished. Either they were abandoned by their parents, or were slain by them or by persons who trafficked in children for reward. No accurate guess can be made of the numbers who died. Illegitimate children were the principal victims, their birth a disgrace and their future without hope. One member of Parliament put the death-rate at thirty thousand illegitimate children per year.[32] Not for the last time in our social history, it took the revelation of a notorious abuse to bring about the first community intervention to protect children from the hands of persons who took them in for reward and then allowed them to die of neglect. Margaret Waters was executed in 1870 for her part in such a baby-farming enterprise,[33] and consequently the Infant Life Protection Act 1872 placed a registration requirement on persons taking in two or more children under one year old for reward for more than twenty-four hours. No enforcement measures were attached and the provision met with the strongest opposition from those who believed that it infringed the fundamental rights of parents to make whatever arrangements they chose respecting their children. It was proclaimed in 1874 that 'I would far rather see even a higher rate of infant mortality prevailing than has ever yet been proved against the factory district or elsewhere . . . than intrude one iota further on the sanctity of the domestic hearth and the decent seclusion of private life. . .'.[34] Others did not object to licensing the child-minders but opposed removing from parents the choice whether to use licensed or unlicensed people. The Act became a dead letter and another sensational trial in 1896 of Mrs Dyer, a baby-farmer who threw the bodies of the babies she murdered into the Thames at Reading, instigated the passage of a more stringent and successful Act in 1897.[35]

In an atmosphere where the infant life protection movement was opposed because it interfered with the parents' choice to decide who was to mind their children, it is not surprising to find great reluctance to intervene to protect children against the parents themselves. Even the reformer Lord Shaftesbury, in reply to a letter seeking his support for legislation to protect children against abuse by their parents, wrote: 'The evils you state are enormous and indisputable, but they are of so private, internal and domestic a character as to be beyond the reach of legislation, and the subject, indeed, would not, I think, be entertained in either House of Parliament.'[36] Yet it had been a long tradition in England for children to be brought up apart from their parents and it was commonplace in Tudor and Elizabethan England for the Poor Law authorities to remove children from vagrant parents and either set them to work or return them to the parish of their birth in order to relieve the burden they imposed on the poor rates. Protection of community funds justified the enforcement of parental obligations to provide for their own children, and in 1868 section 37 of the Poor Law Amendment Act stated:

When any parent shall willfully neglect to provide adequate food, clothing, medical aid or lodging for his child being in his custody, under the age of fourteen years, whereby the health of the child shall have been or shall be likely to be seriously injured, he shall be guilty of an offence . . . and the [Poor Law] guardians . . . shall institute the prosecution and pay the costs thereof out of their funds.

Although going beyond the then current criminal law of assault and murder, in so far as the provision protected against 'neglect' and sought to guard against future injury to a child, there were no provisions for the detection of offences or for the removal of the child from a dangerous environment. Furthermore, since the prosecuting authorities were the Poor Law guardians, the only cases likely to be detected were those of the children of poor persons in receipt of poor relief outside the workhouse. But the wider concerns of the evangelical movement moved from anti-slavery and animal welfare into concern for the moral failing of parents who ill-treated or neglected their children. An historic meeting of the Liverpool Society for the Prevention of Cruelty to Animals in 1882 discussed the suggestion of forming a local society to protect children, and in the following year the Liverpool Society for the Prevention of Cruelty to Children was formed. Various local societies amalgamated into the National Society for the Prevention of Cruelty to Children in 1889, and its activities were instrumental in securing the passage through Parliament of a number of bills designed to strengthen the law against child cruelty. The first, and historically perhaps the most significant, of these was the Poor Law Amendment Act 1889 which provided (in Section 1) that 'where a child is maintained by the guardians of any union and is deserted by its parent' or if the parent was 'imprisoned as the result of an offence against the child' the guardians might resolve 'that such child be under the control of the guardians until it reaches sixteen (if a boy) or eighteen (if a girl)'.

The result of the resolution was to vest in the guardians parental rights over the child in all matters except its religious upbringing. Parents were given the right of appeal to a magistrates' court, which could order the return of the child if it was found not to be in Poor Law care, or if it had not been deserted, or if 'it is for the benefit of the child that it should be either permanently or temporarily under the control of such parent or that the resolution of the guardians should be determined'. These resolutions became known as 'Poor Law adoptions' and form the basis of what is still a unique feature of child welfare law in Britain; namely that, if a child is in the care of a local welfare authority, that authority has (subject to appeal by the parents) power to assume to itself parental rights respecting the child by simple administrative resolution. In no other country in the common law tradition is such a power to be found.

At the same time the reformers sought to extend the protection of the law to children who were not under Poor Law supervision. Section 1 of the Prevention of Cruelty to and Protection of Children Act 1889 (sometimes referred to as 'The First Children's Charter') made it a misdemeanour for anyone over sixteen who had custody, control or charge of a boy under fourteen or a girl under sixteen wilfully to ill-treat, neglect or abandon the child in a manner likely to cause unnecessary suffering or injury to health. In particular, a policeman with a warrant could enter premises where he had reasonable cause to believe an offence was being committed and the child could be removed to a 'place of safety'. If a parent was convicted, the court could commit the child to the charge of a relative or other fit person, who would have 'like control over the child as if he were its parent and shall be responsible for its maintenance, and the child shall continue under the control of such person, notwithstanding that it is claimed by its parent . . . .'.[37] The association with the Poor Law remained, however, inasmuch as until 1904 the prosecuting authority was the Poor Law authority and the place of safety was usually the workhouse. But, as the Act was extended and consolidated,[38] there grew up alongside the protective powers of the Poor Law guardians respecting children in their care a second body of law whereby courts could sanction the removal of children from their homes and commit them into the care of other persons, usually welfare authorities, in an endeavour to protect them from damage they suffered, or might suffer, in their home environment.

Yet, despite the growth of these powers to protect children in their homes, and the activities of the National Society for the Prevention of Cruelty to Children, with which local authorities shared their enforcement power, it seems that, as the twentieth century progressed, concern about child protection decreased, while anxiety over delinquency remained pervasive as ever, so much so that by the early 1960s the Departmental Committee which considered the primary legislative machinery available to deal with child abuse and neglect saw it solely in terms of legislation to deal with juvenile delinquents.[39] It is hard to account for the decline. A possible explanation may be that, as the original basis for concern, namely nineteenth-century Christianity's solicitude for the moral reform of the parents, weakened, a new ground for intervening in family life had to be found. This was to emerge from welfarist concerns for public health and the quality of the nation's human resources, but it faced difficulties in making inroads into the prevalent ideology of family autonomy.[40] Child abuse and neglect thus tended to become overshadowed by other welfare concerns and was eventually submerged by post-war anxiety about juvenile delinquency.[41] Yet, by the end of the 1970s, child protection had dramatically re-emerged in the public consciousness. As in the case of wife-beating, this phenomenon can largely be attributed to the crusading efforts of a single individual, in this instance Henry Kempe. His revelations in 1962,[42] based largely on advances in medicine, especially in radiography,[43] that parents frequently inflict deliberate injuries on their children, should have come as no surprise. Writing of the work of the National Society for the Prevention of Cruelty to Children in 1894, Gertrude Tuckwell mentions as commonplace incidents such as the following:

biting a child's wrist till a wound was made, and then burning the wound . . . forcing the bone ring of a feeding bottle up and down the throat of a three-months-old baby till it bled; . . . leaving a baby unlifted out of its cradle for weeks, till toadstools grew round the child out of its own rottenness . . . keeping the stumps of little amputated legs sore to have the child with its little face puckered up in pain, to excite pity . . .[44]

Once awakened, the extent to which public consciousness was gripped by child abuse and neglect was remarkable and parallels the case of wife-battering. Initially diagnosed by Kempe and his colleagues as the result of pathological character defects in the parents,[45] this was seen by some as an internal threat to the stability of society, a cancer in the heart of its most cherished institution, self-perpetuating in a 'cycle of violence'.[46] Others saw child abuse as a reflection of a violent society, a response to individual injustices and therefore a standing rebuke to an unjust, authoritarian, political system.[47]

The nature and extent of family violence

Alarm over the significance of family violence has been reinforced by claims as to its all-pervasive nature. Straus, investigating the phenomenon of interspousal violence in the United States, devised a physical violence scale of the following items:

K. Throwing things at the spouse
L. Pushing, shoving or grabbing
M. Slapping
N. Kicking, biting, or hitting with the fist
O. Hit or tried to hit with something
P. Beat up
Q. Threatened with a knife or gun
R. Used a knife or gun[48]

Data emerging from his sample of over two thousand couples showed that 3.8 per cent of respondents reported one or more attacks within the past year which fell within categories from N to R on the scale. Straus calculates that the data shows that such violence occurs to about 1.8 million wives in the United States each year, although he surmises that the true incidence might be double this due to under-reporting. He also shows that wives were violent towards their husbands only slightly less often than husbands were to their wives, but that the types of violence used by wives tended to fall within categories K and O more often than in the case of husbands. More recently[49] Straus has shown that violence is more prevalent among unmarried than married couples unless the parties are over thirty, divorced, have high incomes or have cohabited for over ten years. The House of Commons Select Committee on Violence in the Family (1975) quoted an estimate of the Parliamentary Under-Secretary of State in the Welsh Office that there might be about five thousand cases of wife-beating in Wales each year, which is 0.7 per cent of the total number of married women in Wales.[50] Marsden and Owens (1975) estimated that severe violence might be occurring in about 10 per cent of marriages in the United Kingdom.

The true incidence of child abuse is even harder to discover, because, unlike adults, child victims cannot answer questionnaires. Estimates therefore rely on official identification of abuse, and accordingly become heavily influenced by the identification process. Although estimates of the extent of abuse have been made,[51] it is thought better to avoid adding to this speculation. It is enough to know that, like spousal abuse, child abuse occurs sufficiently frequently to be perceived as a significant problem by welfare agencies. It is probable, however, that the extent of child *neglect* is under-observed because of the many inhibitions of welfare agencies against making positive identifications.[52] Nor is it the purpose of this book to attempt an assessment of the competing theories of why family violence occurs. The probability is that all reflect part of the truth. Rather, it is to propose a principled, defensible basis for state intervention in these cases and to relate this to the types of intervention in question.

10
Modern Responses to Family Violence

Violence between adults

As far as adults are concerned, the principle of intervention looks deceptively straightforward. Every person is entitled to equal protection of the law against violent attack. But does the legal obligation go further and require intrusion into family life to detect commission of these crimes? If the answer is no, this immediately marks off family violence from most other types of criminal behaviour. It is suggested that, except in so far as the children might be threatened (an important qualification), *the parties themselves* should determine the 'acceptable' level of violence between them, so that intervention would be conditional on its instigation by one party.[1] Yet this acceptance of the limits of community surveillance over family living is dependent on the accessibility and effectiveness of remedies, for an adult may be suffering unacceptable violence, yet be unwilling to seek intervention because the cost of doing so is too great in terms of effort and possible disruption of the family's life.

Accessibility and appropriateness are, then, key issues to legal response to domestic violence. The most accessible public agency is normally the police. Questions have, however, frequently been raised about the adequacy of their response to domestic violence.[2] They may be reluctant to intervene (unless the assault is extremely serious) for a number of reasons, which include unwillingness to become involved in emotional, domestic issues; the risk of dislocating family ties; lack of enthusiasm to intervene in a case where subsequent charges are unlikely to be pressed[3] or where, if they prosecute, the victim is thought unlikely to testify; bias in favour of the male person; and fear for their own safety.[4] It has therefore been found helpful to establish a multi-agency crisis centre, open (almost) around the clock which can be approached *both* by the public directly and by the police.[5] The reasons for doing this are strong. The prosecution of a victim's spouse or cohabitee, unlike in the case of a stranger, may deprive the victim of a source of income and, in the long or short term, the child of a second parent. Prosecution may even fail to provide the most effective protection, for it may be more important to remove the violent person from the premises, at least temporarily (and not necessarily by imprisonment) and then attempt to work out a longer-term solution to the problem.

English law has developed a variety of remedies which achieve some of these objectives. The most striking has been the injunction. This remedy was originally (and remains) an option available to the High Court when a party to divorce or judicial separation proceedings required protection from the other party. Since 1976, it has been extended to the county courts and may be sought both by spouses or cohabitees (who are defined as men and women 'who are living with each other in the same household as husband and wife') irrespective of whether the claimant seeks any other legal remedy.[6] The injunction can require the respondent not to molest the complainant, to depart from the common home (whoever owns it) and even to keep outside a defined area in which the home is situated. Nor is it necessary to show that physical violence was actually used. Judges will be ready to order an adult out of the home if this is the most reasonable solution to the conflict.[7] If, however, physical violence which has been used against the claimant or a child is likely to be repeated, the court may attach a power of arrest to the injunction (which will then be lodged at a local police station for a short period, usually three months),[8] during which the police may arrest the respondent without warrant where there is reasonable cause to suspect breach of the injunction. Parallel, and somewhat more complex,[9] powers have been conferred on magistrates under the Domestic Proceedings and Magistrates' Courts 1978, but these are limited to conflicts between married people.

There is little doubt that the injunction procedure is capable of being activated with great speed and that the arrest power is potentially very effective. There may even be some cause for concern whether it is not too frequently activated by a spouse, or, at least, his or her lawyer, as part of tactics preceding divorce petitions.[10] It is in its nature a short-term measure, and should be limited to a brief period, such as a month, or, if indefinite, the parties should understand that they are at liberty to seek its revocation, which should not be long delayed.[11] This is sensible, for the parties should be encouraged to take steps towards the ultimate resolution of the dispute. But it is unclear how accessible the remedy is to a spouse who has not already endured so much as to be seriously contemplating divorce. In cases falling short of that situation, the front line agencies are probably the local women's refuge (if available) and the police. Women at a refuge interviewed by Pahl (1982) mostly found the police 'unhelpful', especially if they were married and living together with their husband. They did, however, receive better attention if they had an injunction. There is, moreover, no clearly worked out, standardized, mode of handling such cases. Maidment (1978) discusses schemes in New York City and Washington DC whereby 'intrafamily' offences are subjected to procedures separate from those applicable in routine criminal cases. In the former, all such cases are brought before the family court, and the court itself decides whether it should proceed as a civil matter or be transferred to the criminal justice system. In Washington, such cases are referred to the US Attorney's Office, and this office (after mandatory consultation with the Director of Social Services) will decide whether the civil or criminal route should be taken. The system differs from that in New York inasmuch as, whichever process (civil or criminal) is invoked, the case is not conducted by the complainant but by Corporation counsel.

How far is it justified to treat criminal assaults within the family differently from non-family crime? Parnas, at one time a strong advocate of decriminalization procedures,[12] has now argued for more rigorous use of the criminal law.[13] This recantation mirrors the disillusion felt in the United States about the prospects of acquiring sufficient resources for effective 'therapeutic' intervention in social problems, as well as the doubts, also found in the area of child protection, of the effectiveness of such processes. Furthermore, unequal response of the criminal law has been assailed as failing to underline society's condemnation of domestic violence and denying equal protection of the law to its victims.[14]

The crucial objective should be to achieve a balanced response. It would be as wrong to ignore the familial context of violence where it occurs between adults as it is where violence is inflicted on children. In cases where there are children, the central concern should focus on the viability of the partnership as a context for the future upbringing of the children. This feature alone justifies at least *prima facie* reference to welfare agencies. If the adults wish to continue to provide this, criminal prosecution may do too much or too little. The stigma of prosecution, a severe fine, or imprisonment might seriously undermine the family's potential to function harmoniously. It also may fail to provide the appropriate immediate response, which could be the short-term removal of the offender from the home pending investigation of the family's future. Apart from any appropriate counselling (whatever view is entertained about its effectiveness), the measures could contain any necessary provision for securing the family's accommodation at that time, such as an injunction against disposal of the home or other family property or, if the home is in the public sector, an order to the authority to transfer the tenancy to the occupant partner. Criminal proceedings alone will not necessarily provide any of this.

That so many women and children need to have recourse to women's refuges to escape violent husbands has been seen as a rebuke to existing protective mechanisms and confirmation that domestic violence reflects a social system which supports male authoritarianism.[15] But there must be limitations to any system which eschews overwhelming intrusion in domestic life. There will always be a need for refuges to which, in the absence of available friends or relatives, family members may withdraw, not only in cases where protective measures do not operate swiftly enough, but also to provide a context, free of pressures, where informed decisions can be reached as to what measures, in both the short and the long-term, would be appropriate to the case. Women's (and children's) refuges should not, then, be seen as aberrations, but as integral to the protective machinery. This requires some commitment of public funds. It would be tragic if unwillingness to support these institutions forced over-reliance on the criminal law and enforcement agencies.

Child abuse and neglect: children's rights

Unlike adults, very young children cannot reach out to the community's protective agencies. They cannot, even in theory, set their own limits to the acceptability of the treatment they receive at the hands of their parents. Does this mean that no limits should be set? If we answer negatively, we need to consider the justification for drawing such limits and the implications this has on the relationship between families and the community.

We have observed how intrusions into family life have in the past been impelled by the desire to protect the public purse, to maintain public safety, to remould the moral character of the parents and to improve the quality of the nation's human resources. These are descriptions of social motives, not principles for action, though they may provide the basis for acceptable principles. None of them puts the claim of the child himself, as an individual, as a sufficient or even necessary, justification.[16] If this is done it becomes necessary to develop a theory about what claims children do have and, equally importantly, how they may be realized, for recognition of a claim as valid is empty unless the consequences of its implementation are accepted.

The movement for children's rights attempts to rest the justification for measures concerning children on the realization of the claims of children as individuals. This provides the rationale for proclaiming a 'Bill of Rights' for children. The Royal Commission on Family and Children's Law in British Columbia (Berger Commission) gave three reasons for seeking such a measure.[17] First, it would put in positive form matters that are presently approached in a negative fashion (the threat to remove a child if neglected could be seen as a right of the child not to be neglected). Second, it would encourage the recognition of individual capacities and identities of children in court proceedings. Third, it would introduce the dimension of the child's point of view in decisions affecting their interests. The Commission proceeded to identify twelve 'children's rights', including the right to an environment free from 'physical abuse, exploitation and degrading treatment'. A similar classification has been made by Foster and Freed (1972), who include in the list the right to 'receive parental love and affection' and to be regarded 'as a person'. The Berger Commission goes as far as to suggest that a child whose rights are violated should have a remedy by way of 'judicial declaration' of entitlement to the right which, it would be hoped, would not be ignored by the state authorities.

Sometimes the rights sought for children form part of a programme of political aspirations.[18] It is not always realized what the full implications of attempting to mobilize these rights would be. Since very young children lack the ability to seek the enforcement of these rights there would need to be constant intrusion into family functioning to ensure their realization. Rights of children and family autonomy are antithetical. The balance struck between them reflects a political judgement about the nature we want our society to have. The conflict between principles of personal freedom and attempts to control the quality (and, indeed, values) of the work-force has been central to western, liberal societies at least since the early nineteenth century. In a classic exposition of this theme in France, Donzelot (1980) describes how the method of philanthropy developed as a means of offering assistance and advice to families (thereby transmitting moral values) which could be rejected only at the price of ascription of deviance. Later on, the influence of psychoanalysis on casework techniques exposed families to incursions into their innermost workings, for, by manipulating the members' images of themselves, psychoanalysis in effect imposes prevalent values on families without outwardly appearing (or claiming) to do so. The erosion of family autonomy thus achieved can mark a considerable advance in the realization of some proclaimed children's rights. A right to 'love and affection' might be promoted by casework techniques which improve the psychodynamic relationships within the family. Failure to achieve improvement (or refusal by the family to co-operate with the therapy) could lead to a charge of 'deviance' or even 'madness', and thus justify further intrusion, perhaps even the removal of the child.

Yet the very possibilities inherent in such a process have prompted an attempted reformulation of children's rights *in terms of family autonomy*. Goldstein *et al.* (1980) argue that children have a basic right to 'family integrity' which requires 'the privacy of family life under the guardianship of parents who are autonomous'.[19] Thus the parental right to freedom from state intrusion is proffered as the right of the child, too, and is based on the claim that it is the child's right that the parents be afforded the opportunity to develop psychological ties with the child untrammelled by state intrusion, and, this achieved, that these ties be maintained uninterrupted.[20] Although advanced in terms of a child's rights, this is at bottom a political theory about the relationship between family and state. A theory of children's rights would need plausibly to express claims which, in principle and not merely incidentally, enhance their interests. An uninterrupted parent–child relationship may, as the authors concede, actually damage a child. It cannot therefore in itself constitute a right of a child, although it may be an instrument whereby her rights are advanced. Whether it is such or not depends upon contingent judgements about certain psychoanalytic theories and the desirability of state intervention. In advancing the standard of minimum state intervention, the authors point to the lack of resources of the 'legal system' to respond appropriately in accordance with the child's needs.[21] But whether such resources are made available is a political matter. Yet again, the grounds which the authors propose as the sole justifications for intervention are very narrowly drawn. They are (effectively) confined to cases of death of or abandonment by the parents, sexual abuse resulting in criminal conviction of a parent, serious bodily injury inflicted by a parent and refusal to authorize lifesaving medical care. The reason for excluding emotional damage is that the authors consider the term too imprecise to give 'fair warning' to parents and adequately to control the actions of state officials; furthermore, they argue that knowledge of the causes of and proper treatment for such harm is insufficient to justify the intervention.[22] The concerns here are clearly of social ideology: a concept of fairness to parents and the supposed desirability of limiting state action. As for inadequacy of knowledge of the nature and causes of emotional harm, it may be wondered why, if this is so, the authors themselves rest the cornerstone of their case for uninterrupted parent–child relationships on their supposed indispensability for proper emotional development. If the concept is so imprecise and uncertain, it seems a weak basis for a theory of intervention or non-intervention. If, on the other hand, emotional development is so centrally crucial, it is hard to see why this alone, if denied a child, should be excluded from grounds for intervention and thus from her field of rights.

Thus the equation of children's rights and family autonomy reflects both a political theory about how family life should be organized within itself and *vis-à-vis* the state, and contingent judgements about the (present) efficacy of therapeutic intervention. In so far as it rests on political theory, it is a theory which potentially annihilates the independent status of children's rights. In so far as it rests on contingent judgements, it is open to empirical verification or refutation within an admittedly wide area of subjective assessment. What should be grasped, however, and confronted, is that the ascription of rights to children entails the potential abridgement of other values, in particular those associated with family autonomy. The recognition of these rights, as is the case with *any* rights, demands a price. The extent of the price is essentially a political judgement.

How, then, can the case be made for a set of rights adhering to children alone? It was argued earlier that the justification for providing coercive state mechanisms to divert resources from a former family member to (his) children lay in a presupposition that the adult world owes to the future generation of adults the duty, so far as possible, to ensure that each individual has equal prospects of maximizing his potential during adulthood (the 'equality principle'). This may be regarded as the most fundamental claim of all children. We saw, too, that this principle suffered modification within the context of western political systems. Their political and economic structure would not tolerate the wealth distribution that the principle, if applied absolutely, would entail. How, then, within these constraints, are these claims translated into legal form? Normally it is done by conferring legally enforceable claims on the child's parents. A mother's entitlement to child benefit rests on the conceptualization of the parent as agent for the child. The parent is given the legal right against the state, but the entitlement is premised on the child's needs. The parent is socially, if not legally, a trustee for the child.

But parents are expected to do far more than merely apply family-based state entitlements for the benefit of their children. The social organization of our society entrusts them with the task of introducing them to adult life. But to permit unrestricted parental autonomy would be to negate children's rights. The conflict is resolved by the expectation that parents will do their best for their children. Failure to do so invites social criticism, and specific failures attract legal accountability. The basic principle according to which parents are accountable is that, given existing social and economic restraints, all children should have an equal opportunity to maximize the resources available for them during their childhood (including their inherent abilities) so as to minimize the extent to which they enter adult life affected by avoidable prejudices incurred during childhood. This, it is suggested, is the root principle of children's rights. The extent to which it is implemented is dependent on the inroads which any society is prepared to make on parental (or family) autonomy. The state thus intervenes on behalf of the child against the parents, calling the parents to account for their stewardship. Thus, when intervention happens, the state, far from infringing a child's 'right' to 'family integrity',[23] is in effect enforcing the right conferred on the child against her parents that they secure her claims. The parents' rights over their children, while correctly perceived as rights *vis-à-vis* other individual adults, are in effect duties towards the child.[24]

Grounds for intervention

How far is the principle that children have a right that their parents are to do their best for them in fact realized in English law? The answer primarily lies in the provisions in section 1 of the Children and Young Persons Act 1969 which permit a court to intervene and if necessary order the child's removal if it is satisfied, with respect to a child or young person (that is, a person not yet seventeen), that

(a) his proper development is being avoidably prevented or neglected or his health is being avoidably impaired or neglected or he is being ill-treated; or
(b) it is probable that [condition (a) will be satisfied in a case where a court has found it to be satisfied with respect to another child or young person who is or was a member of the same household as the child in question];
(bb) it is probable that the conditions set out in this paragraph will be satisfied in his case (having regard to the fact that a person convicted of certain offences against children is or may become a member of the same household as the child in question);
(c) he is exposed to moral danger; or
(d) he is beyond the control of his parent or guardian; or
(e) he is not receiving proper full-time education; or
(f) he is guilty of an offence, excluding homicide, and he is in need of care and control which he is unlikely to receive unless the court makes an order. . . .

The most significant provisions in our context are (a), (b) and (bb), which can be seen as the legal expression of the right of every child that there should be no avoidable impediment to or neglect of his 'proper development', or impairment to or neglect of his health, nor should he suffer ill-treatment. The concept of 'proper' development permits the introduction of generally accepted theories about child development, both physical and emotional. We have seen that Goldstein *et al.* (1980) would consider these grounds to be too broad and uncertain and thus threaten a child's 'right' to 'family integrity'. Another fear is that such broadly drawn grounds risk the imposition of uniform standards of child care upon groups which may legitimately differ by class or ethnic origin. Wald (1975) therefore argues for narrowly defined grounds, such as serious physical injury, conditions creating a substantial risk of imminent death, disfigurement or impairment of bodily functions, and sexual abuse. However, he would include serious emotional neglect, strictly defined.[25] Katz (1971), on the other hand, considers it highly desirable that emotional neglect be an independent legal standard for intervention, provided that specific reference is made to the child's mental health.

It is probable that the significance of statutory definitions is exaggerated. Sometimes they will, of course, be important. A clear exclusion of emotional harm, for example, could drastically reduce the scope for intervention. But qualifications such as 'serious', 'substantial' and 'imminent' are capable of very flexible interpretations. Even such apparently straightforward notions as physical injury to children can, as we have seen,[26] be viewed very differently by different groups of people over time. It is therefore inevitable that there is a subjective, interpretative element in any intervention decision. Every such decision may disturb a child's relationship with her parent, and asserts a specific view of the child's rights as against parental freedom, class attitudes or cultural practices. Who makes the decisions and the institutional context in which they are made may be at least as important as statutory words.

The words of the English statute are indeed flexible. But they are applied in a context in which primary identification is usually made in the health services, particularly the health visiting system, which is required to oversee the health of all children under five.[27] Clinical evidence is related to social evidence of the family's function obtained from a variety of sources, and decision-making is usually shared between professionals from medical, social work, police and, sometimes, legal services. Ultimate responsibility for action rests (normally) with local authority personal social services departments which operate within a bureaucratic structure of accountability. The system rests not only on the accountability of workers within the institution, but on the accountability of the department itself to the community, both through its elected representatives at local government level and through its adherence to its legislative charter laid down by Parliament. This charter on the one hand requires that authorities investigate reports suggesting that a child's rights (as defined above) may be violated and institute proceedings if the report is substantiated, while on the other imposes on them a duty to diminish the need for such proceedings by making available appropriate 'advice, guidance and assistance'.[28] Final authorization for coercive intervention must be given by a magistrates' court, consisting of three lay persons usually drawn from the local community. It is, in effect, a system of checks and balances.[29] The concepts of proper development and impairment to health permit, it is suggested, a reasonable balance to be struck *in the context of this decision-making structure* between the social conception of what rights a child should have against her parents and proper respect for the liberal principles which might stand in the way of their realization. However, it is arguable that the term 'avoidable' fails sufficiently to capture the central feature of such intervention, which is that the parents, whether deliberately or otherwise, are responsible for the child's condition. It would be better to specify that the court should expressly be required to find that the parents had failed to act as reasonably competent parents would have done in the relevant circumstances.[30] This permits proper allowance to be made for social diversity and enshrines the liberal principle that, if the parent has done all a reasonable parent could do, no ground exists to displace his trusteeship. It would also reflect the way in which welfare authorities currently exercise their powers in practice.

It is probable that the value of the multi-faceted system would be enhanced by formalizing the link between medical and social input into the decision. This could be done by requiring intervention applications routinely to be submitted jointly by social services and community health services. This would ensure proper prior liaison between the bodies (and assist development of channels of communications between them), a matter of critical importance in case management. The medical input would be important in ensuring that medical personnel were satisfied that the *condition of the child* demanded intervention; the social services input would be (as it now is) directed to the question of parental responsibility for the child's condition and to the provision of proposals for the future management of the case.[31]

The question has arisen whether intervention can be justified on the basis that harm to the child is apprehended in the future, though it has not yet happened. For example, would it be right to remove a child from the mother at the moment of birth in view of the mother's known psychiatric history?[32] At present, intervention by the magistrates' court procedure discussed above is confined to present or past harms unless the child is, or is likely to become, a member of the same household as a child wth respect to whom the conditions are or were satisfied or is likely to join a household containing a person convicted of certain offences against children. But, despite these restrictions on the powers of magistrates' courts, a welfare authority concerned about any child's future may invoke the wardship jurisdiction of the Family Division of the High Court. Once done (and it can be activated by simple application), the Court has jurisdiction to make almost any disposition it wishes based on the judge's appreciation of the child's best interests. The dilemma is simple and obvious: to balance the degree of risk to the child against the likelihood that it may occur. If children are to have rights, even the right to life, such decisions must be taken. But it is suggested that the inherent checks and balances with which child welfare law and procedure operate provide a better context for such decisions than the less controlled jurisdiction of the High Court[33] and should clearly apply in such circumstances.

Child abuse and neglect: investigation and identification[34]

Unlike most people who assault their victims, parents who seriously injure their children normally seek medical help for the child. This provides a point of contact with the family and an opportunity for diagnosis of the cause of injury. Perhaps because this provided the major occasion for identification in the United States, much early literature concerned the physical presenting symptoms of child abuse and discussed the steps medical staff should take in reporting suspicious cases. But, despite the sensitivity which most paediatricians have probably acquired, it is probable that hospital accident departments are poor locations for identification of child abuse. Although clinical evidence may in some cases be sufficient to determine abuse, this is rarely likely to be the case. The injury has to be seen in the context of parental demeanour and family functioning. Quite apart from that, there are many contextual restraints operating on medical staff inhibiting their likelihood of seriously pursuing a case where other explanations are equally as likely as abuse. Hospitals are also unlikely to see cases of neglect until a very serious stage has been reached.

Identification of abuse or neglect may be made in schools and by neighbours. But schools will see only older children and in any case have limited opportunities for observation. Neighbours could be a useful referral source. Yet they are likely to operate in a sporadic fashion, sometimes unwilling to intervene, at other times doing so too readily. And even if they do report their suspicions, the problem of investigation remains.

The British health visiting scheme provides perhaps the most successful agency for investigating child abuse and neglect. The visitors, who have professional nursing qualifications, are under a statutory duty to oversee the health of every child under five. They do this partly through clinics at community health centres but mainly by home visits. However, they have no statutory rights of entry or other coercive powers. Nor have they access to other resources. They represent a classic example of the 'libertarian compromise' between state surveillance and family autonomy. They maintain their routine voluntary surveillance by operating a 'rule of optimism' whereby ambiguous events are normally interpreted favourably to the parents. Perceived failure of parental love, or withdrawal of co-operation, will be occasions for defeating the rule. Their focus of concern is the child, not the family, but their leverage lies in persuasion and example. Yet failure to accept advice thus proffered, for reasons deemed culpable, could lead to referral to social services and, ultimately, coercive intervention.

The process of identification is not, as has been indicated, necessarily straightforward. It is rare that the physical condition of the child alone will be sufficient to permit a conclusion of abuse or neglect[35] because these concepts imply, first, attribution of the cause of the condition to human agency and, second, assessment of the *quality* of the human act. Since it is rare that there is direct evidence of the cause of the condition, heavy reliance is inevitably placed on circumstantial evidence. Sometimes the evidence is of an apparently objective character, as when it is possible to compare a child's weight loss when at home with weight gain when with third parties. Often, however, it is less concrete. In short, a profile of the child's caregivers is built up with the aim of answering the question: are these the kind of people who are likely to abuse or neglect the child?

Identification thus consists largely of a critique of parental competence. The standards by which parental conduct is assessed both by agencies and courts thus becomes central to identification of and response to child abuse and neglect. This is perfectly consistent with the preceding analysis of children's rights in the context of family autonomy. Attention is directed to two matters. Are the child's rights to non-impairment of her health and proper development and to freedom from ill-treatment being infringed, and is the infraction brought about by the behaviour of those agents (normally, the natural parents) whose responsibility it is to promote those rights?

Care proceedings

Apart from short-term emergency measures designed to give immediate protection to the child,[36] coercive intervention must follow court proceedings wherein the court must be satisfied not only that the alleged ground for intervention exists but also that the child is in need of care or control which she is unlikely to receive unless the court makes an order.[37] The objectives of court proceedings in these cases can be stated to include at least the following. First, to impose upon the welfare authorities the discipline of scrutinizing their own case so that they become sensitive to assessing the weight of the evidence upon which they rely and the plausibility of the view they hold. Second, to provide the parents the opportunity to meet allegations made against them as regards their parenting competence. Third, to require the authorities to articulate their strategy for the case and demonstrate that a court order is necessary to secure to the child the degree of care she would not enjoy without the order; and fourth, to provide the community, through the magistrates, the opportunity continually to monitor the line being drawn between the currently held view of children's rights and family autonomy.

The success of the first of these objectives can be assessed by considering how far the discipline informs the routine practices of the relevant agencies. Do they rely excessively on inherently unreliable information? Do they keep systematic records? Do they give the parents adequate opportunity to account for themselves? Do they seek confirmation of suspected features from appropriately qualified personnel? The welfare agencies' liaison with legal services can be important in these matters, and the growing practice of English social services departments to involve a member of the local authority legal department (ideally, someone with experience in this area) at a relatively early stage in cases likely to lead to court action is welcome.[38]

With respect to the second objective, English care proceedings are woefully deficient. The proceedings were designed primarily for cases of juvenile delinquency. In that context it makes sense that the parties to the proceedings should be the child and the local authority, and that the parents, though not parties, should be given the opportunity to meet allegations made against them in the proceedings. But child abuse and neglect cases are quite different. They essentially challenge (on behalf of the child) the parents' competence. The true parties are the local authority and the parents. But since the parents do not have full status as parties, they (technically) should not call their own witnesses to testify as to the child's condition nor cross-examine other witnesses. However, in practice, magistrates' courts invariably allow the parents the fullest freedom to 'state their case' so that they do not feel aggrieved by the court procedure.[39] The most significant handicap of their non-party status, however, is that they do not qualify for legal aid.[40] The child, however, does. The result is that, although the parents will inevitably have approached a lawyer to take 'their' case, when the legal aid certificate is granted, this will be done in the *child's* name, thus constituting the lawyer as a lawyer for the child. How the lawyer proceeds will depend very much on his perception of his role, and whether he perceives any clash of interest between the parents and the child, in which case he may refuse to accept instructions from the parents, leaving them unrepresented, unless they can pay for a lawyer out of their own funds. Often, however, the lawyer will adopt a 'dual' role, putting his view of the child's case and helping the parents to 'present' their case.

That parents should have full party status in care proceedings is so obvious that it is hard to understand why appropriate reform has been so long delayed. The probable explanation is that government is concerned about the escalation in costs. There is, indeed, partial provision in the Children Act 1975 which permits a court (in practice, the clerk), on apprehension of a prospective conflict between the interests of child and parent, to make an order, the effect of which is to appoint a guardian *ad litem* for the child and to entitle the parents to apply for legal aid and 'make representations' to the court (though they still do not become full parties). Since legal aid will still be available for the child, and the guardian *ad litem*, too, might desire legal representation, the potential expense of this reform has inhibited its full implementation. At present it applies only in certain cases where an application is made for the *discharge* of a care order and this is *unopposed* by the local authority,[41] but in 1982 the government announced its intention to implement it fully.

The situation demands a closer examination of the role of the child's lawyer. At present he is subjected to conflicting pressures and loyalties which could make his position invidious. But, even if this were resolved by the presence of a (legal-aided) lawyer for the parents, how is he to discharge his obligation to the child? If the child is old enough to instruct a lawyer, a role can readily be perceived for him, that he should represent the child's wishes to the court. But in most abuse and neglect cases the child is too young to articulate relevant wishes and, even if able to do this, the issues may be too complex to suppose that the child is in a position to appreciate them fully. The lawyer is inevitably left in the position of having to form his own judgement of the child's interests, which he is invariably less informed or competent to do than the welfare authorities. Frequently, therefore, the lawyer has recourse to the 'formal' role of 'testing' the authority's case in court, thus helping to ensure it satisfies the appropriate legal standards of proof.

Yet in most cases this role can be discharged as effectively, or more effectively, by a lawyer acting for the parents. Where the parents oppose the authority, and especially if they are fully represented as parties, there seems little room for a half-hearted reduplication of their lawyer's role by another lawyer. Indeed, the practice of the child's lawyer of 'formally' testing the authority's case could create the misleading impression that the lawyer has somehow come to an informed, independent, judgement that the authority's case should fail. There may, in *some* cases, be room for seeking a 'second opinion' on the welfare agency's assessment of the case and its proposals for the child. This is eventually what the guardian *ad litem*, who is likely to have social work training, will do. In view of the scarcity of resources, this function might reasonably be restricted to cases where the authority proposes removal of the child from home for more than a temporary period, but made compulsory in all such cases. There may also be grounds for appointing a lawyer for the child in cases where the parents choose not to oppose the authority's application, at least if the intention is to remove the child. But in cases contested by parents, the legal representation of the child seems an unnecessary, even unhelpful, extravagance, and this would be even truer if a guardian *ad litem* had been appointed.

The third objective of care proceedings (articulation of a strategy for the child showing the need for court intervention) is theoretically provided for in the English procedure by the fact that a ground for intervention is not, strictly, established unless the court is satisfied that the child is in need of care and control which would not be provided unless an order were made under the Act. Yet this 'care and control' test seems to have little impact in abuse and neglect cases, it seemingly being taken for granted that, once a primary ground is established, the requirement is impliedly fulfilled. The reason is probably that the test simply refers to 'an' order: it is not necessary to show, at this point, that *the* order which is sought (or the plans proposed for the child) is necessary in this way. Indeed, the theoretical criminal model of the proceedings obliges *that* matter to be considered only after the primary grounds for intervention have been upheld. At this point the proceedings become informal, the authority submits to the magistrates the 'home surroundings' report which may rely heavily on information not admissible in the first stage of the proceedings. Some sketch of the authority's plans will be outlined, and one of its officers will usually enter the witness box to answer questions. But this part of the proceedings is usually very desultory. It can be argued that the authority's proposals for the child are indeed relevant information to a court's assessment of the evidence as to whether the child's development is being avoidably prevented or impaired and that the parents are entitled to require the authority to demonstrate plausibly how they are likely to improve matters and how they conceive the parent–child relationship to develop in the future.

Finally, it is thought that a magistrates' court is normally reasonably well placed to oversee the borderline between children's rights and family autonomy. There is a limit to which certainty can be achieved by statutory guidance and there is likely to be some movement back and forth across this line. The lay input into the courts might be valuable here, and this is an added reason why concern might be expressed about the apparently increased resort in cases of abuse and neglect to the wardship jurisdiction of the High Court. Yet the ground for intervention under this jurisdiction is simply the judge's assessment of the child's 'best interests'. Such an open-ended criterion contrasts unfavourably with the more defined grounds available for care proceedings. Furthermore, since wardship proceedings may be instituted by anyone with an interest in the child, the presentation of a case in the High Court is not necessarily subject to the system of institutional checks and balances described above. Although there have been examples of eagerness by Family Division judges to extend their jurisdiction in this area,[42] doubts about this have also been expressed.[43] Any such extension could seriously threaten the delicate balance between family autonomy and children's rights.

Disposal

In the long term, there are only two distinct options in dealing with child abuse and neglect. One is the permanent removal of the child; the other is to attempt behaviour modification of the family, with or without the temporary removal of the child. Successful cases of behaviour modification have been reported with especially chosen families by removal of the whole family into highly intensive therapy centres.[44] But positive results may be achieved less drastically; for example, where the children's safety is threatened by a particular 'visiting' male friend of the mother, she may be persuaded to give up the relationship.

Unlike the case in Canada, where applications might be made for permanent (Crown wardship) or temporary (wardship of a children's aid society) removal of the child, the usual practice in England and Wales is to blur this distinction. The two most common orders are care orders, which vest parental rights in the authority (other than the right to arrange the child's adoption), or supervision orders, which, reflecting the original concerns of this legislation with juvenile delinquency, simply require the authority to 'advise, assist and befriend' the child. The latter order gives the authority no additional powers over the family,[45] except that it may return to court and apply for a care order without having to re-establish the primary grounds. They are accordingly seldom favoured by authorities, although sometimes granted by courts as a compromise between their concern for the child and sympathy towards the parents. A care order, however, gives the authority extensive power over the family. The authority may, on the one hand, remove the child from the home immediately, and permanently; or it may prefer to leave the child at home, under threat of immediate withdrawal, and seek behaviour modification.[46] It is sometimes thought that the experience of court proceedings in themselves are sufficient to achieve the desired improvement in parenting behaviour. .

Practice would be improved if authorities were required to present to the court the chosen option and to justify the decision. It may be that, because supervision orders are thought to be so defective, care orders are sought more frequently than they need be. This means that, at least in some cases, authorities acquire more powers over the children than are necessary. For example, where a care order is made, the authority has complete discretion as to whether or not to allow a parent to see the child.[47] But if supervision orders are to be made more attractive, they should be designed as a measure for controlling the family rather than the child. They might, for example, contain a range of conditions specified by the court, perhaps permitting the authority to remove the child for short periods on their breach and allowing its officers to enter the home without a warrant if they believe the child to be in danger. They might authorize temporary removal of the child, the method and frequency of parental contacts and the procedure for reintroducing the child into the family. Cases resulting in court proceedings are inevitably those where the libertarian compromise of behavioural control by persuasion and co-operation has broken down. The coercion thus exposed may be distasteful to some. It indeed infringes important values. But without it any claim that children have legally recognized rights must be hollow.

PART FOUR: LAW AND SUPPORT

Support for Family Living

> 'There is no doubt at all in my mind . . . that the Government
> believe implicitly . . . in the family and recognize that the family
> needs all the support that society, through the Government, can
> give it' (House of Lords Debates, 1976).[1]

Public policy and families

The above quotation is representative of what has become a
commonplace assertion of government policy in both western and
eastern societies. We have seen[2] how government policy has at various
times seen family living as promoting certain ends of overall social
policy. The proper functioning of the family has been thought to make
important contributions to social stability by preventing juvenile
vagrancy and crime and producing adults who would be well-
adjusted to the values of the current social system. Some have also
claimed that solicitude for family living conceals deeper motives such
as the desire to maintain the dominant economic structure of society
or the division of labour between the sexes.

It would appear that the family is indeed a relatively flexible unit
which has been susceptible to the transmission of broader societal
goals. However, the problem of child care and a woman's uniquely
intimate relationship to it by reason of her reproductive function sets
limits to potential manipulation of family living, at least within the
context of even broadly defined parameters of acceptability of state
action. This raises a second facet of the relationship between state

policy and family life. Non-intervention in the life, at least of 'normal' families, is in our society considered a value in itself. It is true that a non-interventionist stance may be viewed as reflecting an *implicit* policy towards families by reason of the assumptions made about normality,[3] but it would be wrong to discount the idea of non-intervention as an independent value of sufficient weight that it could impede the achievement of other social goals (for example, population control or child health) otherwise considered desirable. This chapter looks at some areas in which state action can, to a greater or lesser degree, be held to promote family life. The topics are necessarily disparate. But they will enable some assessment to be made in conclusion about the present relationship, at least in Britain, between the state and families.

Family living and child care

It is now universally assumed that upbringing within a family is the optimum form of child care for children, and (consequently) for society. This seems to be supported by studies which have compared the conditions and achievements of children in residential settings with family-reared children.[4] It has, however, been argued that the effects of institutionalization, given reasonably high standards, need not seriously inhibit a child's intellectual growth[5] nor need any psychological ill-effects be necessarily irreversible.[6] But it is difficult to disentangle behavioural consequences which are attributable to institutionalization from other possible causal factors, such as pre-institutional experience. From the point of view of policy, however, the issue is almost certainly resolved by economic considerations. Residential care is more expensive than family care, particularly if it is to be of sufficiently high standard.

Family preference in child care is indicated by policies of reticence in removing children from families,[7] and of placing children whose own families have broken down, or who have been removed from their families, in alternative family settings by fostering or adoption. But the removal of children from their family of origin, even if into another family setting, confronts the basic assumption that it is a child's natural parents who are, normally, to provide the child with his family life. These policies come into conflict when parents seek to recover their children who have been placed in an alternative family setting. How can one reconcile the provision of family life for these children with the actual or potential claims of their parents?

A survey by the Association of British Adoption Agencies published in 1973[8] found that some 60 per cent of children under eleven who had been in care for over six months were not likely ever to return to their families.[9] Although 48 per cent were boarded out (8 per cent with relatives and 33 per cent in a foster home), adoption was planned for only 7 per cent. Yet the researchers concluded that one-third of the children needed a substitute home. A variety of reasons appeared to account for the failure to find them an adoptive home. One of the most important was that the child had a sibling, but other associated factors were the child's race and whether he showed behavioural problems. It may also have been that parental opposition was a factor (25 per cent of children needing placement had one or more parent opposed to fostering, whereas this was true with respect to only 6 per cent of those actually boarded out), but some of these objections may have been reasonably based, as where placement might have separated siblings. Only 19 per cent of children needing placement saw at least one parent frequently.

Should these children remain in long-term foster care or should they be adopted into their new homes? In only a small number of cases will the child's contacts with his natural parents continue.[10] This is not necessarily attributable to lack of parental interest. When asked to account for a decline in contact, parents have attributed this to hostility shown by foster-parents, fear of upsetting the child and opposition from social workers.[11] Yet the child's relationship to the foster-parents may suffer similar ambiguities. Packman (1976) has described how the role of the foster-parents has been changing. Before the Children Act 1948 fostering was mainly looked upon as substitute parenthood. Although the law did not recognize any claim the foster-parents might have felt towards the child, fostering operated as *de facto* adoption. After 1948 the claims of the natural parents were given more weight under the influence of the post-war emphasis on the significance of maternal bonding.[12] The policy towards rehabilitating children in their original families seriously threatened the already unprotected position of foster-parents. They were now 'perceived as a species of residential child-care worker, operating from their own homes',[13] a position underwritten by their undertaking, when accepting a child from a local authority, to return the child when required to do so by the authority.

Foster-parents may fear to develop deep attachments to a child in such circumstances. The lack of integration of the children may be emphasized by their retention of their original family name. They remain at risk of further disruption should a foster-parent die or simply desire to return the child.[14] George (1970) showed that 78 per cent of children placed in foster homes when over five were subsequently moved. They remain perpetually vulnerable to parental reclaim. The extent to which children in foster care are at risk of precipitate, unplanned recovery by unsatisfactory parents depends on the legal basis upon which they have been removed from their original home. If this has been done by a care order,[15] the parents can challenge the fostering arrangement only by applying for the order to be discharged. In the Maria Colwell case, in which such an application succeeded and the child was returned, subsequently to die at the hands of her stepfather, the girl's foster-parents, who had cared for her devotedly for six years, had not been informed of the date set for the hearing of the application for discharge.[16] This deficiency has been corrected.[17] A parent who makes persistent, unmeritorious applications for discharge may be restrained from doing so by an order under the wardship jurisdiction of the High Court.

If the child has been received into care by the authority on no authority other than the parents' agreement, then, even if subsequently boarded out in a good foster home, the parents may at any time reclaim the child.[18] If the authority refuses to accede, its legal position is unclear. In *London Borough of Lewisham* v. *Lewisham Juvenile Court Justices*[19] the House of Lords took the view that authorities are under no duty to return the child even if the parents demanded it. On the other hand, the parents are free to 're-possess' the child (if they are able), unless the child has been in care for more than six months, in which case the parents would need to give twenty-eight days' notice before taking back the child.[20] This extraordinary result seems to encourage parents to attempt self-help and authorities to conceal children from them. To prevent such a situation, authorities may, at any time when the child is in their care by parental agreement, pass a resolution assuming upon themselves parental rights over the child. They may do this, however, only if certain conditions are satisfied, and the resolution may be challenged by the parents in a magistrates' court. The conditions are set out in the Child Care Act 1980, s. 3. They include circumstances where a child is abandoned or orphaned, but extend to situations where the parent (or parents) with respect to whom the resolution is passed is, by reason of mental disorder, or 'habits or mode of life', or consistent failure to discharge parental obligations, unfit to have the care of the child.[21] The resolution can be rapidly passed by the authority's social services committee and (subject to the challenge in court) effectively secures the child against reclaim.

But how soon and in what kinds of cases should the resolution procedure be used? It is likely that authorities take different views on these questions. Adcock and White (1982), reporting research into the use of the procedure in four local authorities, observed that resolutions tended to be passed with respect to children who had already been in care more than once within their earliest years. Only 14 per cent had no previous reception into care. These are, then, children whose family life has already been significantly disrupted and for whom, presumably, it is thought there is little chance of improved home circumstances. Over a third (38 per cent) of the resolutions were passed within six months of the current period in care. Resolutions within this period were subject to legal difficulty before the *Lewisham* case, for it was arguable that, once the parents reclaimed the child, the authority lost its jurisdiction to pass a resolution respecting that child. However, the House of Lords held that this was not so. Provided it has physically held on to the child, the resolution may be passed. Although the matter must be regarded as legally settled, the result rests on a dubious reading of the legal provisions[22] and represents an unsatisfactory demarcation between the authorities' powers and the position of parents. When a parent reclaims a child over whom the authority has not yet acquired parental rights, it would be better to regard the position of the authority (and any foster-parent) as analogous to that of a hospital which is temporarily caring for a child admitted by the parents. The hospital has no legal authority to prevent the parent from removing the child and, if it wishes to do this, it must obtain a Place of Safety Order,[23] followed, if appropriate, by care proceedings.

The provisions discussed above are designed to empower a local authority to take appropriate measures to secure the child's interests when these are considered to be in opposition to the wishes of the parents. But they do nothing to improve the status of foster-parents, either against the child's parents or against the authority itself. The concept of 'custodianship' introduced by the Children Act 1975 was intended, in part, to provide a means of enhancing this status and may therefore indicate a partial retreat to the older concept of fostering. The Act provides that 'any person with whom the child has had his home for a period or periods before the making of the application which amount to at least three[24] years and include the three months preceding the making of the application' may apply for custodianship. If the legal guardian of the child (usually the parent) consents, the period is reduced to twelve months, unless the applicant is a relative, in which case it is three months. The application may be made in a magistrates' court, and, if it is successful, the custodianship order vests 'legal custody' of the child in the applicant. This is defined as meaning 'so much of the parental rights and duties as relate to the person of the child including the place and manner in which his time is spent'.[25] A custodianship order can therefore strengthen the relationship between the child and foster-parents. This had been suggested by the Curtis Committee as long ago as 1946[26] and had been reiterated by the Houghton Committee (1972).[27] It can be seen as a form of the 'foster care with tenure' advocated by Goldstein.[28] Like adoption, the effect would be to terminate the foster-parents' entitlement to an allowance from the local authority. In principle, they must support the child as their own. But to overcome financial disincentives, the authority would have discretion to make contributions towards the child, particularly in cases of hardship.

A number of puzzles, however, surround the concept. While it is specifically provided that the custodian's consent will suffice to permit the child to marry under eighteen and that he may not arrange for the child's emigration from the United Kingdom,[29] it is not made clear whether he can change the child's surname, a matter which may well give rise to dispute. It seems likely that, if the child is one over whom the local authority had parental rights (whether by resolution or care order), the custodianship order would transfer most of those rights to the custodian, but that rights respecting the child's property would remain with the authority.

These are, however, soluble issues. What is less explicable is the fact that by 1983 the provisions had not yet been implemented. There is some concern that they could lead to some litigation, and hence increase costs[30] and that they would restrict the flexibility of fostering as a resource for child care. The real problem seems to be the difficulty of resolving the modern role of foster-parents with the presently perceived needs of children for security and continuity in a family setting.

Adoption of children in care

Fostering, even if strengthened by custodianship, does not involve the complete severence of the parental tie. A parent may be forbidden to remove the child from his present surroundings and perhaps be unable to influence day-to-day decisions affecting the child. But he will retain a say in the religious upbringing of a child over whom a local authority has assumed parental rights (but possibly not in the case of the custodian), and may possibly be able to control the surname he bears. He retains rights concerning the child's property. His right to visit the child will be subjected to the authority's discretion, but, where a custodianship order has been made, this can be controlled by the court. In all instances he retains his right to apply to a court for a review of the situation and to argue that it would be in the child's best interests to be returned to him.

It may therefore be thought that greater security would be achieved if the child were adopted. This is clearly the policy of the Canadian welfare authorities with respect to permanent Crown wards. This opportunity is open to the welfare authorities in England too. If they believe that adoption is the best course for a child in their care (whether voluntarily or not), provisions in the Adoption Act 1976[31] will, when implemented, permit them to apply for an order 'freeing' him for adoption even before they have found a placement for him. The Act does not specify any minimum time during which the child must be in care before they may make such an application. When it is made, the parent cannot remove the child from care pending the hearing of the application. If the parent objects to this procedure, the authority must make simultaneous application for the court to dispense with his consent to adoption. The court may do this if the parent cannot be found or is incapable of giving his consent or has persistently failed without reasonable cause to discharge his parental duties or has abandoned or neglected the child, or has persistently ill-treated the child, or has seriously ill-treated him and the child's rehabilitation in the home is unlikely. It may also override his refusal to consent if he is withholding his consent unreasonably. But the court can dispense with the consent only if the child is already placed for adoption or if it is satisfied that 'it is likely' that the child will be placed for adoption.[32] If the child is legitimate, the consent of both his mother and father is necessary; if he is illegitimate, the father's consent is necessary only if he has been granted custody of the child.

Where the consent of both parents is required, and withheld, normally it will not be enough to free the child for adoption to establish a ground of dispensation against one parent alone, but in this case the other parent may be put in a difficult position. Would it be unreasonable for him to withhold his consent to an adoption order? Section 6 of the Adoption Act 1976 states that, in reaching any decision relating to the adoption of a child, 'a court or adoption agency shall have regard to all the circumstances, first consideration being given to the need to safeguard and promote the welfare of the child throughout his childhood.' In *re P. (An Infant: Adoption: Parental Consent)*,[33] the Court of Appeal was undecided whether this section meant that a parent, in deciding whether to give or withhold consent, had to give first consideration to the child's welfare. But there is little at stake in the point because the House of Lords had already held[34] that a reasonable parent would always have regard to his child's welfare and would treat it as decisive when it was reasonable to do so. This open-ended formula leaves a wide measure of discretion in the hands of the trial court, which is very difficult to challenge on appeal.[35] In any event, the power to override a parent's 'unreasonable' objection enhances the opportunity for local authorities to use adoption as a means of attempting to achieve greater security within a home environment for children in their care.

As is the case of custodianship, the provisions for freeing a child for adoption are not yet in force. It remains to be seen how welfare authorities in England and Wales will use these new powers. The legal provisions have not resolved the dilemma which is created when a child is removed from his parents. It is easy to enact that all concerned should pay first consideration to the child's interests. But is this better served by endeavouring to rehabilitate his family so that he can be returned to it, or by finding him a substitute home?

Research by Tizard (1977) compared the progress of children, all of whom had been in institutional care for the first two to seven years of their lives, but who subsequently had either been adopted or been restored to their natural parents. By the time the children reached the age of eight, the adopted children surpassed the restored children (and even a 'control' group of matched children who had never left their families) in intellectual attainments, probably because of greater attention paid to these by the adoptive parents. Emotionally, they appeared more troubled than the control group but less so than the restored children. Even if the findings are accepted, do they establish a sufficient case for preferring substitute placement to restoration? And if substitute placement is preferred, should it be adoption or fostering? Answers to these questions will reflect shifting values. Continuity of relationships is surely a major contribution family life makes to child care, and a familistic policy therefore argues for safeguarding such relationships when formed. Whether adoption or fostering is the better method must surely depend on the circumstances of individual cases. The problem is essentially the same as that which arises after divorce where policy presently discourages total severance of the parental connection. This might seem to favour fostering over adoption. But this need not necessarily be so. Adoption is no longer thought in itself necessarily to preclude the exercise of access by natural parents[36] and legal measures have facilitated the procedure whereby adopted persons may ascertain their true parentage and contact their parents.[37] It has even been urged that adoption agencies should routinely be involved in this process.[38] In these ways a compromise can be reached between the promotion of family living for children, the claims of natural parents and preservation of an individual's links with his biological origins.

For a significant minority of children in care, however, the obstacle to their adoption is not parental objection but unavailability of an adoptive home. The children in Rowe and Lambert's (1973) study who were thought to be in need of a substitute family but for whom none had been found were characterized by their colour, behaviour problems or simply the presence of siblings for whom homes were also required.[39] Those authors suggest a number of ways of helping these children. One of them is that, in some cases, adoption might be subsidized. This had been recommended by the Houghton Committee (1972) despite opposition to the suggestion by most of their witnesses. Objection is based on the tradition that an adopted child should be treated as any other child of the adoptive parents and that it would, accordingly, be wrong to confer benefits on an adoptive home which are denied to natural families. Subsidized adoption was introduced in New York in 1968, and now operates in many other American states. The Children's Bureau of the US Department of Health, Education and Welfare has issued a model Subsidized Adoption Act which specifies certain categories of children as qualifying for subsidized adoption. These include children who have established significant emotional ties with prospective adoptive parents while in their care as a foster-child; and children who are not likely to be adopted due to physical or mental disability, emotional disturbance, high risk of disease, age, sibling relationship, racial or ethnic factors or any combination of these. While the existence of the National Health Service in Britain has made the presence of health difficulties less of an obstacle to adoption in Britain, some of the other factors mentioned in the list of the model Act may nevertheless impede adoption. The Children Act 1975 therefore provides for experimental schemes for subsidized adoption to be tried with the approval of the Secretary of State.

Family living and parental decision-making

A specific feature of the view that non-intervention encourages family living is the belief that proper respect for family life requires the right of parents to make important decisions for or on behalf of their children free from external restraint. Family autonomy becomes an aspect of parental sovereignty. Opportunities to bypass this authority may be viewed as undermining hierarchical authority structure within the family. The strengthening of the individual claims of children has indeed, in recent years, weakened the *formal* authority of parents. The reduction of the age of majority from twenty-one to eighteen in 1970,[40] a measure taken in many jurisdictions, confined a parent's power[41] to impede his child's right to marry to when the child is aged sixteen and seventeen. Even there, parental authority may be bypassed by application to a court. It is by no means clear on what basis a court can authorize a child to marry in face of parental objection that he or she is too young. If courts require even stronger reasons than that, the scope for parental control seems very small indeed.[42] Minors are generally permitted to enforce contracts which are to their benefit (including training and employment contracts) and may acquire a passport in their own name at the age of sixteen. But, as was seen earlier in connection with the weakening of parental involvement in their children's choices over marriage,[43] such measures probably have little impact on social behaviour. Family involvement may be more realistically encouraged in other ways, of which greater consultation with parents over educational methods and curricula is an important aspect.[44]

On sexual matters the question is more difficult. May a child under sixteen obtain contraceptives on prescription without her parent's consent or knowledge? It is expressly provided in England that a minor's consent to medical treatment is sufficient if the minor is over sixteen.[45] This should not be taken as implying that a minor under that age cannot validly consent to medical treatment and it is probable that she can do this if able to exercise a reasonable judgement.[46] But in the case of contraceptives the position is more doubtful because it is an offence for a man to have sexual intercourse with a girl below sixteen unless he is under twenty-four and reasonably believes that she is over sixteen.[47] It is unlikely that the provision of contraceptives to a girl under sixteen can amount to incitement to the offence (if only because it is not the girl who commits the offence), but it is arguable that the girl might be legally unable to consent to this 'treatment', in which case the doctor's action might be a technical assault on her under civil (but not criminal) law. The Department of Health and Social Security has taken the view that doctors need not obtain parental consent when prescribing contraceptives to girls under sixteen. This has been upheld in the High Court.[48] To introduce a parental veto, or even a requirement that the doctor disclose to the parents, risks extensive disruption both to the relationship between doctor and patient and between parent and child. It is hard to believe this is warranted by vague appeals to strengthening family life.

The case of abortion is more complex. Under the Abortion Act 1967, abortion can be performed only if two registered medical practitioners certify either that (a) the continuance of the pregnancy would involve a risk to the life or physical or mental health of the woman or the existing children of her family greater than if the pregnancy were terminated, or (b) there is a substantial risk that the child, if born, would be seriously mentally or physically handicapped. The woman's actual or potential environment may be taken into account in deciding the effect of abortion on her health. There are no special provisions for minors and it seems, therefore, that the same reasoning applies in this case as to other cases of 'medical treatment' as far as parental consent is concerned. So long as the girl is capable of reasonable understanding of the act, her own consent should be sufficient. It may be thought that the implications of abortion are so significant that no child under sixteen can reasonably be held capable of exercising proper judgement about it, in which case the parents should decide. Whether this is so in any given case must depend on its circumstances.

It may also be asked whether, at least in the case of abortion, the parents should have a right to be informed if the girl is under sixteen. The argument would be that the fact that the girl is seeking abortion indicates tensions in her life-style which would benefit from parental guidance and that the possible consequences of the operation on her psychological well-being demand family monitoring. Against this it can be said that, if the matter is being kept secret from the parents in any event, family relationships are likely to be poor and disclosure to the parents potentially further damaging. The proper approach, it is suggested, lies in intensive counselling for the child. Any child in that situation is likely to be undergoing serious psychological stress, which will be exacerbated if it cannot be dealt with within the family. A key issue in the counselling role must be an attempt to divert the problem into the family setting for resolution. It is probable that the parents and child will take the same view as to the desirability or otherwise of abortion. However, to compel such disclosure, still more to give the parents a veto, would confer on family members powers which would override specifically recognized individual rights. Would this really promote the benefits of family living? If abortion is to be allowed at all (which is a separate question), the under-age, but reasonably cognisant, child should, it is thought, be held entitled to the advantage of the legal provision in her own right. This has been the conclusion of the United States Supreme Court, which has held unconstitutional legislative attempts to create a parental veto.[49]

Social and legal measures

Despite Glendon's warning about the unpredictable consequences many social policies have on families,[50] some measures, at least, can be seen to be supportive of family living. Perhaps most important are provisions relating to housing. A family is less likely to stay together if it cannot live together. Of the thirty-five thousand children who came into care in England and Wales at the request or with the agreement of their parents in 1977, 1,100 did so because the family was homeless and 5,600 because of unsatisfactory home conditions. Housing policies can therefore have an important impact, not only on the continued functioning of family living, but even on its formation. Parker and Land (1978) observe that English public housing policy has favoured families (whether with one or two adults) over the single and elderly and hence has been 'mildly pronatalist'. This is contrasted with the private sector, where the presence of children might make obtaining a mortgage, or rented premises, more difficult. However, the British practices of permitting mortgage interest repayments on a dwelling house to be offset against income for tax purposes, and of allowing supplementary benefit authorities to pay mortgage interest, while not specifically directed at helping families, frequently do so. Provisions enhancing the security of the matrimonial dwelling on breakdown of the marriage may also help towards keeping at least the single parent family together at this time.

Beyond facilitation of communal residence for family members, the impact of other social measures is indeed problematic. In so far as family breakdown seems to be associated with (among other things) economic adversity, it might be thought that income assistance strengthens family living. Yet, as has been observed, American studies show no evidence that communities receiving *higher* welfare payments suffer less family breakdown than others.[51] It is possible that the problem may be more closely related to the husband's employment record.[52] The question of income assistance should, then, be seen rather as one of dealing with poverty, of income distribution in general, rather than promotion of family life. Yet, in effecting a certain measure of income distribution through tax and social security laws, states can exhibit certain assumptions about the organization of family life and build these assumptions into the distribution machinery.

Many such assumptions can be found in United Kingdom law. For example, on marrying, a man (not a woman) becomes entitled to deduct an allowance of £2,145 from his income before tax. If the wife is earning, her income is added to his and he is taxed on the aggregated total. But, since this might substantially increase the husband's tax liability and deter her from earning, a further deduction (or relief) of £1,375 is permitted if she is in paid employment.[53] This system operates as a benefit for most people who marry, but as a disadvantage if both earn substantial incomes, for the aggregation of income brings them into a high tax bracket which is not sufficiently compensated for by the reliefs. Since 1971 it has been possible to mitigate the effects of this compulsory aggregation by separate taxation of the wife's *earned* income. Her earned income allowance is replaced by a single person's allowance and the husband loses the married man's allowance. The wife's investment income continues to be aggregated.

There are a number of difficulties in this system. Firstly, i operates regressively (disproportionately benefiting higher income **groups**).[54] Nor is the advantage tied to the inception of a family. Rather, it seems to assume the dependence of the wife on the husband. If only one spouse (no matter which) is the substantial earner, is there a good reason in effect to subsidize (him) to facilitate (his) support for the other?[55] It is possible that the wife had disadvantaged herself on marrying (see the examples given on p. 120), but the economics of shared living (especially the savings in housing costs) may largely, or completely, compensate for this. It may be concluded that the relief should be abolished and the income saved distributed by way of increased cash benefits to families with children. But this solution has disadvantages. Marriage, as we saw, is now more frequently preceding a planned decision at some stage to raise a family. Expenses in preparation for this event may be reasonably incurred, and marriage allowances or rebates might be seen as a contribution towards these, and hence, albeit in a rough and unsystematic way, as encouraging family life. Also, since marriage and child-rearing are increasingly coincidental, financing direct benefits to families with children out of savings from abolishing the allowance effectively pays for those benefits from revenues drawn from families with children. It is also relevant to remember that married people frequently care for the elderly relatives of one or both of the spouses. Marriage remains a useful external indicator that family functions of these kinds are or may be performed, though possibly couples who perform them without marrying should be given similar advantages. There is no reason, however, why the Inland Revenue should continue to regard the husband as the sole, or even the major, breadwinner. Australia and New Zealand have devised a rebate system that is at once progressive (giving greater benefit to the least well off) and non-discriminatory.[56]

The social security system reflects various assumptions about family roles. A married woman may pay the same national insurance contributions as her husband, but she will be entitled to additional dependency benefits only if she can show that the reason her husband is not working is due to some incapacity on his part. Similarly, an increase in unemployment and sickness benefit is payable for a period in which 'some female person' has the care of a child of the beneficiary's family and an addition may be made to a retirement or invalidity pension if a 'female person' caring for the child is residing with the beneficiary unless he has a wife entitled to a pension by virtue of his contributions. However, the discriminatory aspects of these provisions were removed in the Social Security Act 1980, expected to be implemented in 1983.[57] Nevertheless, that it is the woman who performs the household and child-care duties continues to be assumed in the non-contributory invalidity pension. At first a married woman was not entitled to this allowance, since she was deemed dependent on her husband, so her earning disability did not justify benefit. From November 1977 a wife qualifies for the benefit, but not only must she show that she is incapable of paid employment; she must also show that she is 'incapable of performing normal household duties', a qualification not found in the case of men.[58] Even more significantly, the non-contributory invalid care allowance, a benefit premised on the assumption that the beneficiary has had to give up full-time employment in order to care for an invalid relative, is not payable to married women or female cohabitees.[59]

Provisions such as these treat the family as a unit of distribution of finance and of labour. In the same way as the family benefits and the 'cohabitation rule' discussed earlier,[60] they assume the economic benefit accruing to the beneficiary will be passed on within the family circle, as defined. The assumptions about the distribution of labour are more controversial. They have been criticized as ignoring the actual rates of participation in the labour force by married women.[61] The criticism is somewhat overstated because the assumptions are based on *full-time* employment patterns and, as we have seen, only about one-third of employed mothers with dependent children filled full-time jobs.[62] To ignore the division of labour in the home can also raise problems (not insoluble) concerning equity between families. Take the case of the invalid care allowance. If this was payable to a married woman who had given up employment to care for the relative, this might be said unfairly to favour her over the married woman who has not been in such employment but cares for the person nonetheless. Similarly in the case of the invalidity pension: is payment justified on the basis of incapacity to take paid employment if the woman is able to do that which many married women, even though a minority, do in any case without state financial benefit? Such provision would seem to favour women who earn over those who 'choose', or are able, to remain at home, caring perhaps for children or other relatives. On the other hand, payments to all married women who do not earn would amount to the provision of a 'state housekeeping wage', and, while this concept has its advocates, such a scheme would have serious implications for public expenditure.

Can the elements of discrimination in such benefits, then, be removed? It would be possible, for example, to add the rider about inability to perform 'household duties' to the qualification of the *husband* to receive the disability pension. It would mean that a husband who had hitherto devoted little time or skill to these tasks would be denied the pension if he could perform them, the assumption being that he should do this while his wife earns the family income. Owing to the lower level of women's income, such families would be likely to be less well off than families where the woman suffered disability and her husband continued to work. Yet such a solution seems unavoidable if discrimination is to be avoided, and the example illustrates the dilemma created by ignoring (for ideological reasons) inequalities which are current in social organization. The case of the invalid care allowance could be solved by making the allowance payable to all married men and women who care for an infirm relative, whether or not they abandoned employment to do this. A distinction could be drawn between this and a housekeeping wage on the ground that this is an additional undertaking which reduces the burden on state public facilities.

This brief review of tax and social security measures indicates how the state can manipulate the way families function to achieve broad social ends. It also shows that the state's perceptions of social reality, like that of any agent, can be based on incorrect assumptions compounded with substantial ideological input. Some aspects of this have been criticized here. But there remains a limit to the scope of manipulation of family life. The one feature which determines these limits is the assumption that familial organization is the favoured residential context in which children are reared. This is not to belittle the importance of families with regard to other roles, for example, the care of the elderly.[63] But it remains true that on birth almost all children enter a residential family and are thought best served by remaining in it during their childhood. This event has permanent consequences for the parents and the division of labour between them. It is to these matters that the final chapter turns.

12
Family Roles and Social Roles

Day-care and women's employment

The rearing of children puts considerable demands on a community; without the family, it is unlikely that the economic structure of western societies, as presently organized, could tolerate them. A community may be so organized that this burden is borne entirely by families, which can attempt to meet the demands from their own resources, whether financial or human. During the nineteenth century, however, it appeared that in a number of respects, families, left to themselves, were unequal to the task. We have seen the growth of health services designed to supplement this familial role, a development which Donzelot (1980) sees as increasing the power of the wife within the middle-class home because she was the link between the medical profession and family health.[1] The education services, however, have had a profound effect in supplementing or replacing the educative role of parents, and thus providing not only a source of control over child-rearing outside parental control but also a weakening of the family's grip on the children.

School education shows the overlap between education and child care. Day schooling (as distinct from boarding) does not, of course, provide complete day-long care for most children, although, if it did, the call on family members to supplement this for school-age children would be considerably alleviated, at least during school terms. On the other hand, the familial influence on the children's upbringing would be correspondingly weakened. The conflict is acute for the youngest children. In Britain, the state sees its commitment as being primarily to education, and sets the starting age at five. For children under that age, the state assumes no universal obligation, for that would be assuming a child-care rather than an educative role, which is thought more appropriately left to families. Provision for children under five is therefore sporadic. The Department of Education and Science provides nursery education in nursery schools for some 490,000 children in England and Wales, mostly nearly five years old, but the children usually attend either in the morning or afternoon and the facility is not available in school holidays. Other day-care provision is subject to the ultimate responsibility of the Department of Health and Social Security. Local authority day nursery places, available all day throughout the year for children from a few months old to five years, cater only for some 26,000 children and are allocated on a priority basis (favouring, for example, single parent families). There is a scattering of voluntary and community based provision (such as playgroups, which do not, however, cater for full-time employed parents) and privately run facilities, some attached to places of work. Estimates of the number of children cared for privately by child-minders in their own homes varies from 100,000 to 200,000.[2]

Day-care for children under five and especially those under three is therefore primarily seen as a family responsibility. In theory the family seems well placed to perform it. The division of labour will leave one parent (invariably the mother) to perform the task; or else the parents can call on other family members (usually grandparents) to do it.[3] But in practice the picture looks different. Urban changes have probably reduced to insignificance the availability of relatives as a day-care resource. A 1976 survey of three inner-city areas in London found that 73 per cent of mothers wanted some day-care provision for their two-year-olds and 90 per cent wanted it for their three- to four-year-olds. In fact, many mothers with young children are in employment. The Jacksons' (1979) research in a working-class area of Britain showed that 63.7 per cent of mothers with children under five were not in employment, leaving over a third of cases where either the mother or both parents earned. When broken down by ethnic groups, the percentage of mothers in employment was 32 per cent for whites, 22 per cent for Asians and 80 per cent for blacks. Blacks also worked the longest hours. The overwhelmingly dominant reasons why women with young children take employment is financial necessity. An American study recently found no evidence that such women were significantly influenced by attitudes to family roles. Economic need was the real motivation.[4] It is clear that, in many low-income households, the earnings of the wife form a crucial part of family income. The extent to which the earnings of wives are essential to prevent a family falling into officially defined poverty is significant.[5]

The problem of child-care for employed women therefore plays an important part in determining the totality of the family income. It could also be considered important at the ideological level as being the most powerful factor impeding the full equality between the sexes. The following discussion is premised, therefore, not on the assumption that women in any sense 'should' supplement, or replace, a child-care role by employment, but that for many women their perception of the interests of their family and themselves includes their ability to maintain regular paid employment. In times of full employment and of war this usually coincides with the state's perception of its own interests, although in times of high unemployment it becomes an embarrassment to governments.

Child-minding and other responses

These economic facts and their inconsistency with the allocation of full-time child care to the family have led to (or perpetuated) the proliferation of informal day-care arrangements. In the late nineteenth century, long-term private arrangements for the care of children led to the abuse of 'baby-farming' and the first tentative steps in child protection legislation.[6] The modern problem is different, for it concerns mainly day-care arrangements by earning parents.[7] These are subject to weak legislative control. Legislation has imposed registration requirements both as to premises (unless they are a private home) and persons (if the minding takes place in a private home). Local authorities have power to inspect premises of a registered child-minder and, with a warrant, to enter premises where a breach of the registration requirements is suspected.[8]

Recent research in England has drawn attention to the potentially serious adversities faced by daily-minded children, especially those in working-class homes,[9] although it seems that, at least outside the large urban complexes, child-minding is not necessarily predominantly used by working-class people.[10] In order to allow the parents to maintain their work-place schedules, these children may be awakened unusually early and brought home late. Apart from physical tiredness, their time with the minder is unlikely to be intellectually or emotionally rewarding. Both Bryant and the Jacksons observed an unusual degree of passivity and withdrawal in minded children who compared unfavourably with children who attended professional day-care centres. A minder seldom, it seems, plays the role of a substitute mother. The minded child is characteristically abruptly introduced into territory which is not his own, and bound by rules and practices different from those with which he is familiar. His passivity is likely to be encouraged by a minder concerned in going about her daily routines. How far these unhappy early experiences handicap a child in his subsequent educational career has never been assessed, although the Jacksons suggest it may be a significant cause of later behavioural problems.[11]

Whether improving the circumstances of *child-minders* (for example, by paying them more) can assist these *children* is unclear. Bryant *et al.* (1980) urge educating both parents and minders to a greater awareness of the sensitivities of the children (mothers and minders might be encouraged to spend more time at each other's premises), and that local authority supervision should focus more on the condition of the children than (as at present) on the state of the premises. Whatever the right approach, it is clear that child-minding is not a cheap, easy, solution to the problem of child care outside the family.

It seems that no industrialized society has succeeded in establishing arrangements which successfully release the majority of mothers of children under three from most of the demands of child care. Thus it has been stated that in Sweden, in 1974, only 26 per cent of children with employed mothers had access to such facilities, and that the length of time some children spent in them (sometimes ten hours a day) has led to demands for shorter working hours.[12] Even in Denmark, where considerable priority has in the past been given to day-care facilities, demand has 'considerably outstripped the supply'.[13] The shortage of day-care facilities in Hungary led to the introduction, in 1967, of a child-care grant to mothers who were employed for one year before the birth of the child, or who were students, which lasts until the child is three. This may be seen as a pronatalist measure, but is open to criticism for creating inequity between families and (some would argue) reinforcing the sex role stereotype.[14]

Mothers, children and employment

Various statutory measures have attempted to reduce the conflict between the demands of motherhood and those of employment. Unless a woman's pregnancy renders her incapable of doing a particular job (or it is prohibited for pregnant women to do it), once she has been in a job for six months a woman cannot be dismissed for the sole reason of her pregnancy.[15] A woman who has been in continuous service with the same employer for two years, who gives at least three weeks' notice, is entitled to maternity leave from eleven weeks before the expected date of birth and to re-instatement into her position for a period up to twenty-nine weeks from the birth.[16] If these conditions are fulfilled, the woman is entitled to pay from the employer at 90 per cent of her basic wage, less the standard rate of the state maternity allowance, whether or not she is in fact entitled to it.[17] This lasts only for six weeks and is reclaimable by the employer from the government.[18]

The provisions could be criticized as being ungenerous and inflexible.[19] A number of trade union negotiated agreements include the availability of a short period (usually 3–10 days) of paid leave for the father. But such provisions, concentrated as they are at alleviating the position of the woman during the events immediately surrounding childbirth, fail to reach the problem at a deeper level. For most women the advent of children is likely to bring about a permanent restructuring of their employment pattern.[20] A survey of eligible female employees of Barclays Bank in 1976–7 showed that only 10 per cent exercised their right to return to work. Lack of day-care facilities may be the reason for this in possibly one-third of these cases.[21] We have seen the problems of child care during the first three years of a child's life, a period which is extended for a woman who has second or subsequent children. But beyond that age, leaving aside the very real problems of care after school hours and in school holidays,[22] it is the mother who is normally expected to care for her children when they are sick.

Rather, therefore, than to place primary emphasis on seeking to replace the family by community care for young children, it might be better to examine ways of altering employment patterns so as to release family members sufficiently to fulfil child-care roles. The employment protection measures relating to pregnancy and the immediate aftermath of childbirth illustrate statutory intrusions into the labour market to promote these ends. But they could go much further. Sweden offers a striking illustration. A parenthood benefit allows *both parents together* the total of 270 days' absence from work, of which 180 days must be used in connection with the child's birth, but the remaining 90 may be used at any time before the child reaches the age of eight. They may allocate these days between them as they wish. Compensation is on the same basis as sickness benefit. Furthermore, a parent who has been with one employer for six months and who has a child under eight is entitled to insist on a working day of not more than six hours.[23] Some may argue that such provisions do little in themselves to redefine the social role of women as the primary caregivers, for it is likely to be the mother who will take their benefit, especially if the father is the higher earner. In this way the facts that men generally earn more than women and that women assume greater domestic responsibility mutually reinforce each other. Hence it may be suggested that a proportion of the benefit be available *only if* the father takes it. Such indirect inducements may (slowly) bring about a change in expectations among men and their employers that family obligations are to be equally shared.

This approach to the problem of child care raises in a form different from that considered hitherto the relationship between state intervention and family autonomy. For here the political issue, at least on the surface, concerns state intervention in employment, not the family, although the consequences (should) indirectly affect family living. State intervention in employment does indeed confront serious political questions, but it is plausible to suppose that the conflict is less acute than in the case of direct intervention in familial child-care arrangements, at least in families which are not perceived as deviant. Glendon (1981) has vividly described the transference, over the course of this century, of legal controls from an individual's family relations to his or her employment setting. It could be argued, however, that, while the 'new property' which job-related security and benefits represent has taken *some* account of the family context in which the individual employee usually operates (as in health insurance schemes covering the employee and his family), this process has been inhibited when it confronts certain demands of market forces and sex-role conventions. Yet the extent of modern involvement of the state in employment indicates that this may prove a fruitful indirect point of entry into family regulation.

The very possibility of intervention of this kind reveals the integral relationship between the organization of family life and the economic organization of society. A perfect reconciliation of child care with the economic aspirations of both adults of a family may be achievable only under specific economic conditions. In a severe economic reverse, demanding a shake-out of the labour force and greater competitiveness and insecurity in employment, the state is likely to throw the family on its own resources for child care. Conversely, in times of relative economic affluence, family members can be expected to seek to further their interests by mobilizing the earning capacity of each adult; for the poor, this may be a necessity. Sometimes, in times of crisis, the state will demand this, in its own interests. Either case generates a conflict between the ideological and economic structure of society and the assumption of family-based child care. Inevitable compromise is likely to devalue family-based child care, for a mother will be expected to earn, in the former case to maintain self-esteem and the family's economic respectability, and in the latter to contribute to the national effort.

These issues go wider than the concerns of family law, or even family policy, reflecting, as they do, shifts in political values and fluctuations in economic fortune. Is family-based child-rearing consistent with current ideologies of (relatively) free economic dealing, (relatively) low state regulation of employment and (relatively) low public expenditure commitment? But perhaps we can say that one matter should hold as a constant: the principle of commitment to the quality of the environment in which all children are reared. The temptation to undervalue this in face of conflicting demands of the state, or aspirations of the adults, or the privations of poverty, should be resisted. It may be that this is the most sure route to social justice and security for the future.

Notes

Chapter 1

1. Festy (1980), p. 10; Watkins (1981); Finer Report (1974), vol. 1, para. 3.8. In the United States marriage rates have been consistently high since the late nineteenth century: Cherlin (1981), p. 10.
2. *Royal Commission on Human Relationships* (1977), vol. 4, para. 2.6.
3. Similarly in the United States, where despite the consistency of the overall marriage rate, there has been a distinct shift to a later age at marriage in the period 1960 to 1975: Sweet (1977), Table 1; Carter and Glick (1976), p. 407. In Canada, the proportion of brides under twenty fell by 7 per cent between 1974 and 1978: *Ontario Statistics 1980*, Table 4.4
4. Leete (1979), p. 7.
5. *Social Trends 1982*, pp. 34–5; Dunnell (1979).
6. Glick and Spanier (1980), p. 20.
7. Glick and Spanier (1980); Yllo and Straus (1981).
8. Gill (1977), pp. 13–14.
9. See Davenport (1961); Blake (1961); Schlesinger (1968).
10. Festy (1980), p. 6; Agell (1980), p. 15.
11. *Social Trends 1980*, p. 35.
12. *Birth Statistics 1979*, OPCS Series FMI, No. 6, HMSO, 1981.
13. The proportion of children born after pre-marital conception has been steadily declining: Leete (1979), p. 8; Sweet (1977).
14. *Royal Commission on Human Relationships* (1977), vol. 4, para. 2.7.
15. Glendon (1981), pp. 85–6.
16. Rimmer (1981), p. 40.
17. Davids (1980).
18. Sweet (1977); Davids (1980). Leete and Anthony (1979) found no evidence that the care of children lessened a woman's chances of remarrying after divorce.
19. Glendon (1981), p. 86.
20. Gill (1977), pp. 11–12.
21. Gill (1977), p. 20.
22. Gill (1977), pp. 244–5.
23. Gill (1977), pp. 294–5.

24. Crellin *et al.* (1971).
25. Matrimonial Causes Act 1937.
26. Legal Aid Act 1960.
27. Matrimonial Causes Act 1967.
28. See below, pp. 52-3.
29. *New Zealand Official Yearbook 1976*, Section 4D.
30. Matrimonial Proceedings Act 1968 (N.Z.).
31. *Canada Official Yearbook 1975*, pp. 53, 157-8.
32. The 1976 figure refers to decrees granted in the Family Court of Australia only; other courts may have granted some 10,000 decrees in addition: Evatt (1977). The annual number of divorce decrees granted in Australia has declined since 1976.
33. See Glendon (1981), pp. 121-5, pointing out the strain to which canon law has been subjected in the light of social change.
34. Leete (1979), pp. 77-9; Haskey (1982).
35. Weitzman (1981), pp. 143-4; Cherlin (1981), p. 23; Haskey (1982), p. 5.
36. Weitzman (1981), p. 155; Cherlin (1981), p. 29.
37. Leete (1979), pp. 41-4; Cherlin (1981), p. 29.
38. Weitzman (1981), p. 156; Cherlin (1981), p. 29.
39. Homosexual relationships are omitted from this scenario because it seems improbable that they will come within the scope of family law in the foreseeable future. But it is arguable that, in principle, they should be susceptible to some form of legal regulation: see below, pp. 145-51.
40. Morgan (1975), chs. 1 and 5.
41. For example, Bankowski and Mungham (1976); see also Collins (1982).
42. The point is made by Morgan (1975), ch. 5.
43. Mair (1971), chs. 1 and 2; Stone (1977), pp. 86-91.
44. Habbakuk (1950).
45. Krause (1971), pp. 3-5.
46. Matrimonial Causes Act 1857.
47. Matrimonial Causes Act 1923, s. 1.
48. Hansard, *Parliamentary History of England*, vol. xv (1753), cols. 70-1; see also Stone (1977), pp. 35-7.
49. Marriage Act 1816.
50. The Poor Relief (Deserted Wives and Children) Act 1718.
51. Poor Law Amendment Act 1834, s. 57.
52. See MacQueen (1849), pp. 42-3; Stone (1977), p. 633.
53. Parsons (1959), p. 273.
54. Morgan (1975), chs. 1-2.
55. Mitchell (1971); Rowbotham (1972).
56. Firestone (1970).
57. Mitchell (1971), p. 107; Firestone (1970), p. 82; James (1971), pp. 190-8.
58. Washburn (1962), pp. 96-9.
59. Mead (1931), pp. 57-63.
60. Millett (1969), p. 170.
61. Geiger (1968), p. 110.
62. Rowbotham (1972), pp. 159-160; O.M. Stone (1969).

63. Meijer (1971); Rowbotham (1972), ch. 7.
64. Ferge (1978).
65. Scott (1976).
66. Irvine (1980).
67. Laing (1971), p. 78.
68. Holt (1973).
69. Morgan (1975), ch. 3.
70. Glendon (1981), ch. 2.
71. This speculation is suggested by the concluding pages of Glendon (1981).

Chapter 2

1. *Study Commission on the Family* (1982), p. 26.
2. Hart (1976); Wallerstein and Kelly (1980), pp. 26–34; Weiss (1975), chs. 2–3; Cherlin (1981), p. 77. There is some evidence that the incidence of suicide is unusually high among recently separated and divorced people: *The Times*, 25 March 1981; Murch (1980), pp. 167–8 reports that only 26 per cent of fathers and 14 per cent of mothers in his sample avoided ill-health attributable to marriage breakdown; see also Chester (1971).
3. Bloom *et al.* (1979).
4. Rowntree (1964); Christensen (1969).
5. Leete (1979), pp. 74, 77–9.
6. Thornes and Collard (1979), ch. 5.
7. Spanier and Glick (1981).
8. For the United States, see Spanier and Glick (1981), Hampton (1975); for the United Kingdom, see Gibson (1974), Thornes and Collard (1979), p. 73. A new factor, the husband's unemployment, may now be becoming relevant: Maclean and Eekelaar (1983).
9. Sweet (1977); Thornes and Collard (1979), p. 51.
10. Spanier and Glick (1981), p. 334.
11. Makabe (1980); Sepler (1981).
12. Leete (1979), pp. 79–80; Carter and Glick (1976), p. 396.
13. Glenn and Weaver (1977): since no adjustments were made to take into account the lengths of the respective marriages, these findings must be regarded as very tentative.
14. McGregor (1957), pp. 38, 50.
15. Weitzman (1981), p. 143.
16. Leete (1979), pp. 71–3; it should be remembered that breakdown invariably occurs some time before the divorce and that in England and Wales there are restrictions on obtaining divorce within the first three years of marriage.
17. Cherlin (1981), ch. 2.
18. Gill (1977), p. 305.
19. Hart (1976).
20. See pp. 5–6.
21. For a brief survey of European developments and a good discussion of the issues, see Duncan (1979).

22. *Evans* v. *Evans* (1790) 1 Hagg. Const. 35.
23. Morton Report (1956) para. 69 (xxxvi).
24. Devlin (1965), p. 75.
25. Rheinstein (1972), ch. 16.
26. In 1976, 70 per cent of petitioners in England and Wales were wives: Leete (1979), p. 86.
27. Latey Report (1967).
28. Family Law Reform Act 1969, s. 1; Eekelaar (1971), pp. 64–5.
29. See also the failure of attempts to introduce 'western' style family law in Turkey reported by Dror (1959).
30. Mia Kellmer Pringle, *The Needs of Children*, commissioned by the Department of Health and Social Security: see *The Times* (15 February 1980).

Chapter 3

1. Eekelaar (1971), pp. 120–5.
2. *Williams* v. *Williams* [1966] 2 All E.R. 614.
3. Matrimonial Causes Act 1937.
4. Divorce (Scotland) Act 1938.
5. Divorce and Matrimonial Causes (Amendment) Act 1920, s. 4. (N.Z.).
6. *Mason* v. *Mason* [1921] N.Z.L.R. 955, 961 (per Salmond J.).
7. Divorce and Matrimonial Causes (Amendment) Act 1921–2 (N.Z.).
8. Matrimonial Causes (Amendment) Act 1938 (S.A.).
9. Supreme Court (Amendment) Act 1945 (W.A.).
10. Matrimonial Causes Act 1959, ss. 28 (m) and 37 (Aus.).
11. *idem.*
12. Now Divorce Act 1970, c. D–8 (Can.).
13. Divorce Act 1970, section 3.
14. Divorce Act 1970, section 4.
15. Divorce Act 1970, section 9(1) (e) and (f).
16. Mortimer Report (1966).
17. Divorce Reform Act 1969, s. 2(1); subsequently Matrimonial Causes Act 1973, s. 1(2). The new law came into operation on 1 January 1971.
18. The court may nevertheless refuse to grant a decree if satisfied that the marriage has not broken down irretrievably: Matrimonial Causes Act 1973, s. 1(4). It is difficult to see how a court could easily be so satisfied.
19. Matrimonial Causes Act 1973, ss. 5 and 10.
20. Below, pp. 43–4.
21. See below, p. 49.
22. See below, p. 62.
23. Australian Bureau of Statistics, *Divorce* (1976).
24. *New Zealand Official Yearbook 1975*, p. 122.
25. *Judicial Statistics 1979*, Table D 8(b).
26. Law Commission (1966), para. 17.
27. Law Commission (1966), paras. 92–3.
28. *Grant* v. *Grant* (1975) 9 Nfld. & P.E.I.R. 33.

29. *Anderson* v. *Anderson* (1973) 29 D.L.R. (3d) 587 (Alta.); *Smith* v. *Smith* (1972) 6 R.F.L. 70 (N.S.).
30. *Delaney* v. *Delaney* [1972] 1 O.R. 264.
31. *Smith* v. *Smith* [1976] S.L.T. (Notes) 26.
32. *White* v. *White* [1966] S.C. 187.
33. See *Annual Survey of Commonwealth Law* (1967) 568.
34. *Gollins* v. *Gollins* [1964] A.C. 664; *Williams* v. *Williams* [1964] A.C. 698.
35. *Bramley* v. *Bramley* (1974) 48 D.L.R. (3d) 367 (Ont.).
36. *Grime* v. *Grime* (1980) 16 R.F.L. (2d) 365 (Ont.).
37. *Grant* v. *Grant* (1974) S.L.T. (notes) 54; J. B. Stewart (1975) S.L.T. (News) 45.
38. See Brown (1963), p. 645.
39. *Bannister* v. *Bannister* (1980) 10 Fam. Law 240.
40. [1972] 1 W.L.R. 955.
41. [1976] Fam. 32.
42. Divorce (Scotland) Act 1976, s. 1(2) (b).
43. For a discussion of this situation, see Eekelaar (1976), 92 *Law Quarterly Review* 10.
44. This happened in *Richards* v. *Richards* [1972] 3 All E.R. 695; *Welfare* v. *Welfare* (1978) 8 Fam. Law 55; *Dowden* v. *Dowden* (1978) 8 Fam. Law 106. See Finlay (1975).
45. Cretney (1979), pp. 167–8.
46. *Ash* v. *Ash* [1972] Fam. 135.
47. *Storey* v. *Storey* (1973) R.F.L. 170 (P.E.I.).
48. *Pheasant* v. *Pheasant* [1972] Fam. 202.
49. *Rauch* v. *Rauch* (1976) 61 D.L.R. (3d) 633 (Ont.).
50. But in Scotland connivance has been retained as a bar with respect to the condition based on adultery: Divorce (Scotland) Act 1976, s. 1(3).
51. Matrimonial Causes Act 1973, s. 1(2) (a). This additional requirement is not found in the reformed Scottish law: *ibid.*, s. 1(2) (a).
52. Compare *Cleary* v. *Cleary* [1974] 1 W.L.R. 73 with *Carr* v. *Carr* [1974] 1 W.L.R. 1534.
53. See Eekelaar (1974), 90 *Law Quarterly Review* 292.
54. Riddell Lecture (1970).
55. Below, pp. 52–4.
56. Cretney (1979), p. 111.
57. Divorce Act, R.S.C. 1970, c. D–8, s. 4(1).
58. Family Proceedings Act 1980, s. 39(2) (N.Z.).
59. Family Law Act 1975, s. 48(2) (Aus.).
60. This point has gained significance after the decision of the House of Lords in *Richards* v. *Richards* [1983] 3 W.L.R. 173, that disputes over the occupation of the home are not necessarily to be decided on the basis of what is best for the children; see below p. 137.
61. Senator Murphy, Address to Sydney University Law School, 7 August 1973 (Attorney-General's Department), p. 8.
62. Family Law Act 1975, s. 49(2) (Aus.).
63. *In the Marriage of Lane* (1976) 10 A.L.R. 204 (where the husband's 'basic kindliness inhibited him from that ultimate total rejection of his wife

required by the Act'); *In the Marriage of Falk* (1977) 3 Fam. L.R. 11, 238.
64. *Mouncer* v. *Mouncer* [1972] 1 All E.R. 289; *Adeoso* v. *Adeoso* [1981] 1 All E.R. 107.
65. Divorce Act 1970, s. 9(3) (b) (Can.); Family Proceedings Act 1980, s. 40 (N.Z.).
66. Family Law Act 1975, s. 50 (Aus.); Matrimonial Causes Act 1973, s. 2(5).
67. Contrast the Canadian cases of *Crawford* v. *Crawford* [1976] 3 W.W.R. 767 and *Nolan* v. *Nolan* (1977) 75 D.L.R. (3d) 662 (Ont.).
68. *Macrae* v. *Macrae* (1967) 9 F.L.R. 441.
69. *M.* v. *M.* [1967] N.Z.L.R. 931.
70. *Lachman* v. *Lachman* (1970) 12 D.L.R. (3d) 221; *Norman* v. *Norman* (1973) 32 D.L.R. (3d) 262.
71. *Santos* v. *Santos* [1972] Fam. 247; see House of Lords Debates, vol. 304, cols. 1082ff. Parliament reiterated this intention when it applied the basic structure of the English Act to Scotland, for there the separation grounds are expressed as being applicable where 'there has been no cohabitation' between the parties: Divorce (Scotland) Act 1976, s. 1(2)(d) and (e).
72. *In the Marriage of Todd (No. 2)* (1976) 1 Fam. L.R. 11, 186.
73. Davis *et al.* (1982) found that 99 per cent of petitioner and 92 per cent of respondent parents sought legal advice. Probably many fewer people see lawyers where no children are involved, especially if respondents: Eekelaar and Maclean (1983).
74. Elston *et al.* (1975).
75. Hahlo (1975), p. 59.
76. Elston *et al.* (1975), p. 609.
77. Matrimonial Causes Rules 1977, Rule 48.
78. See Gibson (1980), p. 620.
79. Matrimonial Causes Act 1973, s. 1(3); see *Grenfell* v. *Grenfell* [1978] 1 All E.R. 561.
80. Murch (1980), p. 213.
81. Matrimonial Causes Rules 1977, Rule 48(4).
82. Matrimonial Causes Rules 1977, Rule 95(1). The role of welfare officers is considered in detail in chapter 4.
83. See *Noble* v. *Noble* [1963] 3 All E.R. 887.
84. Murch (1980), ch. 13, suggests that the special procedure has instigated steps towards an inquisitorial system. It is thought to be more correct, historically, to view these measures as residual instances of a system which was originally overwhelmingly inquisitorial.
85. O'Neill (1974); Gibson (1980), p. 620.
86. These are elaborated in detail by Mnookin and Kornhauser (1979).
87. Murch (1980), p. 22–3.
88. Winks (1980); see also Smith (1981), arguing for legislative intervention to permit 'dual' representation.
89. See Crouch (1982).
90. See Davis (1980), pp. 34–5.
91. Finer Report (1974), paras. 4.330–4.334.

92. The term 'conciliation' is used in contrast to 'reconciliation' where the objective is to restore cohabitation between the parties. Attempts to institutionalize reconciliation have been notably unsuccessful: see Bates (1978).
93. Family Proceedings Act 1980, s. 9(3) (N.Z.).
94. See Smith (1981), with respect to California.
95. Family Law Act 1975, s. 16(2). The extent to which the facility is used varies widely, from constituting 65 per cent of the service's work in Launceston to 10 per cent in Melbourne: Ruddock Report (1980), vol. 1, para. 10.34.
96. Smith (1981).
97. Family Law Act 1975, s. 14(5) (Aus.).
98. *Report of the Royal Commission on Courts* (1978), para. 484.
99. Family Proceedings Act 1980, s. 9(3).
100. See *Practice Direction (Pre-Trial Review: Financial Provisions)* [1980] 1 W.L.R. 245 (this experiment was later discontinued); Family Law Regulations, Reg. 96 (Aus.). An attempt to resolve custody and access disputes by conciliation before a registrar, in the presence of both parties, a welfare officer and (where appropriate) the children, was introduced in the Principal Registry of the Family Division in London on 1 January 1983: see *Practice Direction* [1982] 2 All E.R. 988. Various procedures have been introduced locally in England; for one in Bristol, see G. M. Parmiter, *Law Society's Gazette* (25 February 1981).
101. Family Proceedings Act 1980, ss. 13–15 (N.Z.).
102. Ruddock Report (1980), vol. 1, para. 7.48.
103. Eekelaar (1982a); Murch (1980), p. 160. See also the comment in the Ruddock Report (1980), vol. 1, para. 10.62 on welfare officer investigations in Australia: 'The current thinking of the counselling service and the court itself is that resources should be diverted away from the reporting function towards a conciliation service which would strive to make early contact with the parties.'
104. See, for example, Freeman (1982) and, in general, Abel (1982).
105. *Edgar* v. *Edgar* [1980] 1 W.L.R. 1410. Once an agreement has been incorporated in a court order, even proof of exploitation will be insufficient to set it aside: *Tommey* v. *Tommey* [1982] 3 All E.R. 385.
106. See note 73 above.
107. See Barrington Baker *et al.* (1977), paras. 4.20–4.
108. See MacDougall (1982).
109. See Rwezaura (1982); Merry (1982), p. 32.
110. This perspective will be developed later; see below pp. 171–6.
111. This is required before a divorce may be granted under the so-called 'administrative' procedure in Denmark: see Munck (1982). Davis (1983) has proposed alterations to the legal aid scheme and method of paying barristers to increase recognition of pre-trial negotiation and so to encourage settlements.
112. Some thirty-seven states have done this, according to Sepler (1981).
113. Glendon (1981), p. 33.
114. See Baxter (1977); Tottie (1980); Schmidt (1982).

Chapter 4

1. Haskey (1983). These figures refer to children under sixteen when the divorce petition is filed, thus excluding children under sixteen when their parents separated. Nor, when teenage unemployment is high, can it be assumed that dependency ceases at sixteen.
2. Above, pp. 9–10.
3. Rimmer (1981), pp. 39–40.
4. Crellin *et al.* (1971).
5. Ferri (1976).
6. Rutter (1972), p. 108.
7. Finer Report (1974), vol. 2, Appendix 12 (Norman Murchison, drawing on Douglas *et al.* (1968)).
8. Ferri (1976), p. 130.
9. Compare Zill's finding of emotional disturbance in 14 per cent of children aged between seven and eleven in divorced households (cited in Cherlin (1981), p. 79).
10. See, for example, Albert J. Solnit, *Newsweek* (11 February 1980).
11. Below, pp. 111–17.
12. Greenberg and Wolf (1982). But since the data did not include the economic circumstances of the families prior to the separation, the poorer performance may be attributable to other factors.
13. Eekelaar (1982a), p. 63; the same percentage has been found in California: Weitzman and Dixon (1979), p. 504.
14. Eekelaar and Clive (1977), Table 12; Maidment (1976). Interestingly, one-third of the fathers in Chambers's study about whom information about visits was known no longer visited their children: Chambers (1979), pp. 127–8.
15. Chambers, *ibid*.
16. See below, p. 700.
17. Davis *et al.* (1983).
18. *Cook* v. *Cook* [1978] 1 W.L.R. 994.
19. Wallerstein and Kelly (1980), p. 133.
20. Goldstein, Freud and Solnit (1973), p. 38: 'A "visiting" or "visited" parent has little chance to serve as a true object for love, trust and identification, since this role is based on his being available on an uninterrupted day-to-day basis.'
21. Littner (1973): the author was writing as Director of the Child Therapy Training Program of the Chicago Institute for Psychoanalysis.
22. Richards and Dyson (1982), p. 64; Richards (1982).
23. [1973] 2 All E.R. 81.
24. [1981] Fam. 31.
25. Maidment (1981a); Eekelaar (1973), p. 230.
26. *Jussa* v. *Jussa* [1972] 2 All E.R. 600.
27. Eekelaar and Clive (1977), para. 5.6.
28. *Practice Direction* [1980] 1 W.L.R. 301.
29. For a full discussion see Folberg and Graham (1979).

30. See for example *Conrad* v. *Conrad* (1973) 7 N.S.R. (2d) 684 (custody granted to husband; one year later, on receipt of welfare report, transferred to wife); *H.* v. *D.* [1974] 2 N.Z.L.R. 481 (eighteen months from hearing to final judgment); *Talsky* v. *Talsky* (1976) 62 D.L.R. (3d) 267 (Ontario litigation lasting three years).
31. See also Maidment (1976) and Gosse and Payne (1975), in whose samples no such cases were found.
32. Eekelaar (1982a).
33. See especially Patricia Morgan (1975); Clarke and Clarke (1976), chs. 1 and 15.
34. See below, pp. 196–7.
35. Rutter (1976), pp. 163, 167.
36. Rutter (1972), pp. 102–11.
37. No such instances were found by Eekelaar and Clive (1977) or Maidment (1976); there were less than three hundred new references made to the Official Solicitor in matrimonial cases in 1979: Stone (1982), pp. 64–5.
38. Matrimonial Causes Rules 1977, Rules 95 and 115.
39. Family Law Act 1975, ss. 62(a) and 65 (Aus.).
40. American enthusiasm for legal representation for children (for example, Landsman and Minow (1978)) should be treated with caution in the English context due to divergent traditions and economic circumstances between the professions in the two countries. For a fuller discussion of problems concerning legal representation for children, see below, p. 182.
41. Eekelaar (1982a); Murch (1980), p. 164.
42. Murch (1980), ch. 16, puts forward many valuable suggestions on how a role like this might be performed, emphasizing the necessity to involve both parents openly in the process.
43. Eekelaar (1982a).
44. Wilkinson (1981), ch. 8.
45. *re W. (J.C.)* [1964] Ch. 202.
46. [1981] Fam. 31; but see above, p. 71.
47. *re L.* [1962] 3 All E.R. 1 (C.A.); *Champion* v. *Champion* (1966) 1 S.A.S.R. 594; *Talsky* v. *Talsky* (1976) 62 D.L.R. (3d) 267 (S.C. Can.).
48. *J.* v. *C.* [1970] A.C. 697, 713–14.
49. See especially *S.* v. *S.* (1976) Fam. Law 148.
50. [1962] 3 All E.R. 1.
51. *S. (BD)* v. *S. (DJ)* [1977] 1 All E.R. 656; see also *re K.* [1977] Fam. 179.
52. *Dyment* v. *Dyment* [1969] 2 O.R. 748.
53. *Seddon* v. *Seddon* (1862) 2 Sw. & Tr. 640; *Handley* v. *Handley* [1891] p. 124.
54. *Stark* v. *Stark* [1910] P. 190.
55. (1967–8) 11 F.L.R. 247; see also *McManus* v. *McManus* [1970] A.L.R. 186 (N.S.W.).
56. [1968] W.A.R. 177.
57. [1973] 2 All E.R. 993.
58. (1975) Sol. Jo. 610.
59. *Gilbert* v. *Gilbert* (1979) 10 R.F.L. (Ont. Co. Ct.).
60. *Tam* v. *Tam* (1978) 24 N.S.R. (2d) 252 (Nova Scotia).
61. *Yeoman* v. *Yeoman* (1979) 13 B.C.L.R. 10 (B.C.).

62. *Case* v. *Case* (1975) 18 R.F.L. 132.
63. [1926] Ch. 676.
64. See *J.* v. *C.* [1970] A.C. 668, 715.
65. See *re C (M.A.)* [1966] 1 All E.R. 838; *Conrad* v. *Conrad* (1973) 7 N.S.R. (2d) 284; *Talsky* v. *Talsky* (1976) 62 D.L.R. (3d) 267.
66. [1970] A.C. 668.
67. *re W.* [1971] A.C. 682, 703–4.
68. *O'Connor* v. *A. & B.* [1971] 2 All E.R. 1230, 1232, 1240.
69. (1976) 6 Fam. Law 75; see also *D.* v. *M.* (*minor: custody appeal*) [1982] 3 All E.R. 897, 902.
70. *Barnett* v. *Barnett* [1972–3] 2 A.L.R. 19.
71. *Berger* v. *Berger* (1975) 17 R.F.L. 216.
72. Bates (1976).
73. (1976) 62 D.L.R. (3d) 267.
74. Mnookin (1975), pp. 264–5.
75. See, for example, Prentice (1979); *Lovell* v. *Lovell* (1950) 81 C.L.R. 513 (High Court of Australia), approved *In the Marriage of Rose* (1976–7) 12 A.L.R. 107 (Family Court of Australia). In *re W. (a minor)* (1983) 13 Fam. Law 47 the trial judge's clearly expressed 'bias' towards the mother was qualified by the Court of Appeal, which, nevertheless, allowed his decision to stand.
76. It is possible that some of these agreements were prompted by legal advice that 'that is what the court would order'. But it is impossible to know how far this is so. It is unlikely to be a significant factor: see Weitzman and Dixon (1979), pp. 505–8.
77. This was the conclusion of Weitzman and Dixon (1979).
78. Mnookin (1975), pp. 289–91.
79. Pp. 71–2.
80. *re Lori Lee Sullivan* (1969) 1 N.B.R. (2d) 948.
81. (1973) 8 R.F.L. 247 (Sask.).
82. *re B (a minor)* [1975] 2 All E.R. 449.
83. Paula Weiss (1979).
84. Adoption Act 1976, s. 14 (3) and 15 (4).
85. *re S.* [1977] Fam. 173. The onus was, however, put differently in *re D.* (1980) 10 Fam. Law 246, creating uncertainty, and the outcome of such adoption applications seems to depend mainly on the attitude of individual judges: see Rawlings (1982) 45 *Modern Law Review* 637.
86. Enrolment of Deed (Change of Name) Regulations 1974; such provisions are common in jurisdictions which, unlike England and Wales, require formal approval of changes of name.
87. *Re T.* [1963] Ch. 238.
88. Matrimonial Causes Rules 1977, Rule 92(8).
89. *D.* v. *B.* [1979] Fam. 38, 50; *R.* v. *R.* [1977] 1 W.L.R. 1256.
90. *W.* v. *A.* [1981] 1 All E.R. 100.
91. *North* v. *North* [1978] 6 W.W.R. 75 (B.C.).
92. *re J.* [1973] Fam. 106.
93. See above, p. 71.
94. See above, p. 70.

95. Fast and Cain (1966).
96. Maidment (1975), pp. 182, 196–7.
97. See Report by Justice, *Parental Rights and Duties in Custody Suits* (1975), Appendix; Payne and Kallish (1981).

Chapter 5

1. Chambers (1979), pp. 48–9.
2. House of Commons Debates Written Answers 27 July 1979. Beckerman and Clark (1982) found that the incidence of poverty of single parent families in 1974–6 was 58.8 per cent, twice the national average, and the incidence, taking into account benefits, was 12.3 per cent, compared to 2.6 per cent of all non-pensioner households.
3. Ferri (1976), pp. 49–50; see also Finer Report (1974), vol. 1 paras. 5.19–20.
4. Henderson Report (1975), vol. 1, 198–200.
5. Glendon (1981), pp. 86, 134. Forty-two per cent of mother–child families were below the poverty level in 1978. Sixty-two per cent of New York City's mother–child families were in receipt of welfare benefits in 1979, compared to 4.6 of two-adult families: *New York Times* (14 February 1982).
6. See also Chambers (1979), p. 54.
7. *Study Commission on the Family* (1981), p. 12.
8. Equal Opportunities Commission, *Fourth Annual Report* (1979), p. 70.
9. Where 58 per cent of all American mothers of school-age children were in the labour force in 1978: Weitzman (1981), p. 171.
10. Glendon (1981), p. 130; Chambers (1979), p. 54.
11. In the United States the ratio of women's to men's full-time earnings is very similar: Glendon (1981), p. 130.
12. Law Commission (1980), pp. 32–3; Glendon (1981), pp. 130–1; Rimmer and Popay (1982), pp. 21, 49.
13. Law Commission (1980), p. 34.
14. Manners and Rauta (1981), pp. 3–8.
15. See further below, p. 119.
16. Glendon (1981), p. 94, who points out that the same holds true in France; Weitzman (1981a), p. 1188.
17. See above, p. 29. Hence Maclean and Eekelaar (1983) found that, in 1981, only 1 in 5 of persons divorced since 1971 had savings over £500 at the time of divorce.
18. Eekelaar and Maclean (1983).
19. Scottish Law Commission (1981), pp. 72–4, read in conjunction with Doig (1982). Almost identical findings with respect to England were made by Eekelaar and Maclean (1983).
20. The figure for child-support orders is close to that of a national sample, where it was found that some 80 per cent of divorced mothers in the United States had child support orders in their favour, though such orders were much more likely the higher the mother's socio-economic status: Sorensen and MacDonald (1982).

21. Weitzman and Dixon (1979), p. 496; Weitzman (1981), p. 46. Data from the Institute of Law Research and Reform at the University of Alberta more closely approximate the Californian than the Scottish figures. Only 18 per cent of wives with dependent children received support awards on divorce, but 65 per cent of cases contained awards for children: Alberta Institute of Law Research and Reform (1981), vol. 1, 14. In Sweden, alimony was awarded in favour of only 10 per cent of wives divorcing in 1971, and half of these were limited to a period of not more than four years: Agell (1979), p. 159.
22. McGregor, Blom Cooper and Gibson (1970). A pilot study reported by Gibson (1982) revealed that 85 per cent of the sample magistrates' courts maintenance orders were for amounts below the recipients' supplementary benefit entitlement. See also Finer Report (1974), vol. 2, Appendix 7.
23. Chambers (1979), p. 7. The wives questioned in the Alberta study indicated that about one-third of husbands were excellent payers, about 15 per cent were 'fair' payers, under a quarter poor payers and a quarter non-payers. But the report fails to relate this data to the duration of the order: Alberta Institute of Law Research and Reform (1981), vol. 1, p. 16.
24. Glendon (1981), p. 70.
25. See below, pp. 123–4.
26. Sorensen and Macdonald (1982); Hoffman (1977), p. 74; Cherlin (1981), p. 82.
27. For example in England and Wales: Matrimonial Causes Act 1973, s. 28(1); in Australia the order may be continued in 'special circumstances': Family Law Act 1975, s. 82(4).
28. For example, in Canada: see *Lowe* v. *Lowe* (1976) 20 R.F.L. 216 (B.C.).
29. Kamerman and Kahn (1978), p. 447; Glendon (1981), p. 135.
30. Glendon (1981), p. 135.
31. Finer Report (1974), para. 5.56; below, pp. 123–4.
32. See pp. 171–6.
33. See generally Finnis (1980).
34. Houlgate (1980), p. 99.
35. Williams (1962); Jencks *et al.* (1972).
36. Goldthorpe *et al.* (1980); Bowles (1973).

Chapter 6

1. [1943] 2 All E.R. 579.
2. [1953] P. 266.
3. Above, note 1.
4. Morton Report (1956), paras. 687–701.
5. Married Women's Property Act 1964.
6. Matrimonial Homes Act 1967.
7. Matrimonial Proceedings and Property Act 1970; subsequently Matrimonial Causes Act 1973, s. 24; see below, p. 108.
8. *re Roger's Question* [1948] 1 All E.R. 328.

9. *National Provincial Bank* v. *Ainsworth* [1965] A.C. 1175.
10. *re John's Assignment Trusts, Niven* v. *Niven* [1970] 2 All E.R. 210.
11. *re Densham* [1975] 3 All E.R. 726.
12. Waters (1975).
13. *Gissing* v. *Gissing* [1971] A.C. 886 at 909 per Lord Diplock. This, it is suggested, represents the majority view in this case.
14. [1971] 3 All E.R. 866.
15. *Pettitt* v. *Pettitt* [1970] A.C. 777; *Gissing* v. *Gissing* [1971] A.C. 886; *Murdoch* v. *Murdoch* (1973) 41 D.L.R. (3d) 367 (S.C. Can.).
16. See the analysis in *Rathwell* v. *Rathwell* (1978) 83 D.L.R. (3d) 289 (S.C. Can.) *per* Dickson J. and *Pettkus* v. *Becker* (1981) 19 R.F.L. (2d) 165 (S.C. Can.).
17. See Zuckerman (1978).
18. See for example Matrimonial Property Amendment Act 1968 (N.Z.); *Haldane* v. *Haldane* [1977] A.C. 673 (P.C.); Family Law Reform Act 1975, s. 1 (Ont.) (now Family Law Reform Act 1978, s. 8); Family Law Act 1975, s. 79(4) (b) (Aus.).
19. For attempts, see Rosen (1974); Pottick (1978). See Bailey (1980), p. 196, for a discussion of judicial difficulties over such a provision in Australia.
20. Zuckerman (1978), p. 49; *H.* v. *H.* [1975] Fam. 9, *per* Sir George Baker P.
21. The point is technical. If the spouses are joint *legal* owners, the mother may be able to postpone sale (if sought by the husband) but usually only temporarily while she arranges alternative accommodation: *re Evers's Trust, Papps* v. *Evers* [1980] 1 W.L.R. 1327. If the husband only is the legal owner, he may be able to defeat the mother's right to occupy by appointing a second trustee to participate in the sale: see Stephen Freeman: Note on *Williams and Glyn's Bank* v. *Boland* [1981] A.C. 487, in (1980) 43 *Mod. Law Rev.* 692, 695.
22. Gray (1977), p. 278.
23. Eekelaar (1971), p. 101.
24. Pedersen (1965). A study in Denmark has shown that most Danes prefer this system to separation of property, but a considerable number favour confining the community to property acquired after marriage: I. M. Pedersen, International Society on Family Law, Newsletter (1976), p. 22.
25. Kahn-Freund (1971), pp. 34–5; see also Kiralfy (ed.) (1972), chs. 4 (A. Colomer) and 5 (E. D. Graue).
26. Draft discussion document on a Uniform Marital Property Act, National Conference of Commissioners on Uniform State Laws, 1 January 1982.
27. See Holland (1978); Shone (1979).
28. Matrimonial Property Act 1976 (N.Z.) as amended by Matrimonial Property (Amendment) Act 1980 (N.Z.).
29. If alimony was to be ordered, 83 per cent still thought the property should be shared, but 25 per cent thought that the husband should receive more than half: Working Paper, Matrimonial Property (April

1974), Institution of Law Research and Reform, Edmonton, Appendix A, 66.

30. Manners and Rauta (1981), pp. 12–13.
31. Weitzman (1981), Part 1.
32. See *Leatherdale* v. *Leatherdale* (1980) 19 R.F.L. (2d) 148 (Ont.); *Young* v. *Young* (1981) 21 R.F.L. (2d) 388 (Ont.).
33. Scottish Law Commission (1981), para. 3.83.
34. Weitzman (1981a), p. 1200.
35. See *Fielding* v. *Fielding* [1978] 1 W.L.R. 1146; Bailey (1980).
36. *Harnett* v. *Harnett* [1973] Fam. 156, 165; *Sander* v. *Sander* (1967) 41 A.L.J.R. 140 (H.C., Aus.).
37. Law Commission (1980), pp. 27–8.
38. Gray (1977), pp. 325–33.
39. Deech (1977).
40. Eekelaar (1979); Law Commission (1980), pp. 37–9.
41. Deech (1982).
42. Barrington Baker *et al.* (1977).
43. Family Law Act 1975, s. 72 (Aus.).
44. Bailey (1980); Kovacs (1980).
45. Family Proceedings Act 1980, s. 64 (N.Z.).
46. Law Com. No. 103.
47. Weitzman and Dixon (1980); Weitzman (1981), p. 46.
48. Law Commission (1981).
49. The failure of the Law Commission to deal with the option of property entitlement based on partnership is probably due to its earlier rejection of the idea in 1973. (The Law Commission: *Family Law: First Report on Family Property: A New Approach*; Law Com. No. 52, paras. 46–60.) But that rejection was based on the expectation, as yet unrealized, that a system of automatic co-ownership of the matrimonial home will be introduced and a probably over-optimistic confidence in leaving matters to be settled according to the court's sense of equity.
50. See above, p. 92; Eekelaar and McLean (1983) found that, in 1981, in no case in their nationally representative sample of people divorced after 1971 was a former wife who had no children in the marriage receiving any maintenance.
51. Family Proceedings Act 1980, s. 65(3) (N.Z.).
52. On the uncertain interaction between the one-third 'rule' and the 'net result' approach see *Wachtel* v. *Wachtel* [1973] Fam. 72, *Shallow* v. *Shallow* [1979] Fam. 1 and *Slater* v. *Slater* (1982) 12 Fam. Law 153.
53. *Ette* v. *Ette* [1965] 1 All E.R. 341; *Wright* v. *Bye* (1975) 5 Fam. Law 44; *Wilkinson* v. *Wilkinson* (1979) 10 Fam. Law 48; *Slater* v. *Slater* (1982) 12 Fam. Law 153.
54. *Brown* v. *Brown* (1981) 11 Fam. Law 247; *Macey* v. *Macey* (1982) 3 F.L.R. 7.
55. Law Commission (1981), paras. 24–5.
56. See, for example, *Cann* v. *Cann* [1977] 3 All E.R. 957; Barrington Baker *et al.* (1977), para. 3.30.
57. Some other measure, such as the median, might be more appropriate.

The figure might be fixed from time to time by administrative order.
58. Maclean and Eekelaar (1983).
59. Below, p. 134.
60. Law Commission (1980), para. 71. They seem to have had some success: see above, pp. 91–2.
61. *Hanlon* v. *Hanlon* [1978] 1 W.L.R. 592.
62. *Harvey* v. *Harvey* [1982] Fam. 82.
63. *Mullard* v. *Mullard* (1982) 12 Fam. Law 62.
64. *Hulley* v. *Thompson* [1981] 1 All E.R. 1128.
65. See Deech (1982), pp. 634–5.
66. Matrimonial Causes Act 1973, s. 28.
67. See for example *Harvey* v. *Harvey* [1982] Fam. 82, 89.
68. See above, pp. 95–6.
69. *Roberts* v. *Roberts* [1970] P. 1.
70. Law Commission (1981), paras. 40–1.
71. Compare, however, the Scottish Law Commission (1981), paras. 2.98 and 3.188, arguing that only the resources of the parties are relevant, thus excluding those of a second partner.
72. See below, pp. 149–50.
73. Eekelaar (1979), pp. 266–7; *Wright* v. *Bye* (1975) 5 Fam. Law 44; *Shallow* v. *Shallow* [1979] Fam. 1; *Stockford* v. *Stockford* (1982) 3 F.L.R. 53 (in the first two cases there were no children in competition with those of the former family, but in *Stockford* there were children in both families).
74. See *Roberts* v. *Roberts* [1970] P. 1. This is not a 'rule', but an application of common sense: *Tovey* v. *Tovey* (1978) 8 Fam. Law 80; *Stockford* v. *Stockford* (1982) 3 F.L.R. 53.
75. Krause (1981), pp. 436, 443.
76. Finer Report (1974), vol. 1, paras. 4.188–9.
77. This concept is explained below, p. 125.
78. Agell (1979), pp. 163–4; see also, for New Zealand, Social Security Amendment Act 1980, Schedule 20.
79. Pp. 205–7.
80. See Scottish Law Commission (1981), paras. 3.102–3.
81. 'I take [section 15 of the Family Law Reform Act 1978] to mean that unless there are valid health or psychological reasons that the mother should remain in the home, the mother is required to hire a babysitter or place the child in day care and resume her former employment or its equivalent': *re Moosa and Moosa* (1980) A.C.W.S. (2d) 110 (Ontario County Court); see also *Osborn* v. *Sparks* (1982) 12 Fam. Law 146.
82. *Downing* v. *Downing* [1976] Fam. 288.
83. Matrimonial Causes Act 1973, ss. 27, 29.
84. Weitzman and Dixon (1980).
85. Law Commission (1980), para. 64.
86. Weitzman (1981).
87. See Family Law Act 1975, s. 72 (Aus.); Family Proceedings Act 1980, s. 64 (N.Z.); Scottish Law Commission (1981), para. 3.43; Law Commission (1981), para. 17; Law Reform Commission of Canada (1976), 42. For a more cautious approach, see Berger Report (1975).

88. Eighty-five per cent of wives in Todd and Jones's (1972) survey had been in employment *at some time* during the marriage.

89. Glendon (1981), p. 129.

90. Glendon (1981), pp. 132–3.

91. Scottish Law Commission (1981), para. 3.94.

92. Above, p. 104.

93. Deech (1980), p. 304.

94. Muller-Freienfels (1979).

95. Matrimonial Property Act 1976, s. 8(1) (N.Z.).

96. Glendon (1981), p. 67; Weitzman (1981a), pp. 1212–14.

97. Where, however, the procedure is to defer final order until the benefits become payable: Ruddock Report (1980), vol. 1, paras. 5.99–109.

98. Scottish Law Commission (1981), paras. 3.91–9.

99. Such compensation was denied in the California case, *in re the Marriage of Sullivan*, 134 Cal. App. 3d. 484; 184 Cal. Rptr. 796 (1982). But see the dissent of Associate Justice Ziebarth and the discussion of earning capacity as an asset.

100. The Law Commission (1981), para. 25, raised the question that data on children's needs might be made available 'as an administrative measure'.

Chapter 7

1. For a fuller discussion, see Eekelaar (1976).

2. Henderson Report (1975), vol. 1.

3. Finer Report (1974), vol. 1, paras. 5190 and 5.141.

4. Chambers (1979), pp. 261–7.

5. 912 House of Commons Debates, col. 284 (25 May 1976).

6. See the table set out in Krause (1981), pp. 459–61.

7. However, entitlement to AFDC triggers entitlement to various other welfare benefits.

8. Agell (1979), p. 178.

9. Agell (1979), p. 179.

10. Liljestrom (1978), p. 23.

11. Ogus and Barendt (1982), pp. 227–36.

12. Social Security Amendment Act 1973 (N.Z.); see [1975] N.Z.L.J. 6. The provisions are based on the McCarthy Report (1972), especially chapters 22 and 35.

13. Social Services Amendment Act 1977, introducing a new Part IVAAA into the Social Services Act 1947–77 (Aus.).

14. Ruddock Report (1980), vol. 1, para. 5.17.

15. See above, p. 120.

16. Ogus and Barendt (1982), pp. 227–8.

17. Social Security Amendment Act 1973, s. 6, (N.Z.), inserting s. 27C into the Social Security Act 1964 (N.Z.).

18. Ogus and Barendt (1982), pp. 209–11, 236.

19. Social Security Pensions Act, 1975, s. 19(3): this includes caring for children or the elderly or incapacitated.

20. See Social Services Act 1947–77, s. 83 AAD, inserted by Social Services Amendment Act 1977, s. 3 (Aus.).
21. Social Security Act 1964, s. 27B (2) (c) (N.Z.). This had been recommended by the McCarthy Report, which argued that legal aid was available and that the legal process was not 'as destructive of the chances of reconciliation as some submissions argued': McCarthy Report (1972), ch. 35, para. 5. This was, however, abandoned in 1981 in favour of a scheme similar to that proposed by the Finer Committee: Social Security Amendment Act 1980 (N.Z.).
22. Finer Report (1974), vol. 1, paras. 4. 206–09.
23. Finer Report (1974), vol. 1, para. 4. 199–202.
24. House of Commons Debates, vol. 898, col. 62 (20 October, 1975).
25. Ruddock Report (1980), vol. 1, para. 5.29.
26. Atkin (1981).
27. See further Eekelaar (1976).
28. Social Security Amendment Act 1980 (N.Z.); Atkin (1981).
29. Above, p. 115.
30. Maclean and Eekelaar (1983). Krause (1981), p. 472, has suggested that part of a debtor's payments should go directly to the former family, but this would be limited to bringing the family up from AFDC level to the federally-defined poverty line.
31. Finer Report (1974), vol. 1, para. 4.215.
32. Atkin (1981), p. 50.
33. Krause (1981), chs. VII and VIII.
34. Finer Report (1974), vol. 1, para. 5.200.
35. Finer Report (1974), vol. 1, para. 4.156.
36. Finer Report (1974), vol. 1, para. 4.170.
37. Kovacs (1974), pp. 67, 78–9.
38. Alberta Institute of Law Research and Reform (1981).
39. Chambers (1979); Weitzman (1981) p. 1256.
40. Marsden (1973), p. 195, reporting separated wives' accounts of husbands entering into hire-purchase commitments and 'buying cars and radiograms while their children went hungry'.
41. Chambers (1979), pp. 90 *et seq.*
42. Chambers (1979), p. 101.
43. Krause (1981), pp. 422–31.
44. Provision for agreed attachment of earnings orders is made in English legislation: Attachment of Earnings Act 1971, s. 3(1)(d).
45. Above, p. 130.
46. Only 18 per cent of the men were subject to wage-attachment at the time of the research: Chambers (1979), p. 154. In Sweden, attachment is used in over 25 per cent of cases: Agell (1979), p. 181.
47. See Chambers (1979), pp. 258–61. See further the French system, introduced in 1973, discussed by Glendon (1981), p. 71.
48. See above, pp. 91–2.
49. Finer Report (1974), vol. 1, para. 6.84.
50. See further, p. 169 below.
51. Hoath (1981).

52. *re Holliday (a bankrupt), ex p. the trustee of the bankrupt* v. *The bankrupt and another* [1980] 3 All E.R. 385; *Dennis* v. *McDonald* [1981] 2 All E.R. 632.
53. See above, pp. 102–4.
54. [1981] A.C. 487.
55. The Law Commission here reiterated their earlier call for a scheme of automatic co-ownership of the matrimonial home which would confer on a spouse whose name did not appear on the conveyance rights against third parties, but only upon registration of the requirement that disposition of the home required that spouse's consent: Law Commission (1978), paras. 1.310–364.
56. Discussed further in the first edition of this work, pp. 240–3.
57. Crane and Levin (1966–7), p. 256.
58. Only a debtor's family's 'wearing apparel and bedding' to a value of £100 is exempt from execution: County Courts Act 1959, s. 124; Protection from Execution (Prescribed Value) Order 1980.
59. Law Commission (1978), Book Three.
60. See Joint Family Homes Act 1964, ss. 22, 23 (N.Z.).
61. *Walker* v. *Walker* [1978] 1 W.L.R. 533.
62. See below, p. 169.
63. *Richards* v. *Richards* [1983] 3 W.L.R. 173, overruling *Samson* v. *Samson* [1982] 1 W.L.R. 282.
64. See editorial in *The Times* (2 July 1983).

Chapter 8

1. In this context, 'the unmarried' means persons who are not married *to each other*.
2. Since the Housing Act 1980 the housing authority can no longer transfer a tenancy from the father to the mother to keep her and the child in the home because she needs a court order, which can be made only if the parties are married.
3. Domestic Proceedings and Magistrates' Courts Act 1978, s. 50(5).
4. Affiliation Proceedings Amendment Act 1972, s. 2(1).
5. *Haroutanian* v. *Jennings* (1977) 121 Sol. Jo. 163; *Osborn* v. *Sparks* (1982) 12 Fam. Law 146.
6. Guardianship of Minors Act 1971, s. 9.
7. See Law Commission (1982), paras. 10.55–9.
8. *Tremble* v. *Gordon* 430 U.S. 762 (1977).
9. European Convention on the Status of Children Born out of Wedlock (1975).
10. Finlay (1979), pp. 307–12.
11. For example, Children's Law Reform Act 1977, s. 1 (Ont.).
12. Law Commission (1979).
13. Law Commission (1982).
14. Family Proceedings Act 1980, s. 81 (N.Z.); originally the order was restricted to a five-year period: Domestic Proceedings Act 1968, s. 53 (N.Z.); see Atkin (1981).

15. The period is one year in Manitoba and Newfoundland: Family Maintenance Act 1978, s. 11(1) (Man.); Family Maintenance Act 1973, s. 10A (Nfld.).
16. Family Law Reform Act 1978, ss. 1(b) and 14(b) (Ont.).
17. See Bala (1980), p. 112.
18. The Law Commission (1982), paras 6.6–11, suggested that courts be given the power to make property orders in favour of children if the parents were not married to each other. The Commission's attitude to this proposal is ambivalent. On the one hand, they argue that the courts should have the same 'extended range of powers' whether or not the parents are married (para. 6.8); on the other, they defend the property proposal on the ground that, as the order would be in favour of the child, not the parent, it is unlikely to be frequently made (para. 6.6). Yet the importance of property orders for the mother–child family after divorce is well known. Why should they be less so where the parents were not married? Would the technicality that the orders would be in favour of the child deter courts from making them?
19. This was the conclusion of the Law Commission (1982).
20. O. M. Stone (1977), p. 19.
21. Law Commission (1982), paras. 10.60–6.
22. Law Commission (1982), paras. 7.25–33.
23. Law Commission (1982), paras. 4.39–40.
24. As is the case in Norway: Krause (1971), p.181.
25. Law Commission (1982), para. 10.45.
26. See Krause (1981), ch. IX.
27. P. 133.
28. *Upfill* v. *Wright* [1911] 1 K.B. 506, 510; *Diwell* v. *Farnes* [1959] 2 All E.R. 379, 384.
29. Where a child was born, consideration has (artificially) been found in the mother's undertaking not to bring support proceedings: *Ward* v. *Byham* [1956] 1 W.L.R. 496, and in moving from a secured tenancy into the father's flat: *Tanner* v. *Tanner* [1975] 1 W.L.R. 1346.
30. Contrast *Diwell* v. *Farnes*, note 28 above.
31. Pp. 102–4.
32. *Cooke* v. *Head* [1972] 2 All E.R. 38; *Richards* v. *Dove* [1974] 1 All E.R. 888; *Eves* v. *Eves* [1975] 1 W.L.R. 1338; *Bernard* v. *Josephs* [1982] 3 All E.R. 162.
33. *Andrews* v. *Parker* [1973] Qd. R. 93, referred to in (1977) 93 *Law Quarterly Review* 386.
34. *Marvin* v. *Marvin* 557 P. 2d. 106 (1976).
35. Family Law Reform Act 1978, ss. 52(1) & 54 (Ont.); Newfoundland, Prince Edward Island and New Brunswick have enacted similar legislation; see Bala (1980), p. 92.
36. Family Law Reform Act 1978, s. 1(b) (Ont.).
37. These examples are all drawn from the model contracts set out in Weitzman (1981), ch. 12.
38. See Weitzman (1981), pp. 356–9.
39. Family Law Reform Act 1978, s. 18(4) (Ont.).
40. See above, p. 145.

41. *Pascoe* v. *Turner* [1979] 2 All E. R. 945; see also *Greasley* v. *Cooke* [1980 3 All E.R. 710.

42. See above, p. 120.

43. Hence the limitation of remedies in quasi-contract: see Birks (1974); *Holli* v. *Kost* (1972) 7 R.F.L. 77. The same limitation exists in Swedish law: Agell (1980), p. 26.

44. It is one year in Tasmania (Maintenance Act 1967, s. 16 (Tas)), two years in British Columbia (Family Relations Act 1978, definition of 'spouse') and five years in South Australia (Family Relationships Act 1975, s. 11) and Ontario (Family Law Reform Act 1978, s. 14(b)(i)). For Canada, see further Bala (1980); for Australia, see Bailey (1978).

45. See especially Deech (1980).

46. See Agell (1980), p. 24; (1980a).

47. *Gammans* v. *Ekins* [1950] 2 K.B. 328.

48. *Dyson Holdings* v. *Fox* [1976] Q.B. 503; see also *Helby* v. *Rafferty* [1979] 1 W.L.R. 13; *Carega Properties* v. *Sharratt* [1979] 1 W.L.R. 928.

49. I am indebted to the discussion in the unpublished D.Phil. thesis for Oxford University by D. S. Rosettenstein.

50. But the Court of Appeal has refused to extend this doctrine to a case of desertion of a cohabitee: *Colin Smith Music* v. *Ridge* [1975] 1 All E.R. 290.

51. Housing Finance Act 1972, Sch. 3, para. 2.

52. Housing (Homeless Persons) Act 1977, s. 1(1)(a); see further Pearl (1978).

53. See above, p. 127.

54. Social Security Amendment Act 1973, s. 6, inserting s. 27C(1) into the Social Security Act 1964 (N.Z.).

55. Agell (1980), p. 29.

56. See Rosettenstein, note 49 above.

57. Pearl (1980), p. 337.

58. Domestic Proceedings and Magistrates' Courts Act 1978, s. 25 (maintenance orders cease to have effect after the parties have been living together for six months).

59. Administration of Estates Act 1925, s. 46; Family Provision (Intestate Succession) Order 1972.

60. Inheritance (Provision for Family and Dependants) Act 1975, s. 1: the deceased must have been supporting the claimant 'otherwise than for full valuable consideration': *re Wilkinson* [1978] Fam. 22. Maintenance will be awarded only if the cohabitant needs it: *re Coventry* [1980] Ch. 461.

61. Glendon (1981), pp. 20–8.

62. Glendon (1981), p. 26.

63. See above, p. 105.

64. *re Beaumont* [1980] Ch. 408; *Kourkey* v. *Lusher* (1982) 12 Fam. Law 86.

Chapter 9

1. Above, p. 17.

2. Pinchbeck and Hewitt (1969), ch. 2.

3. For accounts of the history of cruelties committed against children, see de Mause (1974) and Radbill (1974). Some of these descriptions might appear less horrifying if set against the general attitudes to pain and suffering of those ages.
4. Observe the attitudes to savage punishments in Maxim Gorki, *Childhood* (1913).
5. Shorter (1976), pp. 62–3; *Holmes* v. *Holmes* [1755] 2 Lee 116.
6. See J. S. Mill, *The Subjection of Women* (1869).
7. See McGregor (1957).
8. 16 & 17 Vic., c. 30.
9. *R.* v. *Lapworth* [1931] 1 K.B. 117.
10. Freeman (1978), pp. 73–4.
11. *Jamieson* v. *Jamieson* [1952] A.C. 525, 545.
12. *Russell* v. *Russell* [1897] A. C. 395.
13. *Fisher* v. *Fisher* (1861) 2 Sw. & Tr. 410, rejected in *Sidney* v. *Sidney* (1865) 4 Sw. & Tr. 178.
14. *King* v. *King* [1952] 2 All E.R. 584.
15. Poor Law (Amendment) Act 1868.
16. McGregor (1957), pp. 22–3.
17. Married Women (Maintenance in the Case of Desertion) Act 1886; Summary Jurisdiction (Married Women) Act 1895; Summary Jurisdiction (Separation and Maintenance) Act 1925; Matrimonial Causes Act 1937.
18. Freeman (1979), part 2.
19. Gelles (1974); Freeman (1978), p. 77.
20. See further, Eekelaar *et al.* (1982).
21. Robert Pashley Q.C., *Pauperism and the Poor Law* (1852), pp. 364–5, quoted in Sidney and Beatrice Webb (1910), pp. 132–3.
22. Cited in Longmate (1974), p. 90.
23. Sidney and Beatrice Webb (1910), p. 45.
24. Pinchbeck and Hewitt (1973), p. 508.
25. An Act for the better Regulation of the Parish Poor Children, etc. 7 Geo. III, c. 39.
26. See Curtis Report (1946), paras. 139–40.
27. Pinchbeck and Hewitt (1973), p. 508.
28. Local Government Act 1929, s. 1.
29. Sidney and Beatrice Webb (1910), p. 188.
30. DHSS, *Health and Personal Social Services Statistics for England, 1978.*
31. Curtis Report (1946), p. para. 32.
32. House of Commons Debates, col. 1486 (6 March 1872).
33. The circumstances are described in Housden (1955), pp. 130ff.
34. *Transactions of the National Association for the Promotion of Social Science* (1874), pp. 574–5, cited in Pinchbeck and Hewitt (1973), p. 359.
35. Infant Life Protection Act 1897.
36. Pinchbeck and Hewitt (1973), p. 622.
37. Prevention of Cruelty to and Protection of Children Act 1889, s. 5(2).
38. Children Act 1908; Children and Young Persons Acts 1932–3.
39. Committee on Children and Young Persons (Ingleby Committee),

Cmnd. 1191 (1960) (**HMSO**); for a fuller account, see Eekelaar *et al.* (1982).

40. See Dingwall *et al.* (1983), pointing out how British health visiting, which relies on voluntary co-operation for its surveillance of family health, rests on a compromise between welfarist concern and family autonomy.
41. For a similar account of developments in the United States, see Pfohl (1977).
42. Kempe (1962).
43. Caffey (1946).
44. Cited in Pinchbeck and Hewitt (1973), p. 628.
45. Kempe (1962); Steele and Pollock (1968).
46. Fontana and Besharov (1977).
47. Gil (1975), (1978); van Stolk (1972).
48. Straus (1978).
49. Yllo and Straus (1981).
50. *Report of the Select Committee on Violence in Marriage*, vol. 1, para. 7 (1975) (HMSO).
51. Usually in Annual Reports of the National Society for the Prevention of Cruelty to Children. See also Hall (1975); MacKeith (1975); *First Report from the Select Committee on Violence in the Family, Session 1976–7*, H.C. 329–i, para. 25 (HMSO).
52. See Dingwall *et al.* (1983); below, p. 180.

Chapter 10

1. Maidment (1978), p. 110.
2. See, more fully, Freeman (1978), pp. 83–6; Maidment (1978), pp. 111–15.
3. If the offence is common assault only, the police cannot bring charges but the victim may do so: *Nicholson* v. *Booth* (1888) 52 J.P. 662. This 'rule' should be abolished.
4. In the United States, police intervention in domestic violence is a frequent cause of injury and death for the police: see Parnas (1971).
5. For an account of this in Canada, see Bell (1978) and Jaffe and Thompson (1978).
6. Domestic Violence and Matrimonial Proceedings Act 1976, s. 1; *Davis* v. *Johnson* [1979] A.C. 264.
7. *Walker* v. *Walker* [1978] 1 W.L.R. 533 (C.A.).
8. *Lewis* v. *Lewis* [1978] Fam. 60; *Practice Note* [1981] 1 All E.R. 224.
9. *McCartney* v. *McCartney* [1981] 1 All E.R. 597; *Horner* v. *Horner* [1982] 2 W.L.R. 914.
10. *Practice Note* [1978] 1 W.L.R. 925, expressing concern at the increase in *ex parte* applications, 50 per cent of which appeared to be unmeritorious. But see p. 137 above.
11. *Hopper* v. *Hopper* [1978] 1 W.L.R. 342 (C.A.).
12. Parnas (1971).
13. Parnas (1978).

14. Marcus (1981).
15. Freeman (1979), p. 146.
16. This is not to argue that the motives of many individuals concerned with child welfare are not centred on the claims of individual children.
17. Berger Report (1975), Part 3; see also *The Rights of Children* (London, National Council for Civil Liberties, 1972).
18. See, for example, Gross and Gross (1977).
19. Goldstein *et al.* (1980), p. 9. Dickens (1981) points to the 'neo-conservative' political context in which this theory took hold. See also Freeman (1983).
20. Goldstein *et al.* (1980), p. 10.
21. Goldstein *et al.* (1980), pp. 11–12.
22. Goldstein *et al.* (1980), p. 77.
23. This term is used by Goldstein *et al.* (1980) for 'the three liberty interests of direct concern to children' (parental autonomy, the right to autonomous parents, and privacy).
24. Beck *et al.* (1978); Dingwall *et al.* (1983).
25. See also Mnookin (1975); Morris *et al.* (1980), p. 132, would entirely exclude emotional harm as a ground for intervention.
26. Above p. 156.
27. See below, p. 180.
28. Children and Young Persons Act 1969, s. 2(1); Children and Young Persons Act 1963, s. 1(1).
29. For a full description of the operation of this system, see Dingwall *et al.* (1983).
30. Dingwall *et al.* (1983), p. 229.
31. Dingwall *et al.* (1983), pp. 235–6. On this analysis, an Australian proposal to remove the power to initiate proceedings from the welfare agency and vest it in an 'independent official' is misguided: Law Reform Commission of Australia, Discussion Paper 12, *Child Welfare* (1979).
32. See Freeman (1980); Morris *et al.* (1980), p. 132, would exclude intervention where harm was 'merely apprehended'.
33. See below, p. 184.
34. For a full discussion of the following, see Dingwall *et al.* (1983).
35. See Gelles (1979), p. 65.
36. In England this is usually done by Place of Safety Orders which may be granted, on application (usually, but not necessarily, by a social worker), by a magistrate for a maximum period of twenty-eight days.
37. Children and Young Persons Act 1969, s. 1.
38. Dingwall *et al.* (1983), pp. 168–72.
39. See *R.* v. *Gravesham Juvenile Court, ex p. B* (1982) 12 Fam. Law 207. The courts have also been generous in allowing parents to appeal against care orders, although, technically, not being parties, they have no independent right to do so: *Southwark London Borough Council* v. *C.* [1982] 2 All E.R. 636. Dingwall *et al.* (1983), pp. 239, 262.
40. In 1982 the government announced its intention to extend legal aid to the parents. They would not, however, acquire full party status.
41. Children Act 1975, s. 64; Hoggett (1981), pp. 95–6.

42. See especially *re CB* [1981] 1 All E.R. 16.
43. In *re E. (Minors)*, *The Times* (25 January 1983); Eekelaar *et al.* (1982).
44. Van Rees (1978); Lynch and Roberts (1982).
45. A condition may be attached to the order requiring the child to attend for medical examination. Can this bind the parent? It is apparently little used.
46. Provision exists for six-monthly reviews by the authority of cases of children in their care and for parents to apply for discharge of care orders: for details, see Hoggett (1981), p. 176.
47. *A. v. Liverpool City Council* [1982] A.C. 363. Provision has been made in the Health and Social Services and Social Security Adjudications Act 1983 enabling termination of access to a child in care to be referred to a court. The significance of this measure would be considerably weakened if the suggestion made in the text for more powerful supervision orders were adopted. This proposal carries the advantage that such arrangements would normally be part of the authority's plans for the child rather than an externally imposed requirement on the authority's case management. On the analysis of this book, case management decisions are properly located with the authority rather than the courts, although it is right that the most serious decisions should be presented to and defended before a tribunal. There is little reason to suppose that courts are better placed to appreciate the children's interests than the authorities and thus a shift of primary responsibility for such decisions from social services departments to the courts would, it is thought, be misguided.

Chapter 11

1. House of Lords Debates, vol. 371, col. 1361 (1976) (Lord Wells-Pestell).
2. See above, pp. 19–24.
3. Land (1978).
4. See Dinnage and Kellmer Pringle (1967).
5. Tizard and Rees (1976).
6. Clarke and Clarke (eds) (1976), pp. 10, 130.
7. See above, p. 180.
8. Rowe and Lambert (1973).
9. A study of about half the foster-children in San Francisco found that 62 per cent of these children, too, were expected to remain in foster care until maturity: Mnookin (1975), p. 275.
10. Frequent contact was maintained with the natural parents of only 10 per cent of the children boarded out in Rowe and Lambert's study. This corresponds to the 14 per cent found by George (1970). See also Mnookin (1975), p. 275.
11. Aldgate (1976); Shaw and Lebens (1976).
12. See above, p. 20.
13. Packman (1976), p. 138.
14. Tizard (1977), pp. 209–10.

15. See above, pp. 185–6.
16. See Field-Fisher Report (1974), para. 35.
17. Magistrates' Courts (Children and Young Persons) Rules 1970, Rule 14(3) (bb).
18. Child Care Act 1980, s. 2(3).
19. [1980] A.C. 273.
20. Child Care Act 1980, s. 13(2) (b).
21. For more detailed consideration of these conditions, see Hoggett (1981), pp. 160–1.
22. The judgments rest on the fallacy that, if reclaim terminated the authority's right to keep the child under Child Care Act 1980, s. 2, the authority would have no lawful basis for caring for the child. But that would not follow. The authority would be in the same position as any third party temporarily caring for a child.
23. See above, p. 181. There may be a technical objection in so far as, strictly, a Place of Safety Order should only be issued if any of the conditions set out in Children and Young Persons Act 1969, s. 1 (see above p. 176), *presently* apply to the child. However, such orders are regularly granted with respect to children who are temporarily in safe places (hospitals, children's homes) and it is probable that, if challenged, the provisions will be interpreted so that the specified conditions will be held presently to apply to a child despite the child's actual temporary withdrawal from them.
24. The period may be altered by resolution of each House of Parliament: Child Care Act 1980, s. 3(9).
25. Children Act 1975, ss. 33, 86.
26. Curtis Report (1946), para. 425, seeking a means to make possible a stable relation short of adoption between a good foster-parent and a child.
27. Houghton Report (1972), ch. 6.
28. Goldstein (1976), p. 602.
29. Children Act 1975, s. 86 and Schedule 3, para. 7.
30. See DHSS, *The Cost of Operating the Unimplemented Provisions of the Children Act 1975* (October 1980).
31. This Act was not in effect by March 1983; many of its provisions simply consolidate existing legislation and reference is made to the 1976 Act for convenience.
32. Adoption Act 1976, ss. 16(2), 18 and 27.
33. [1977] 1 All E.R. 182.
34. *re W.* [1971] A.C. 682; see also *re H.* [1977] 2 All E.R. 339.
35. *re D. (an infant: parent's consent)* [1977] 1 All E.R. 145.
36. *re J (Adoption Order: Conditions)* [1973] Fam. 106; *re S (A Minor: Adoption Order: Access)* [1976] Fam. 1.
37. Children Act 1975, s. 26; Adoption Act 1976, s. 5. For an account of the use made by adoptees of their 'right to know' about their origins, see Day and Leeding (1980).
38. Triseliotis (1973).
39. Rowe and Lambert (1973), pp. 95–6.

40. Family Law Reform Act 1969, s. 1.
41. The power is not very extensive; a marriage contracted without parental consent remains valid, although one of the parties will probably be guilty of making false statements.
42. Compare *re an Infant* (1963) 6 F.L.R. 12 (Victoria); *re Z* (1970) A.L.R. 914; *re Fox* [1973] 11 R.F.L. 100 (Ont.); for New Zealand, see 4 *Recent Law* 167 (Webb). Applications in England and Wales are made to magistrates and are not reported.
43. Above, p. 33.
44. This is enjoined in the Education Act 1966, s. 8, requiring that, so far as 'compatible with the provision of efficient instruction and training and the avoidance of unreasonable public expenditure, pupils are to be educated in accordance with the wishes of their parents'. See *The Secondary school curriculum and examinations, with special reference to the 14 to 16 year age group*, H.C. Paper 116–1 (1982): *The Times* (17 February 1982). See also Craven *et al.* (1982), pp. 31–2.
45. Family Law Reform Act 1969, s. 8.
46. See Skegg (1973); contrast Samuels (1983).
47. Sexual Offences Act 1956, ss. 5 and 6, Criminal Law Act 1967, sch. 2.
48. See *Gillick* v. *West Norfolk and Wisbech A.H.A.*, *The Times*, 27 July 1983.
49. *Planned Parenthood of Missouri* v. *Danforth* 428 U.S. 52 (1976). In *re P (a Minor)* (1982) 80 L.G.R. 301, a girl of fifteen in care of a local authority desired abortion against her parents' wishes and was made a ward of court. The court permitted the abortion, not on the basis that she could consent to it, but because the judge thought this was in her best interests. Since the issue had been placed within the court's 'paternal' jurisdiction, which can override a child's wishes, this reasoning was probably inevitable. But it does not follow that, had an abortion been performed on her in compliance with the Abortion Act 1967, the lack of her parents' consent would have made it unlawful. See Freeman (1982), 146 *Justice of the Peace* 370.
50. Glendon (1981), p. 137.
51. Glendon (1981), pp. 135–6. Above, p. 96.
52. Maclean and Eekelaar (1983).
53. Rates are as at 1980/81.
54. This is avoided in Australia and New Zealand by a system of fixed sum rebates.
55. This happens in Australia and New Zealand, too, where the rebate diminishes in proportion to the earnings of the other spouse. In Britain, the Chancellor of the Exchequer has argued for the continuation of favourable tax treatment to married people on the basis of 'the mere fact of a spouse's financial dependence'. He rejected on the grounds of administrative complexity arguments that such treatment should be given only if one of the spouses had specific home responsibilities (such as the care of children or relatives) or was incapacitated or had completed bringing up the children. *The Taxation of Husband and Wife* (Cmnd. 8093, HMSO, 1980).
56. The Chancellor of the Exchequer has put forward a system of mandatory

independent taxation, but favours continuing allowances instead of a rebate (or cash allowance) system, which is rejected on the ground that it would increase public expenditure. A non- (or partially) earning spouse would be entitled to transfer his or her single allowance to the benefit of the earner, thus retaining the tax advantages of marriage for the one-earner family: *The Taxation of Husband and Wife* (Cmnd. 8093, HMSO, 1980).

57. Ogus and Barendt (1982), pp. 368–9.
58. Ogus and Barendt (1982), pp. 166–7.
59. Ogus and Barendt (1982), p. 178; Parker and Land (1978), pp. 340–1.
60. See above, pp. 149–50.
61. Parker and Land (1978); Land (1978).
62. See above, p. 89.
63. See Land (1978); Rossiter and Wicks (1982).

Chapter 12

1. Donzelot (1980), p. 20.
2. See Equal Opportunities Commission, '*I want to work . . . but what about the kids*' (1978); Jackson and Jackson (1979), pp. 175, 182. Nationally, there is demand for about twice as many day-care places as are available: Rimmer and Popay (1982), p. 50.
3. In West Germany in 1975 it has been reported that 45.6 per cent of children whose mothers were in employment were looked after by grandparents: Neidhardt (1978), p. 235.
4. Gordon and Kammeyer (1980). In Canada, of the women economically active in 1973 (some 38 per cent of all married women), about 9 per cent had children under two, 12 per cent had children between two and five, 16 per cent had children over five and the rest had no children under sixteen: Statistics Canada 1977, *Perspective Canada II*.
5. Land (1978), p. 261; above, p. 89.
6. See above, pp. 162–3.
7. Private, longer-term, fostering continues, however. It is subject to somewhat unsatisfactory supervision: see Holman (1973); Hoggett (1981), pp. 25–29.
8. Nurseries and Child-minders Regulation Act 1948; Health Services and Public Health Act 1968, s. 60.
9. Jackson and Jackson (1979).
10. Bryant *et al.* (1980).
11. Jackson and Jackson (1979), pp. 184–6.
12. Liljestrom (1978), pp. 43–5.
13. Vedel-Petersen (1978), p. 311; nor does the Soviet Union achieve institutional day-care for the majority of children under three: Glendon (1981), p. 133.
14. Ferge (1978).
15. Employment Protection (Consolidation) Act 1978, s. 60.
16. Employment Protection (Consolidation) Act 1978, s. 33. The date of return can be extended in certain circumstances.

240 NOTES TO PAGES 209–210

17. The maternity allowance is an insurance-based benefit payable from eleven weeks before the child's birth until seven weeks afterwards.
18. Employment Protection (Consolidation) Act 1978, ss. 34, 39.
19. See Equal Opportunities Commission (1979), pp. 10–14.
20. For a good discussion, see Law Commission (1980), para. 54.
21. Equal Opportunities Commission (1979), p. 15.
22. See Simpson (1978). Some 20 per cent of employed women leave their children alone after school and 27 per cent during the holidays.
23. Agell (1979), pp. 173–4.

BIBLIOGRAPHY

Abel, Richard (ed.) (1982) *The Politics of Informal Justice*, vols. 1 and 2 (New York, The Academic Press).

Adcock, Margaret and Richard White (1982) 'The Use of Section 3 Resolutions', 6 *Adoption and Fostering* 9.

Agell, Anders (1979) 'Social Security and Family Law in Sweden', in A. Samuels (ed.), *Social Security and Family Law* (U.K. Comparative Law Series No. 4).

Agell, Anders (1980) 'The Swedish Legislation on Marriage and Cohabitation: A Journey without a Destination', *Scandinavian Studies in Law* 11.

Agell, Anders (1980a) 'Cohabitation without Marriage in Swedish Law', in John M. Eekelaar and Sanford N. Katz (eds), *Marriage and Cohabitation in Contemporary Societies* (Toronto, Butterworths).

Alberta Institute for Law Research and Reform (1981) *Matrimonial Support Failures: Reasons, Profiles and Perceptions of Individuals Involved* (Edmonton, University of Alberta).

Aldgate, Jean (1976) 'The Child in Care and his Parents', 2 *Adoption and Fostering* 29.

Armitage, Andrew (1978) in Sheila B. Kamerman and Alfred J. Kahn, *Family Policy: Government and Families in Fourteen Countries* (New York, Columbia University Press).

Atkin W. R. (1981) 'Liable Relatives: The New State Role in Ordering Maintenance', 5 *Otago Law Review* 48.

Bailey, Rebecca (1978) 'Legal Recognition of *de facto* Relationships', 52 *Australian Law Journal* 174.

Bailey, Rebecca (1980) 'Principles of Property Distribution on Divorce – Compensation, Need or Community?', 54 *Australian Law Journal* 190.

Bala, Nicholas (1980) 'Consequences of Separation for Unmarried Couples: Canadian Developments', 6 *Queen's Law Journal* 72.

Bankowski, Z. and Geoff Mungham (1976) *Images of Law* (London, Routledge and Kegan Paul).

Barrington Baker, W., John Eekelaar, Colin Gibson and Susan Raikes (1977) *The Matrimonial Jurisdiction of Registrars* (Oxford, SSRC Centre for Socio-Legal Studies).

Barry, B. M. (1977) 'Justice between Generations', in P. M. S. Hacker and J.

Raz (eds), *Law, Morality and Society* (Oxford University Press).

Bates, F. (1976) 'The Changing Position of the Mother in Custody Cases: Some Comparative Developments', 6 *Family Law* 125.

Bates, F. (1978) 'Counselling and Reconciliation Provisions: An Exercise in Futility', 8 *Family Law* 248.

Baxter, Ian F. G. (1977) 'Recent Developments in Scandinavian Family Law', 26 *International and Comparative Law Quarterly* 150.

Beck, C., G. Glavis, S. Glover, M. Jenkins and R. Nardi (1978) 'The Rights of Children: A Trust Model', 46 *Fordham Law Review* 669.

Beckerman, Wilfred and Stephen Clark (1982) *Poverty and Social Security in Britain since 1961* (Oxford University Press).

Bell, Garry L. (1978) 'Inter-Spousal Violence, Discovery and Reporting', in John M. Eekelaar and Sanford N. Katz (eds), *Family Violence: An International and Interdisciplinary Study* (Toronto, Butterworth).

Berger Report (1975) *Report of the Royal Commission on Family and Children's Law* (Victoria, Government of British Columbia).

Birks, Peter (1974) 'Restitution for Services', *Current Legal Problems* 13.

Blake, J. (1961) *Family Structure in Jamaica* (New York, The Free Press).

Bloom, Bernard L., Stephen W. White and Shirley J. Asher (1979) 'Marital Disruption as a Stressful Life Event', in George Levinger and Oliver C. Moles (eds), *Divorce and Separation* (New York, Basic Books).

Bowlby, John (1951) *Maternal Care and Mental Health* (Geneva, World Health Organization).

Bowlby, John (1973) *Separation: Anxiety and Anger* (London, The Hogarth Press).

Bowles, S. (1973) 'Understanding Unequal Economic Opportunity', 62 *American Economic Review* 346.

Bradbrook, Adrian J. (1971) 'The Role of Judicial Discretion in Child Custody Adjudication in Ontario', 21 *University of Toronto Law Journal* 402.

Brown, L. Neville (1963) 'Cruelty without Culpability', 26 *Modern Law Review* 625.

Bryant, Bridget, Miriam Harris and Dee Newton (1980) *Children and Minders* (London, Grant McIntyre).

Caffey, J. (1946) 'Multiple fractures of the long bones of infants suffering from chronic haematoma', 56 *American Journal of Roentology* 163.

Carter, Hugh and Paul C. Glick (1976) *Marriage and Divorce: A Social and Economic Study* (Cambridge, Harvard University Press).

Chambers, David L. (1979) *Making Fathers Pay: the Enforcement of Child Support* (University of Chicago Press).

Cherlin, A. J. (1981) *Marriage, Divorce, Remarriage: Trends in the United States* (Cambridge, Harvard University Press).

Chester, R. (1971) 'Health and Marriage Breakdown: experience of a sample of divorced women', 25 *British Journal of Preventive Medicine* 231.

Chester, R. (1971a) 'The Duration of Marriage to Divorce', 22 *British Journal of Sociology* 172.

Chester R. (1971b) 'Contemporary Trends in the Stability of English Marriage', 3 *Journal of Biosocial Science* 389.

Christensen, H. T. (1969) 'Cultural Relativism and Pre-marital Sex Norms',

25 *American Sociological Review* 31.

Clarke, Ann M. and A. D. B. Clarke (eds) (1976) *Early Experience: Myth and Evidence* (London, Open Books).

Collins, Hugh (1982) *Marxism and Law* (Oxford, Clarendon Press).

Cooper, David (1971) *The Death of the Family* (Harmondsworth: Penguin Books).

Crane, F. R.and J. Levin (1966–7) 'The Rationalization of Family Property Law', 9 *Journal of the Society of Public Teachers of Law* 238.

Craven, Edward, Lesley Rimmer and Malcolm Wicks (1982) *Family Issues and Public Policy* (London, Study Commission on the Family).

Crellin, Eileen, M. L. Kellmer Pringle and P. West (1971) *Born Illegitimate* (London, National Foundation for Educational Research in England and Wales).

Cretney, S. M. (1979) *Principles of Family Law* (3rd edn) (London, Sweet and Maxwell).

Crouch, Richard (1982) 'Divorce Mediation and Legal Ethics', 16 *Family Law Quarterly* 219, reprinted in John M. Eekelaar and Sanford N. Katz, *The Resolution of Family Conflict: Comparative Legal Perspectives* (Toronto, Butterworth, forthcoming).

Curtis Report (1946) *Report of the Committee on the Care of Children*, Cmnd. 6922 (London, HMSO).

Davenport, W. (1961) 'The Family System in Jamaica', 10 *Social and Economic Studies* 420.

Davids, Leo (1980) 'Family Change in Canada 1971–76', 42 *Journal of Marriage and the Family* 177.

Davis, Gwynn (1980) *Research to Monitor the Bristol Courts Family Conciliation Service* (University of Bristol, Department of Social Administration).

Davis, Gwynn, Alison MacLeod and Mervyn Murch (1982) 'Special Procedure in Divorce and the Solicitor's Role', 12 *Family Law* 39.

Davis, Gwynn (1983) 'Conciliation and the Professions', 13 *Family Law* 6.

Davis, Gwynn, Alison MacLeod and Mervyn Murch (1983) 'Undefended Divorce: Should Section 41 of the Matrimonial Causes Act 1973 be Repealed?', 46 *Modern Law Review* 121.

Day, Cyril and Alfred Leeding (1980) *Access to Birth Records* (London, Association of British Adoption and Fostering Agencies).

Deech, Ruth (1977) 'The Principles of Maintenance', 7 *Family Law* 229.

Deech, Ruth (1980) 'The Case against Legal Recognition of Cohabitation', in John M. Eekelaar and Sanford N. Katz (eds), *Marriage and Cohabitation in Contemporary Societies* (Toronto, Butterworths).

Deech, Ruth (1982) 'Financial Relief: The Retreat from Precedent and Principle', 98 *Law Quarterly Rev.* 621.

de Mause, Lloyd (1974) 'The Evolution of Childhood', in Lloyd de Mause (ed.), *The History of Childhood* (New York, The Psychohistory Press).

Devlin, Patrick (1965) *The Enforcement of Morals* (Oxford University Press).

Dickens, Bernard (1981) 'The Modern Function and Limits of Parental Rights', 97 *Law Quarterly Review* 462.

Dingwall, Robert, John Eekelaar and Topsy Murray (1983) *The Protection of Children: State Intervention and Family Life* (Oxford, Basil Blackwell).

Dinnage, R. and M. L. Kellmer Pringle (1967) *Residential Child Care: Facts and Fallacies* (London, Longmans).

Doig, Barbara (1982) *The Nature and Scale of Aliment and Financial Provision on Divorce in Scotland* (Edinburgh, Central Research Unit, Scottish Office).

Donzelot, Jacques (1980) *The Policing of Families: Welfare versus the State* (London, Hutchinson).

Douglas, J. W. B., J. M. Ross and H. R. Simpson (1968) *All Our Future* (London, Peter Davies).

Dror, Yo (1959) 'Law and Social Change', 33 *Tulane Law Review* 749.

Duncan, William (1979) *The Case for Divorce in the Irish Republic* (Dublin, Irish Council for Civil Liberties).

Duncan, William (1980) 'Supporting the Institution of Marriage in the Republic of Ireland', in John M. Eekelaar and Sanford N. Katz (eds), *Marriage and Cohabitation in Contemporary Societies* (Toronto, Butterworths).

Dunnell, K. (1979) *Family Formation 1976* (Office of Population, Censuses and Surveys, London, HMSO).

Eekelaar, John (1971) *Family Security and Family Breakdown* (Harmondsworth: Penguin Books).

Eekelaar, J. M. (1973) 'What are Parental Rights?', 89 *Law Quarterly Review* 210.

Eekelaar, J. M. (1976) 'Public Law and Private Rights: The Finer Proposals', *Public Law* 64.

Eekelaar, John and Eric Clive, with Karen Clarke and Susan Raikes (1977) *Custody after Divorce* (Oxford, SSRC Centre for Socio-Legal Studies).

Eekelaar, J. M. (1979) 'Some Principles of Financial and Property Adjustment on Divorce', 95 *Law Quarterly Review* 253.

Eekelaar, John, Robert Dingwall and Topsy Murray (1982) 'Victims or Threats? Children in Care Proceedings', *Journal of Social Welfare Law* 68.

Eekelaar, John (1982a) 'Children in Divorce: Some Further Data', *Oxford Journal of Legal Studies* 63.

Eekelaar, John and Mavis Maclean (1983) *Financial Provision on Divorce: A Re-appraisal* (Oxford, SSRC Centre for Socio-Legal Studies).

Elkin, Meyer (1973) 'Conciliation Courts – The Reintegration of Disintegrating Families', 22 *The Family Co-ordinator* 63.

Elston, E., J. Fuller and M. Murch (1975) 'Judicial Hearings of Undefended Divorce Petitions', 38 *Modern Law Review* 609.

Engels, F. (1884) *The Origin of the Family, Private Property and the State* (London, Lawrence and Wishart, 1972 edn.).

Equal Opportunities Commission (1979) '*I want a baby . . . but what about my job?*' (Manchester, Equal Opportunities Commission).

Ermisch, J. F. (1981) 'Economic Opportunities, Marriage Squeezes and the Propensity to Marry: An Economic Analysis of Period Marriage Rates in England and Wales', 35 *Population Studies* 347.

Evatt, The Hon, Justice (1977) 'Developments in Family Law in Australia', Paper presented to the Commonwealth Law Conference, Edinburgh.

Fast, I. and A. C. Cain (1966) 'The Step-parent role: Potential for Disturbances in Family Functioning', 36 *American Journal of Orthopsychiatry* 485.

Ferge, Zsusza (1978), in Sheila B. Kamerman and Alfred J. Kahn (eds), *Family Policy: Government and Families in Fourteen Countries* (New York: Columbia University Press).

Ferri, Elsa (1976) *Growing up in a One-Parent Family* (London, National Foundation for Educational Research in England and Wales).

Festy, Patrick (1980) 'Aspects démographiques de la formation de la famille en Europe occidentale', in John M. Eekelaar and Sanford N. Katz (eds), *Marriage and Cohabitation in Contemporary Societies* (Toronto, Butterworths).

Field-Fisher Report (1974) *Report of the Committee of Inquiry into the Care and Supervision provided for Maria Colwell* (London, Department of Health and Social Security).

Finer Report (1974) *Report of the Committee on One-Parent Families*, vols. 1 and 2, Cmnd. 5629 (London, HMSO).

Finlay, H. A. (1975) 'Reluctant but Inevitable: The Retreat of Matrimonial Fault', 38 *Modern Law Review* 153.

Finlay, H. A. (1979) *Family Law in Australia*, 2nd edn (Sydney, Butterworths).

Finnis, John (1980) *Natural Law and Natural Rights* (Oxford, Clarendon Press).

Firestone, Shulamith (1970) *The Dialectic of Sex* (New York, William Morrow).

Folberg, H. Jay and Marva Graham (1979) 'Joint Custody of Children following Divorce', 12 *University of California Davis Law Review* 523.

Fontana, V. J. and D. J. Besharov (1977) *The Maltreated Child* (Charles C. Thomas).

Foster, Henry H. and Doris J. Freed (1972) 'A Bill of Rights for Children', 6 *Family Law Quarterly* 343.

Fox, R. (1967) *Kinship and Marriage* (Harmondsworth, Penguin Books).

Freeman, M. D. A. (1978) 'The Phenomenon of Wife-Battering and the Legal and Social Response in England', in John M. Eekelaar and Sanford N. Katz (eds), *Family Violence: An International and Interdisciplinary Study* (Toronto, Butterworths).

Freeman, M. D. A. (1979) *Violence in the Home* (London, Saxon House).

Freeman, M. D. A. (1980) 'Removing Babies at Birth: A Questionable Practice', 10 *Family Law* 131.

Freeman, M. D. A. (1982) 'Questioning the De-Legalization Movement in Family Law: Do we really want a Family Court?', Paper presented to the Fourth World Conference of the International Society on Family Law, Harvard, June 1982, reprinted in John M. Eekelaar and Sanford N. Katz, *The Resolution of Family Conflict: Comparative Legal Perspectives* (Toronto, Butterworths, forthcoming).

Freeman, M. D. A. (1983) 'Freedom and the Welfare State: Child-Rearing, Parental Autonomy and State Intervention', *Journal of Social Welfare Law* 70.

Geiger, H. (1968) *The Family in Soviet Russia* (Cambridge, Harvard University Press).

Gelles, Richard (1974) *The Violent Home* (Beverly Hills, Sage Publications).

Gelles, Richard (1979) *Family Violence* (Beverly Hills, Sage Publications).

George, V. (1970) *Foster Care: Theory and Practice* (London, Routledge and Kegan Paul).

Gibson, C. (1974) 'The Association between Divorce and Social Class in England and Wales', 25 *British Journal of Sociology* 79.

Gibson, C. (1980) 'Divorce and the Recourse to Legal Aid', 43 *Modern Law Review* 609.

Gibson, C. (1982) 'Maintenance in the Magistrates' Courts in the 1980s', 12 *Family Law* 138.

Gil, David G. (1975) 'Unraveling Child Abuse', 45 *American Journal of Orthopsychiatry* 347.

Gil, David G. (1978) 'Societal Violence in Families' in John M. Eekelaar and Sanford N. Katz (eds) *Family Violence: An International and Interdisciplinary Study* (Toronto, Butterworths).

Gill, Derek (1977) *Illegitimacy, Sexuality and the Status of Women* (Oxford, Basil Blackwell).

Glendon, Mary Ann (1977) *State, Law and Family* (Amsterdam, North-Holland).

Glendon, Mary Ann (1981) *The New Family and the New Property* (Toronto, Butterworths).

Glenn, Norval D. and Charles N. Weaver (1977) 'The Marital Happiness of Remarried Divorced Persons', 39 *Journal of Marriage and the Family* 331.

Glick, Paul C. and Graham B. Spanier (1980) 'Married and Unmarried Cohabitation in the United States', 42 *Journal of Marriage and the Family* 19.

Goldstein, Joseph, Anna Freud and Albert J. Solnit (1973) *Beyond the Best Interests of the Child* (New York, The Free Press).

Goldstein, Joseph (1976) 'Foster Care and Adoption in an Ideal Placement System', in F. Bates (ed.) *The Child and the Law* (New York, Oceana Publications).

Goldstein, Joseph, Anna Freud and Albert J. Solnit (1979) *Before the Best Interests of the Child* (New York, The Free Press) (1980) (London, Burnett Books).

Goldthorpe, John H. *et al.* (1980) *Social Mobility and Class Structure in Modern Britain* (Oxford, Clarendon Press).

Gordon, Henry A. and K. C. W. Kammeyer (1980) 'The Gainful Employment of Women with Small Children', 42 *Journal of Marriage and the Family* 327.

Gorecki, Jan (1980) 'Moral Premises of Contemporary Divorce Laws: Western and Eastern Europe and the United States', in John M. Eekelaar and Sanford N. Katz (eds), *Marriage and Cohabitation in Contemporary Societies* (Toronto, Butterworths).

Gosse, R. and J. Payne (1975) 'Children of Divorcing Spouses', in Law Reform Commission of Canada, *Studies in Divorce* (Ottawa, Information Canada).

Gray, Kevin J. (1977) *The Reallocation of Property on Divorce* (Abingdon, Professional Books Ltd).

Greenberg, D. and D. Wolf (1982) 'The Economic Consequences of Experiencing Parental Marital Disruption', 4 *Children and Youth Services Review* 141.

Gross, Beatrice and R. Gross (1977) *The Children's Rights Movement* (New York, Anchor Press/Doubleday).

Habbakuk, H. J. (1950) 'Marriage Settlements in the Eighteenth Century', 32 *Transactions of the Royal Historical Society* 50.

Hahlo H. R. (1975) 'Reform of the Divorce Act 1968 (Canada)', in Law Reform Commission of Canada, *Studies in Divorce* (Ottawa, Information Canada).

Hall, M. H. (1975) 'A View from the Emergency and Accident Department', in Alfred White Franklin (ed.), *Concerning Child Abuse* (London, Churchill Livingstone).

Hampton, Robert (1975) 'Marital Disruption: Some Social and Economic Consequences', in Greg J. Duncan and James Morgan (eds), *Five Thousand American Families – Patterns of Economic Progress* (University of Michigan, Institute of Social Research).

Hart, Nicky (1976) *When Marriage Ends: A Study of Status Passage* (London, Tavistock Publications).

Haskey, John (1982) 'The proportion of marriages ending in divorce', 27 *Population Trends* 4.

Haskey, John (1983) 'Children of divorcing couples', 31 *Population Trends* 20.

Henderson Report (1975) *Poverty in Australia: Report of the Commission of Inquiry into Poverty* (Canberra, Australian Government Publishing Service).

Hetherington, E. M., M. Cox and R. Cox (1979) 'Family Interaction and the social, emotional and cognitive development of children following divorce', in V. Vaughan and T. Brazelton, *The Family: Setting Priorities* (New York, Science and Medicine).

Hoath, David C. (1981) 'The Council Tenant and the Housing Act 1980: Some Implications for Members of his Family', 11 *Family Law* 195.

Hoffman, Saul (1977) 'Marital Instability and the Economic Status of Women', 14 *Demography* 67.

Hoggett, Brenda (1981) *Parents and Children* (London, Sweet and Maxwell).

Holland, W. H. (1978) 'Reform of Matrimonial Property Law in Canada', 1 *Canadian Journal of Family Law* 3.

Holman, Robert (1973) *Trading in Children* (London, Routledge and Kegan Paul).

Holt, John (1973) *Freedom and Beyond* (Harmondsworth, Penguin Books).

Houghton Report (1972) *Report of the Departmental Committee on the Adoption of Children*, Cmnd. 5107 (London, HMSO).

Houlgate, Lawrence D. (1980) *The Child and the State: A Normative Theory of Juvenile Rights* (Baltimore, Johns Hopkins University Press).

Housden, L. G. (1955) *The Prevention of Cruelty to Children* (London, Jonathan Cape).

Illich, Ivan (1971) *Deschooling Society* (Harmondsworth, Penguin Books).

Irvine, Elizabeth (1980) *The Family in the Kibbutz* (London, Study Commission on the Family, Occasional Paper No. 4).

Irving, Howard H., Michael Benjamin, Peter E. Boehm and Grant MacDonald (1981) 'A Study of Conciliation Counselling in the Family Court of Toronto: Implications for Socio-Legal Practice', in Howard H. Irving (ed.), *Family Law: An Interdisciplinary Perspective* (Toronto: Carswells).

Jackson, Brian and Sonia Jackson (1979) *Childminder* (London, Routledge and Kegan Paul).

Jaffe, Peter and Judy Thompson (1978) 'The Family Consultant Service with the London (Ontario) Police Force', in John M. Eekelaar and Sanford N. Katz (eds), *Family Violence: An International and Interdisciplinary Study* (Toronto, Butterworths).

James, Selma, 'The American Family: Decay and Rebirth', in Edith Hoshina Altbach (ed.) *From Feminism to Liberation* (Cambridge Schenkman Publishing Co.).

Jencks, C. *et al.* (1972) *Inequality: A Reassessment of the Effect of Family and Schooling in America* (New York, Basic Books).

Kahn-Freund, Otto (1971) *Matrimonial Property: Where do we go from here?* Joseph Unger Memorial Lecture, University of Birmingham.

Kamerman, Sheila B. and Alfred J. Kahn (eds) (1978) *Family Policy: Government and Families in Fourteen Countries* (New York, Columbia University Press).

Katz, Sanford N. (1971) *When Parents Fail* (Boston, Beacon Press).

Kempe, C. Henry (1962) 'The Battered Child Syndrome', 181 *Journal of the American Medical Association* 17.

Kiralfy, A. K. R. (ed.) (1972) *Comparative Law of Matrimonial Property* (Leiden: A. W. Sijthoff).

Kovacs, Dorothy (1974) 'Getting Blood out of Stones: Problems of Enforcement of Maintenance Orders in Magistrates' Courts', 1 *Monash Law Review* 67.

Kovacs, Dorothy (1980) 'Matrimonial Property Reform in Australia: The "Home and Chattels" Expedient. Studies in the Art of Compromise', 6 *University of Tasmania Law Journal* 227.

Krause, Harry D. (1971) *Illegitimacy: Law and Social Policy* (Indianopolis: Bobbs Merrill).

Krause, Harry D. (1981) *Child Support in America: The Legal Perspective* (Charlottesville: The Michie Co.).

Laing, R. D. (1971) *The Politics of the Family and other Essays* (London, Tavistock Publications).

Land, Hilary (1978) 'Who care for the Family?', 7 *Journal of Social Policy* 257.

Landsman, Kim J. and Martha L. Minow (1978) 'Lawyering for the Child: Principles of Representation in Custody and Visitation Disputes arising from Divorce', 87 *Yale Law Journal* 1126.

Latey (1967) *Report of the Committee on the Age of Majority*, Cmnd. 3342 (London, HMSO).

Law Commission (1966) *Reform of the Grounds of Divorce: The Field of Choice*, Cmnd. 3123 (London, HMSO).

Law Commission (1973) *Family Law: First Report on Family Property: A New Approach*, Law Com. No. 52 (London, HMSO).

Law Commission (1978) *Family Law: Third Report on Family Property: The Matrimonial Home (Co-ownership and Occupation Rights) and Household Goods*, Law Com. No. 86 (London, HMSO).

Law Commission (1979) *Family Law: Illegitimacy*, Working Paper No. 74 (London, HMSO).

Law Commission (1980) *Family Law: The Financial Consequences of Divorce: The*

Basic Policy, Law Com. No. 103 (London, HMSO).
Law Commission (1981) *Family Law: The Financial Consequences of Divorce*, Law Com. No. 112 (London, HMSO).
Law Commission (1982) *Family Law: Illegitimacy*, Law Com. No. 118 (London, HMSO).
Law Commission (1982a) *Property Law: The Implications of Williams and Glyn's Bank v. Boland*, Law Com. No. 115 (London, HMSO).
Law Reform Commission of Canada (1976) *Family Law: Enforcement of Maintenance Orders/Obligations*, Study Paper (Ottawa, Information Canada).
Law Reform Commission of Canada (1976a) *Family Law* (Ottawa, Information Canada).
Law Society (1979) *A Better Way Out* (London, The Law Society).
Layard, R. (1978) *The Causes of Poverty*, Royal Commission on the Distribution of Income and Wealth, Background Paper No. 6 (London, HMSO).
Leete, Richard (1979) *Changing Patterns of Family Formation and Dissolution in England and Wales 1964–76* (London Office of Population, Censuses and Surveys, HMSO).
Leete, Richard and Susan Anthony (1979) 'Divorce and Remarriage: A Record Linkage Study', *Population Trends* No. 16 (London, HMSO).
Liljestrom, Rita (1978) in Sheila B. Kamerman and Alfred J. Kahn (eds), *Family Policy: Government and Families in Fourteen Countries* (New York: Columbia University Press).
Littner, Ner (1973) 'The Effects on a Child of Family Disruption and Separation from one or both Parents', 11 *Reports of Family Law* 1.
Longmate, Norman (1974) *The Workhouse* (London, Temple Smith).
Lynch, Margaret A. and Jacqueline Roberts (1982) *Consequences of Child Abuse* (London, Academic Press).
MacDougall, Donald J. (1982) 'Negotiated Settlement of Family Disputes', Paper presented to the Fourth World Conference of the International Society on Family Law, reprinted in John M. Eekelaar and Sanford N. Katz, *The Resolution of Family Conflict: Comparative Legal Perspectives* (Toronto, Butterworths, forthcoming).
MacKeith, Ronald (1975) 'Speculations on some possible long-term effects', in Alfred White Franklin (ed.), *Concerning Child Abuse* (London, Churchill Livingstone).
Maclean, Mavis and John Eekelaar (1983) *Children and Divorce: Economic Factors* (Oxford, SSRC Centre for Socio-Legal Studies); *Journal of Social Policy* (forthcoming).
MacQueen, John Fraser (1849) *The Rights and Liabilities of Husband and Wife*.
Maidment, Susan (1975) 'Access Conditions in Custody Orders', 2 *British Journal of Law and Society* 182.
Maidment, Susan (1976) 'A Study in Child Custody', 6 *Family Law* 195 and 236.
Maidment, Susan (1978) 'The Law's Response to Marital Violence: A Comparison between England and the USA', in John M. Eekelaar and Sanford N. Katz (eds), *Family Violence: An International and Interdisciplinary*

Study (Toronto, Butterworths).

Maidment, Susan (1981) *Child Custody: What Chance for Fathers?* (London, National Council for One-Parent Families).

Maidment, Susan (1981a) '*Dipper* v. *Dipper*: Custody Revisited', 44 *Modern Law Review* 341.

Mair, Lucy (1971) *Marriage* (Harmondsworth, Penguin Books).

Makabe, Tomoko (1980) 'Provincial Variations in Divorce Rates: A Canadian Case', 42 *Journal of Marriage and the Family* 171.

Manners, A. J. and Rauta, I. (1981) *Family Property in Scotland* (London, HMSO).

Marcus, Maria L. (1981) 'Conjugal Violence: The Law of Force and the Force of Law', 69 *California Law Review* 1657.

Marsden, D. (1973) *Mothers Alone* (Harmondsworth, Penguin Books).

Marsden, Dennis and David Owens (1975) 'The Jekyll and Hyde Marriages', *New Society* 8 May 333.

McCarthy Report (1972) *Social Security in New Zealand: Report of the Royal Commission of Inquiry* (Wellington, Government Printer).

McGregor, O. R. (1957) *Divorce in England: A Centenary Study* (London, Heinemann).

McGregor, O. R., L. Blom-Cooper and C. Gibson (1970) *Separated Spouses* (London, Duckworth).

Mead, Margaret (1931) *Growing up in New Guinea* (London, Routledge and Kegan Paul).

Meijer, M. J. (1971) *Marriage Law and Policy in the Chinese People's Republic* (Hong Kong University Press).

Merry, Sally E. (1982) 'The Social Organization of Mediation in Non-Industrial Societies: Implications for Informal Community Justice in America', in Richard L. Abel (ed.), *The Politics of Informal Justice* (New York, Academic Press), vol. 2.

Millett, Kate (1969) *Sexual Politics* (London, Rupert Hart-Davis).

Mitchell, Juliet (1971) *Women's Estate* (Harmondsworth, Penguin Books).

Mnookin, Robert (1975) 'Child Custody Adjudication: Judicial Functions in the Face of Indeterminacy', 39 *Law and Contemporary Problems* 226.

Mnookin, Robert and L. Kornhauser (1979) 'Bargaining in the Shadow of the Law: The Case of Divorce', 88 *Yale Law Journal* 950; 32 *Current Legal Problems* 65.

Mnookin, Robert (1982) 'Divorce Bargaining: The Limits of Private Ordering'. Paper presented to the Fourth World Conference of the International Society on Family Law, reprinted in John M. Eekelaar and Sanford N. Katz (eds), *The Resolution of Family Conflict: Comparative Legal Perspectives* (Toronto, Butterworths, forthcoming).

Moore, Kristin A. and Linda J. Waite (1981) 'Marital Dissolution, Early Motherhood and Early Marriage', 60 *Social Forces* 20.

Morgan, D. H. J. (1975) *Social Theory and the Family* (London, Routledge and Kegan Paul).

Morgan, Patricia (1975) *Child Care: Sense and Fable* (London, Temple Smith).

Morris, Allison, Henri Giller, Elizabeth Szwed and Hugh Geach (1980) *Justice for Children* (London, Macmillan).

Mortimer Report (1966) *Putting Asunder* (SPCK).

Morton Report (1956) *Report of the Royal Commission on Marriage and Divorce*, Cmnd. 9678 (London, HMSO).

Muller-Freienfels, W. (1979) 'The Marriage Law Reform of 1976 in the Federal Republic of Germany', 28 *International and Comparative Law Quarterly* 184.

Munck, Noe (1982) 'Compromise as the Aim of Danish Divorce Procedures', Paper presented to the Fourth World Conference of the International Society on Family Law, reprinted in John M. Eekelaar and Sanford N. Katz, *The Resolution of Family Conflict: Comparative Legal Perspectives* (Toronto, Butterworth, forthcoming).

Murch, Mervyn (1980) *Justice and Welfare in Divorce* (London, Sweet and Maxwell).

Neidhardt, Friedhelm (1978) in Sheila B. Kamerman and Alfred J. Kahn (eds), *Family Policy: Government and Families in Fourteen Countries* (New York, Columbia University Press).

Nozick, Robert (1975) *Anarchy, State and Utopia* (New York, Basic Books).

O'Donovan, Katherine (1982) 'Wife Sale and Desertion as Alternatives to Judicial Marriage Dissolution', Paper presented to the Fourth World Conference of the International Society on Family Law, reprinted in John M. Eekelaar and Sanford N. Katz, *The Resolution of Family Conflict: Comparative Legal Perspectives* (Toronto, Butterworths, forthcoming).

Ogus, A. I. and E. M. Barendt (1982) *The Law of Social Security* (London, Butterworths).

O'Neill, F. T. (1974) 'Divorce: A Judicial or Administrative Process', 4 *Family Law* 71.

Packman, Jean (1976) *The Child's Generation* (Oxford and London, Basil Blackwell and Martin Robinson).

Pahl, Jan (1982) 'The Police Response to Battered Women', *Journal of Social Welfare Law* 337.

Parker, R. and H. Land (1978) in Sheila B. Kamerman and Alfred J. Kahn (eds), *Family Policy: Government and Families in Fourteen Countries* (New York, Columbia University Press).

Parnas, R. I (1971) 'Police Discretion and Diversion of Incidents of Intrafamily Violence', 36 *Law and Contemporary Problems* 539.

Parnas, R. I. (1978) 'The Relevance of Criminal Law to Interspousal Violence', in John M. Eekelaar and Sanford N. Katz (eds), *Family Violence: An International and Interdisciplinary Study* (Toronto, Butterworths).

Parsons, T. and R. F. Bales (1955) *Family, Socialization and Interaction Process* (New York, The Free Press).

Parsons, T. (1959) 'The Social Structure of the Family', in Ruth Nanda Anshen (ed.), *The Family: Its Function and Destiny* (New York, Harper Brothers).

Payne, Julien D. and Kenneth L. Kallish (1981) 'A Behavioural Science and Legal Analysis of Access to the Child in the Post-Separation/Divorce Family', 13 *Ottawa Law Review* 215.

Pearl, David (1978) 'The Legal Implications of a Relationship outside Marriage', 37 *Cambridge Law Journal* 252.

Pearl, David (1980) 'Cohabitation in English Social Security Legislation', in John M. Eekelaar and Sanford N. Katz (eds), *Marriage and Cohabitation in Contemporary Societies* (Toronto, Butterworths).

Pearson, Jessica (1982) 'Custody Mediation in Denver: Shorter and Longer Term Effects' Paper presented to the Fourth World Conference of the International Society on Family Law, reprinted in John Eekelaar and Sanford N. Katz (eds), *The Resolution of Family Conflict: Comparative Legal Perspectives* (Toronto, Butterworths, forthcoming).

Pedersen, I. (1965) 'Matrimonial Property Law in Denmark', 28 *Modern Law Review* 137.

Pfohl, S. J. (1977) 'The Discovery of Child Abuse', 24 *Social Problems* 310.

Pinchbeck, Ivy and Margaret Hewitt (1969) (1973) *Children in English Society*, vols. 1 and 2 (London, Routledge and Kegan Paul).

Pizzey, Erin (1974) *Scream Quietly or the Neighbours will hear* (Harmondsworth, Penguin Books).

Pottick, F. J. (1978) 'Tort Damages for the Injured Homemaker: Opportunity Cost or Replacement Cost?', 50 *Univ. of Colorado Law Review* 59.

Prentice, Beverly (1979) 'Divorce, Children and Custody: A Quantitative Study of Three Legal Factors', 2 *Canadian Journal of Family Law* 351.

Radbill, Samuel X. (1974) 'A History of Child Abuse and Infanticide', in Ray E. Helter and C. Henry Kempe (eds), *The Battered Child*, 2nd edn. (University of Chicago Press).

Rheinstein, Max (1972) *Marriage Stability, Divorce and the Law* (University of Chicago Press).

Richards, M. P. M. (1982) 'Post-Divorce Arrangements for Children: A Psychological Perspective', *Journal of Social Welfare Law* 133.

Richards, M. P. M. and M. Dyson (1982) *Separation, Divorce and the Development of Children: A Review* (Cambridge, Child-Care and Development Group).

Rimmer, Lesley (1981) *Families in Focus* (London, Study Commission on the Family).

Rimmer, Lesley and Jennie Popay (1982) *Employment Trends and the Family* (London, Study Commission on the Family).

Rosen, Harvey (1974) 'The Monetary Value of a Housewife: A Replacement Cost Approach', 33 *American Journal of Economics and Society* 65.

Rosen, Rhona (1979) 'Children of Divorce: An Evaluation of Two Common Assumptions', 2 *Canadian Journal of Family Law* 403.

Rossiter, Chris and Malcolm Wicks (1982) *Crisis or Challenge: Family Care, Elderly People and Social Policy* (London, Study Commission on the Family).

Roussel, Louis and Odile Bourgignon (1978) *Générations nouvelles et mariage traditionnel* (Paris, Presses Universitaires France).

Rowbotham, Sheila (1972) *Women, Resistance and Revolution* (New York, Pantheon Books).

Rowe, June and Lydia Lambert (1973) *Children Who Wait* (London, Association of British Adoption and Fostering Agencies).

Rowntree, G. (1964) 'Some Aspects of Marriage Breakdown in Britain in the last Thirty Years', 18 *Population Studies* 147.

Ruddock Report (1980) *Family Law in Australia: A Report of the Joint Select Committee on the Family Law Act*, vols. 1 and 2 (Canberra, Australian

Government Publishing Service).

Rutter, Michael (1972) *Maternal Deprivation Re-assessed* (Harmondsworth, Penguin Books).

Rutter, Michael (1976) 'Parent–child separation; psychological effects on the children', in Ann M. Clarke and A. D. B. Clarke (eds), *Early Experience: Myth and Evidence* (London, Open Books).

Rwezaura, Barthazar (1982) 'Some Aspects of Mediation and Conciliation in the Settlement of Matrimonial Disputes in Tanzania', Paper presented to the Fourth World Conference of the International Society on Family Law, reprinted in John M. Eekelaar and Sanford N. Katz (eds), *The Resolution of Family Conflict* (Toronto, Butterworths, forthcoming).

Samuels, Alec (1983) 'Can a Minor (under 16) Consent to a Medical Operation?' 13 *Family Law* 30.

Schlesinger, B. (1968) 'Family Patterns in the English-speaking Caribbean', 30 *Journal of Marriage and the Family* 136.

Schmidt, Torben Svenne (1982) 'The Scandinavian Law of Procedure in Matrimonial Causes', Paper presented to the Fourth World Conference of the International Society on Family Law, reprinted in John M. Eekelaar and Sanford N. Katz, *The Resolution of Family Conflict* (Butterworths, Toronto, forthcoming).

Scott, Hilda (1976) *Women and Socialism* (London, Allison and Busby).

Scottish Law Commission (1981) *Family Law: Report on Aliment and Financial Provision*, Scot. Law Com. No. 67 (London, HMSO).

Sepler, Harvey J. (1981) 'Measuring the Effects of No-Fault Divorce Laws across Fifty States: Quantifying a Zeitgeist', 15 *Family Law Quarterly* 65.

Shaw, Martin and Kathryn Lebens (1976) 'Children between Families', 2 *Adoption and Fostering* 17.

Shone, M. A. (1979) 'Principles of matrimonial property sharing: Alberta's new Act', 17 *Alberta Law Review* 143.

Shorter, Edward (1976) *The Making of the Modern Family* (London, Collins).

Simpson, Robin (1978) *Day Care for School Age Children* (Manchester, Equal Opportunities Commission).

Skegg, P. D. (1973) 'Consent to Medical Procedures in Minors', 36 *Modern Law Review* 370.

Smith, Elizabeth J. (1981) 'Non-Judicial Resolution of Custody and Visitation Disputes', in H. H. Irving (ed.) *Family Law: An Interdisciplinary Perspective* (Toronto, Carswell).

Sorensen, Annemette and Maurice MacDonald (1982) 'Does Child Support Support Children?' 4 *Children and Youth Services Review* 53.

Spanier, Graham B. and Paul C. Glick (1981) 'Marital Instability in the United States: Some Correlates and Recent Changes', 30 *Family Relations* 329.

Steele, B. F. and C. B. Pollock (1968) 'A Psychiatric Study of Parents who Abuse their Children', in C. Henry Kempe and Ray A. Helfer (eds), *The Battered Child* (University of Chicago Press).

Stone, Lawrence (1960–1) 'Marriage among the English Nobility in the Sixteenth and Seventeenth Centuries', 3 *Comparative Studies in Society and History* 182.

Stone, Lawrence (1977) *The Family, Sex and Marriage in England 1500–1800* (London, Weidenfeld and Nicolson).

Stone, O. M. (1969) 'The New Fundamental Principles of Soviet Family Law and their Social Background', 18 *International and Comparative Law Quarterly* 392.

Stone, O. M. (1977) *Family Law* (London, Macmillans).

Stone, O. M. (1982) *The Child's Voice in the Court of Law* (London, Butterworths).

Stott, D. H. (1977) 'Children in the Womb: the Effect of Stress', *New Society* 19 May 329.

Straus, Murray A. (1978) 'Wife-Beating: How Common and Why?', in John M. Eekelaar and Sanford N. Katz (eds), *Family Violence: An International and Interdisciplinary Study* (Toronto, Butterworths).

Study Commission on the Family (1981) *Family Finances* (London, Study Commission on the Family).

Study Commission on the Family (1982) *Values and the Changing Family* (London, Study Commission on the Family).

Sweet, James A. (1977) 'Demography and the Family', 3 *Annual Review of Sociology* 363.

Thornes, Barbara and Jean Collard (1979) *Who Divorces?* (London, Routledge and Kegan Paul).

Tizard, Barbara and Judith Rees (1976) 'A Comparison of the Effects of Adoption, Restoration to the Natural Mother and Continued Institutionalisation on the Cognitive Development of Four-Year-Old Children', in Ann M. Clarke and A. D. B. Clarke (eds), *Early Experience: Myth and Evidence* (London, Open Books).

Tizard, Barbara (1977) *Adoption: A Second Chance* (London, Open Books).

Todd, J. E. and L. M. Jones (1972) *Matrimonial Property* (London, HMSO).

Tottie, Lars (1980) 'The Elimination of Fault in Swedish Divorce Law', in John M. Eekelaar and Sanford N. Katz (eds), *Marriage and Cohabitation in Contemporary Societies* (Toronto, Butterworths).

Triseliotis, John (1973) *In Search of Origins* (Boston, Beacon Press).

Trost, Jan (1980) 'Cohabitation without Marriage in Sweden', in John M. Eekelaar and Sanford N. Katz (eds), *Marriage and Cohabitation in Contemporary Societies* (Toronto, Butterworths).

van Rees, Rob (1978) 'Five Years of Child Abuse as a Symptom of Family Problems', in John M. Eekelaar and Sanford N. Katz (eds), *Family Violence: An International and Interdisciplinary Study* (Toronto, Butterworths).

van Stolk, Mary (1972) *The Battered Child in Canada* (McClelland and Steward).

Vedel-Petersen, Jacob (1978) in Sheila B. Kamerman and Alfred J. Kahn (eds), *Family Policy: Government and Families in Fourteen Countries* (New York, Columbia University Press).

Wald, Michael (1975) 'State Intervention on behalf of "Neglected" Children: A Search for Realistic Standards', 27 *Stanford Law Review* 985.

Wallerstein, Judith and Joan Berlin Kelly (1980) *Surviving the Breakup* (London, Grant McIntyre).

Washburn, S. L. (ed.) (1962) *The Social Life of Early Man* (London, Methuen).

Waters, D. (1975) 'Matrimonial Property Disputes – Resulting and Constructive Trusts – Restitution', 53 *Canadian Bar Review* 366.

Watkins, Susan Cotts (1981) 'Regional Patterns of Nuptiality in Europe 1870–1960', 35 *Population Studies* 199.

Webb, Sidney and Beatrice (1910) *English Poor Law Policy* (London, Longmans Green).

Weiss, Paula Barran (1979) 'The Misuse of Adoption by the Custodial Parent and Spouse', 2 *Canadian Journal of Family Law* 141.

Weiss, Robert S. (1975) *Marital Separation* (New York, Basic Books).

Weitzman, Lenore J. and Ruth B. Dixon (1979) 'Child Custody Awards: Legal Standards and Empirical Patterns for Child Custody, Support and Visitation After Divorce', 12 *University of California Davis Law Review* 47.

Weitzman, Lenore J. and Ruth B. Dixon (1980) 'The Alimony Myth: Does No-Fault Divorce make a Difference?', 14 *Family Law Quarterly* 141.

Weitzman, Lenore J. (1981) *The Marriage Contract: Spouses, Lovers and the Law* (New York: The Free Press).

Weitzman, Lenore J. (1981a) 'The Economics of Divorce: Social and Economic Consequences of Property, Alimony and Child Support Awards', 28 *UCLA Law Review* 1181.

Wilkinson, Martin (1981) *Children and Divorce* (Oxford, Basil Blackwell).

Williams, B. (1962) 'The Idea of Equality', in Peter Laslett and W. G. Runciman (eds), *Philosophy, Politics and Society*, 2nd series (Oxford, Basil Blackwell).

Winks, Patricia L. (1980) 'Divorce Mediation: A Nonadversary Procedure for the No-Fault Divorce', 19 *Journal of Family Law* 615.

Yee, L. M. (1979) 'What really happens in child support cases: an empirical study of establishment and enforcement of child support orders in the Denver district court', 57 *Denver Law Journal* 21.

Yllo, Kersti and Murray A. Straus (1981) 'Interpersonal Violence among Married and Cohabiting Couples', 30 *Family Relations* 339.

Zuckerman, A. A. S. (1978) 'Ownership of the Matrimonial Home – Common Sense and Reformist Nonsense', 94 *Law Quarterly Review* 26.

INDEX